Textual Amulets from Antiquity to Early Modern Times

Bloomsbury Studies in Material Religion

Series editors: Birgit Meyer, David Morgan, S. Brent Plate, Crispin Paine, Amy Whitehead, and Katja Rakow

Bloomsbury Studies in Material Religion is the first book series dedicated exclusively to studies in material religion. Within the field of lived religion, the series is concerned with the material things with which people do religion, and how these things – objects, buildings, landscapes – relate to people, their bodies, clothes, food, actions, thoughts and emotions. The series engages and advances theories in 'sensuous' and 'experiential' religion, as well as informing museum practices and influencing wider cultural understandings with relation to religious objects and performances. Books in the series are at the cutting edge of debates as well as developments in fields including religious studies, anthropology, museum studies, art history, and material culture studies.

Buddhism and Waste
Edited by Trine Brox and Elizabeth Williams-Oerberg

Christianity and Belonging in Shimla, North India
Jonathan Miles-Watson

Christianity and the Limits of Materiality
Edited by Minna Opas and Anna Haapalainen

Figurations and Sensations of the Unseen in Judaism, Christianity and Islam
Edited by Birgit Meyer and Terje Stordalen

Food, Festival and Religion
Francesca Ciancimino Howell

Islam through Objects
Edited by Anna Bigelow

Material Devotion in a South Indian Poetic World
Leah Elizabeth Comeau

Museums of World Religions
Charles D. Orzech

Qur'anic Matters
Natalia K. Suit

The Religious Heritage Complex
Edited by Cyril Isnart and Nathalie Cerezales

Textual Amulets from Antiquity to Early Modern Times

The Shape of Words

Edited by
Christoffer Theis and Paolo Vitellozzi

BLOOMSBURY ACADEMIC
LONDON • NEW YORK • OXFORD • NEW DELHI • SYDNEY

BLOOMSBURY ACADEMIC
Bloomsbury Publishing Plc
50 Bedford Square, London, WC1B 3DP, UK
1385 Broadway, New York, NY 10018, USA
29 Earlsfort Terrace, Dublin 2, Ireland

BLOOMSBURY, BLOOMSBURY ACADEMIC and the Diana logo are trademarks of Bloomsbury Publishing Plc

First published in Great Britain 2023
Paperback edition published 2024

A catalogue record for this book is available from the British Library.

Library of Congress Control Number: 2022936795.

ISBN: HB: 978-1-3502-5453-4
PB: 978-1-3502-5457-2
ePDF: 978-1-3502-5454-1
eBook: 978-1-3502-5455-8

Series: Bloomsbury Studies in Material Religion

Typeset by Deanta Global Publishing Services, Chennai, India

London, British Museum, EA 56241. Inscribed amulet. Image licensed by the Trustees of the British Museum

Contents

List of Figures ix
Preface xi
List of Contributors xiii

1 Textual Amulets from a Transcultural Perspective
Christoffer Theis and Paolo Vitellozzi 1

2 Writing on Magical Gems: Reflections on Inscribed Gemstone Amulets of the Imperial Period
Paolo Vitellozzi 10

3 Of Comprehensible and Incomprehensible Inscriptions: Remarks on Some Gems with Multi-headed Gods
Christoffer Theis 34

4 Agency and Efficacy in Syriac Amulets across the Ages
Nils Hallvard Korsvoll 56

5 Demons in Runic and Latin Amulets from Medieval Scandinavia *Rudolf Simek* 69

6 Magic Letters: Unintelligible Prophylactic Formulas
Edina Bozoky 80

7 The Materiality of Talismans from Early Modern Spain: Morisco (and Old-Christian) Cases
Esther Fernández Medina 90

8 Talismans and Engravers of Talismans in the Seventeenth-Century Ottoman Society According to the Journal of Evliyā Çelebi
Özlem Deniz Ahlers 100

9 Small Letters against Great Misfortunes: A Glance at Safavid Amulet Culture *Sarah Kiyanrad* 112

10 Final Remarks: Toward a Transcultural View of Magical Writing
Christoffer Theis and Paolo Vitellozzi 132

Figures

2.1	Perugia, MANU. Green chalcedony amulet showing Chnoubis	13
2.2	Paris, BN. Red jasper amulet showing Hercules and the Nemean lion	15
2.3	London, BM. Hematite inscribed amulet	17
2.4	Perugia, MANU. Agate inscribed amulet	18
2.5	Perugia, MANU. Green jasper amulet showing an anguipede	19
2.6	Perugia, MANU. White chalcedony amulet	20
2.7	Berlin, ÄM. Carnelian amulet showing a series of magical symbols encircled by an *ouroborus* snake	23
2.8	Perugia, MANU. Hematite inscribed amulet	25
2.9	St. Petersburg, SHM. Sardonyx amulet showing a flying Perseus	27
2.10	Perugia, MANU. Black chalcedony amulet showing Hermanubis and the dead Osiris	29
2.11	London, BM. Jasper amulet showing a mummy surrounded by an inscription	30
2.12	Berlin, ÄM. Green jasper amulet showing a scarab encircled by an *ouroborus* snake	32
2.13	Malibu, J. P. Getty Museum. Agate inscribed amulet	33
3.1	Ann Arbor, Michigan, Kelsey Museum of Archaeology, 26059. Hematite amulet with a two-headed deity	37
3.2	Amduat 892. Two-headed god	38
3.3	Gem Kassel, Staatliche Kunstsammlung, 176. Sard with a two-headed, four-winged figure	39
3.4	Cambridge, MA: Harvard Art Museum, 2012.1.144. Jasper amulet showing an anthropomorphic deity with seven snake heads	40
3.5	London, British Museum, G 191 (EA 56191). Hematite amulet with a composite figure of the *Trikephalos* type	42
3.6	Stelae Harer Family Trust Collection, no. 111. Serpentine stela with a three-headed deity	43
3.7	London, British Museum, Inv. G 525 (EA 56525). Obsidian amulet showing Osiris as a three-headed mummy	45
3.8	Paris, Bibliothèque Nationale, 2170. Lapis lazuli amulet with an antropomorphic deity	46

3.9 New York, Metropolitan Museum of Art, 41.160.642. Lapis lazuli amulet with a four-headed sitting figure 48

3.10 New York, American Numismatic Society, no. 25. Hematite amulet showing a standing deity with four ram heads 49

3.11 Gem depicted by Gabra, showing a figure with four ram heads 50

3.12 Paris, Bibliothèque Nationale, Fr 2896. Yellow jasper amulet with an anthropomorphic, seated deity 51

7.1 Madrid, Real Academia de la Historia. "Herce" 95

7.2 Granada, Biblioteca EEA. مجموعة مؤلفات في الأمداح النبوية [Maŷmūʿat mu'allafāt fī l-amdāḥ al-nabawiyya] 97

8.1 Istanbul, Halûk Perk Museum. Seal of Bedūh with numeric values 107

8.2 Istanbul, Halûk Perk Museum. Three sides of the seal ring of ᶜAlį Rıża 108

9.1a New York, MMA. *Firdausī's Parable of the Ship of Shi'ism*, Folio 18v from the Shāhnāma of Shah Ṭahmāsb 113

9.1b New York, MMA. *Firdausī's Parable of the Ship of Shi'ism*, Folio 18v from the Shāhnāma of Shah Ṭahmāsb 114

9.2a Munich, BSB. Silver amulet case and scroll from gazelle skin 116

9.2b Munich, BSB. Silver amulet case and scroll from gazelle skin 117

9.2c Munich, BSB. Silver amulet case and scroll from gazelle skin 117

9.3 New York, MMA. Miniature Qur'an, Iran or Turkey 118

9.4a New York, MMA. Mail shirt, Iran, *c.* 1500–1600 120

9.4b New York, MMA. Mail shirt, Iran, *c.* 1500–1600 121

9.5 Washington, DC, Freer Gallery of Art. Portrait of a Jewish girl in elaborate costume; Antoin Sevruguin (1851–1933) 126

9.6 Washington, DC, Freer Gallery of Art. Portrait of two women in elaborate costume; Antoin Sevruguin (1851–1933) 127

9.7 New York, MMA. Detail of *Bahram Gur in the Yellow Palace on Sunday*, Folio 213 from a Khamsa (Quintet) of Niẓāmī 128

9.8 New York, MMA. Young man with jewelry (amulet?) 129

Preface

Amulets are used in many cultures for protective, apotropaic, and other beneficial purposes. The supposed power of an amulet, which was thought to derive from the synergy between potent shapes and powerful media, was often enhanced by adding further elements, such as images, symbols, or complex texts that are the transformation of prayers, incantations, and other orally performed speech acts. Describing such speech acts through the analysis of the function of written words on amulets is the core topic of this volume, which aims essentially at comparing such artifacts and their different forms over time and space from a multidisciplinary perspective. The time range stretches from Roman Egypt to the Middle Ages and the Modern period, and provides an overview on these types of artifacts in the Mediterranean world and beyond, including Europe, Iran, and Turkey. Each chapter is dedicated to a specific typology of textual amulets, with a chronological and geographical approach.

This volume originates from the international conference "Textual Amulets in a Transcultural Perspective," held at the University of Heidelberg, April 9–10, 2018. Since the original organizers of the conference, Laura Willer and Konrad Knauber, decided not to proceed with the publication of the proceedings, they entrusted the editors to accomplish the task. Thus, the majority of the lectures given at the conference are now accessible to the readers, who could not take part in the meeting.

Our special thanks to the Collaborative Research Center 933 "Material Text Cultures" at the Ruprecht-Karls-University of Heidelberg, which supported the conference in 2018 both financially and intellectually. We would also like to thank our friends and colleagues Laura Willer and Konrad Knauber, for their efforts in organizing the conference and for giving us the opportunity to share the results. A special thanks goes also to the CRC 933 chairman Prof. Dr. Ludger Lieb for providing financial means for the publication of some pictures in this volume as well as for drawings. We are also especially grateful to the following institutions and people who have generously supplied images, permissions, and other materials: Mathilde Avisseau-Broustet (Département des monnaies, médailles et antiques de la Bibliothèque Nationale de France), Svetlana Adaxina and Zhanna Etsina (State Hermitage Museum, St. Petersburg),

Kenneth Lapatin (The J. Paul Getty Museum of Malibu), Maria Angela Turchetti and Tiziana Caponi (Museo Archeologico Nazionale dell'Umbria), and Olivia Zorn (Ägyptisches Museum und Papyrussammlung, Berlin). Lastly, we wish to express our gratitude to Flavia A. Tulli, for her invaluable help in navigating through the waters of a foreign language.

Christoffer Theis and Paolo Vitellozzi
Leipzig and Perugia, autumn 2021

Contributors

Özlem Deniz Ahlers works as a research associate at the Johannes Gutenberg-University of Mainz, Germany. Her research interests focus on Turkish and Ottoman language and culture.

Edina Bozoky is professor emeritus of Medieval History at the University of de Poitiers, France, and member of the CESCM (Centre d'études supérieures de civilisation médiévale). Among her research interests are the Catharism, Medieval hagiography, and legends and lore of the Middle Ages. She is the author of *Le Livre secret des Cathares* (1997), *Charmes et prières apotropaïques* (2004), *La politiques des reliques de Constantin à Saint-Louis* (2007), *Attila et les Huns: Vérités et légendes* (2012), and *Miracle! Récits merveilleux des martyrs et des saints* (2013).

Esther Fernández Medina is currently an independent researcher. She studied magical health and gender issues among Morisco and Old-Christian women in sixteenth-century Spain. Her research interests focus on Aljamiado literature and Inquisitorial archives. Using such documents, she investigates the practices of the Moriscos related to health, magic, and experimental science as intertwined areas. At the moment she is working on a catalog of magical booklets from Granada.

Sarah Kiyanrad works as a research associate at Ludwig Maximilians-University of Munich, Germany. Her research interests focus on Iranian history and culture, on which she has published extensively since 2013. She is the author of *Gesundheit und Glück für seinen Besitzer: Schriftragende Amulette im islamzeitlichen Iran (bis 1258)* (2017).

Nils Hallvard Korsvoll is associate professor at the University of Agder, Norway. His research focuses on history of religion, ritual, popular religion, magic, and material culture. His publications include articles on liturgy in ancient amulets and the use of biblical references in ancient magic.

Rudolf Simek is professor emeritus and chair of Medieval German and Nordic Studies at the University of Bonn, Germany. Simek researches a wide variety of topics connected to the Middle Ages: Germanic religion and mythology (including Old Norse religion and mythology), Vikings and the Viking Age, Old Norse literature, and medieval science (including astronomy) and popular religion. Simek has published a number of notable works on these subjects, several of which have been translated into multiple languages. Among his most famous monographs are *Die Wikinger* (1998), *Götter und Kulte der Germanen* (2004), *Runes, Magic and Religion: A Sourcebook* (with John McKinnell and Klaus Düwel 2004), *Die Germanen* (2006), *Die Edda* (2007), *Die Schiffe der Wikinger* (2014), *Vinland! Wie die Wikinger Amerika entdeckten* (2016), *Die Geschichte der Normannen. Von Wikingerhäuptlingen zu Königen Siziliens* (2018), and *Monster im Mittelalter* (2019).

Christoffer Theis is research associate at the University of Leipzig, Germany, and member of the Young Academy of Sciences and Literature, Mainz. His wide research interests focus on ancient Egyptian and Near Eastern religion, magic and ritual, loanwords, and language contacts, for which he received a number of awards. His ongoing research project "Egyptian Loanwords in Ancient Near Eastern Languages" will compile for the first time all real or just proposed Egyptian loanwords in other languages of the Ancient Near East.

Paolo Vitellozzi is a postdoctoral scholar of Classics at the University of Perugia, Italy. He works as a teacher of Greek and Latin and as a private art advisor. His interests focus on engraved gems, but he has also published on ancient magic and religion. Among his previous publications are *Gemme e Cammei della Collezione Guardabassi nel Museo Archeologico Nazionale dell'Umbria a Perugia* (2010) and *Tesori di una collezione privata* (2017).

1

Textual Amulets from a Transcultural Perspective

Christoffer Theis and Paolo Vitellozzi

1. Introduction

In many cultures some objects were and are worn for protective, apotropaic, and other beneficial purposes. This volume aims at comparing such artifacts, generally called amulets, and their different forms over time and space from a multidisciplinary perspective. The time span of the objects examined in the chapters ranges from ancient Egypt through to the Arabic period in the Mediterranean world and to various medieval examples, thus providing an overview of their use in different cultures. The investigations focus on inscribed amulets, where words or complex texts are employed to enhance the supposed efficacy of the material components, while a comparative analysis of the praxeology of these amulets examines how they were produced, and how they were worn and used in the rituals that lie behind their making, as well as the special purpose(s) of their inscriptions. A strong emphasis is placed on the material aspects and on how these were selected according to ritualistic purposes. The textual content (words, prayers, magical formulas and symbols)[1], as well as other features of the amulets, are examined from a systematic and phenomenological perspective, in order to determine possible approaches toward an anthropology of writing in ritual contexts.

This volume is the result of the "Textual Amulets in a Transcultural Perspective" workshop, held on April 9–10, 2018, at Heidelberg University Library, organized by Laura Willer and Konrad Knauber.

The main aim of this scientific meeting was to reach a consensus on the argument that in many cultures, texts were and still are used for protective, apotropaic, and sundry other beneficial purposes, together with specific material components. Researchers from different areas at the workshop took a closer look at the typology, praxeology, and mindset associated with these customs, focusing on the connection between text and materiality of inscribed amulets.

Here are their contributions which illustrate the methods and observations shared, providing a fresh view of these phenomena from broader lines of perspective. The cultures surveyed thrived from antiquity to modern times over an area stretching from the Middle East to Scandinavia. With this volume, the editors would like to make the results of the workshop available to a broader audience. For various reasons, not all the presentations given at the workshop could be included in the publication; other contributions will be published in further volumes.

The amulets discussed in the chapters are often an important source to understand the influence of different cultures, not only in antiquity but also in Arabic and medieval times by using elements of different ages and origin. Among the many questions that connect the contributions with one another there are some that could be defined as the general topic: What defines an amulet? How are they generally acknowledged? How were they used? The chapters therefore provide an analysis of amulets in the different cultures of Europe and Asia based on their chronological and geographical similarities following two main lines of thought. The first is an outline into research and definition(s) on textual amulets, while the second is the comparison and collection of different similarities throughout the ages and cultures. It becomes evident that, although many differences might be observed in the use of textual amulets among the various peoples over time, specific lines, traditions, and meanings appear to be recurring elements. Therefore, a short theoretical foreword will be provided by summarizing the content of the volume.

2. Textual Amulets and Their Materiality

Approaching textual amulets from the point of view of their materiality has been theorized in some recent studies.[2] The manufacture of these ritual devices, seen as essential to the expressivity of practice,[3] can be examined in reference to the interrelatedness between the physical objects and the texts they carry. Texts, which are the core topic of the amulet, can be understood both from a material angle and a linguistic point of view,[4] by analyzing the speech acts that are conveyed by the texts through the application of the heuristic models provided by the most recent studies that have arisen from the application of Austin and Searle's Speech Acts theory[5] to magical language.[6]

Therefore, an outline into research on textual amulets, which includes the problems of definition(s) and material agency (assemblages, performance of manufacture, and the materiality of writing itself), has to be presented accompanied by a theoretical premise which will provide the central theme linking together the various chapters. Reference should also be made to the transcultural appearances of amulets since many of the ideas and applications known from Egypt and Mesopotamia can also be found in adjacent cultural areas, as well as in other times in Europe and elsewhere, not only in contemporary finds but also in areas far apart in time, therefore placing them in an intercultural framework. A talisman (from Greek τέλεσμα to Arabic طِلَسْم), according to Ṭašköprüzāde, *Miftāḥ* I. 277.3, is a kind of "indissoluble knot," as well as the anagram of مُسَلِّط "bestowing power,"[7] whose use in magical actions is clearly explained by the latter meaning.[8] For this explanation, we can also point out the tradition by Pseudo-Aristoteles, *Kitāb Sirr al-Asrār* 156.4–157.6 as well as Pseudo-Maǧrīṭī, *Ġāyat al-Ḥakīm* 7,[9] who both talk about the power of such artifacts.

Most of the contributions deal with "magic," but the exact meaning of this word and what lies within it are still subject to a lively debate.[10] Therefore, we shall not delve too much into this discussion since, at least in many cultures, there seems to be no meaningful distinction between magical lore and religious practices. Magic will thus be understood as an element of religion where the interrelation of the two becomes clear, despite the opposition often set up between them, solely by the fact that the somewhat blurred dividing line between these categories can only be drawn artificially.[11] No final answers can be offered to these and other questions, but the volume wishes to include and examine amulets with their pictures and texts from different perspectives and thus take a first step toward their holistic analysis.

3. Summary of the Contributions

In his chapter "Writing on Magical Gems: Reflections on Inscribed Gemstone Amulets of the Imperial Period," Paolo Vitellozzi explores the function of writing on one of the most significant types of amulets of the Roman Imperial period, commonly known as "magical gems." Since these artifacts are defined essentially by the interaction of medium (the stones), image and text, the discussion focuses on how writing was used to achieve the purposes that the amulets were thought to serve, with special regard to ritual contexts as well as to material aspects. Part of the chapter concentrates on the nature of the inscribed texts (magical names, prayers, requests), in order to understand the needs of the people who believed in their power. The chapter also contains a general overview of the many writing techniques (graphic figures, pseudo-writing, cryptography), and the position the texts have within the reduced space of the amulets. This leads the author to a series of reflections on the importance of writing in a society where literate people were a small minority. Anthropological and linguistic questions, such as those regarding the formulary, are also discussed in order to understand the relationship between the dominant Graeco-Roman tradition in the Imperial age and the other Mediterranean cultures. In fact, gemstone amulets can well be regarded as precious documents showing the circulation of religious beliefs and culture among the many populations of the Mediterranean, as well as that of the interaction among different cultural models.

Chapter 3, "Of Comprehensible and Incomprehensible Inscriptions: Remarks on Some Gems with Multi-headed Gods," by Christoffer Theis also focuses on gems from late antiquity, often referred to as "magical"; these objects show many different Egyptian, Greek, Jewish, Mesopotamian, and/or Near Eastern elements. Based on their assumed period of origin between the second and fourth or even fifth centuries AD, these artifacts thus form a veritable treasure trove for the tradition—and thus a *longue durée*—of motifs and symbols. The number of images on gems shows that even in late antiquity, beings from different cultures enjoyed certain popularity as a motif, even though they were hardly mentioned or depicted in sources in epichoric cultures in this period. The focus of the contribution are gems showing beings or gods with more than one head or face, whose study in antiquity is so far a *desideratum* of research. There is virtually no consensus on a name or names for multi-headed beings, since all the epithets and names are confused; even the number of heads is inconsequential. Among the various names of the intercultural framework of gems, Egyptian, Jewish, and Greek influences are preserved, which, when found together, create new beings. The question arises, how were the labels of the gems actually conceived or arranged together? Was it a decision of the stone cutter what text to write down on the gems, and if so, what intention can we recognize? Or were the labels selected by the customer? The aim is to provide answers to the aforementioned questions relying on a corpus of gems with depictions of gods with multiple heads, namely those accompanied by an inscription, focusing on the inscribed texts, their understanding and their relationship with their religious and cultural background.

Nils Hallvard Korsvoll examines "Agency and Efficacy in Syriac Amulets across the Ages." The Syriac amulets, known from antiquity up to the Early Modern period, from Iran to China, provide a clear view of the development of apotropaic practices over time and space, and lying within the same linguistic tradition. Self-designations and operative verbs are used to identify the material source of the amulets' efficacy. Despite the many benefits of using the Syriac amulets to study textual amulets from a transcultural perspective, their restricted number and their temporal and spatial distribution, as well as issues of survival and representation, hinder historical inquiry and therefore remain a challenge. The examination shows that while it is difficult to pinpoint a specific locus of agency, there are certain trends and tendencies in the many corpora. First, there is a shift from the domestic context in the late-antique corpus to a clerical or monastic one in the medieval and early modern body of texts. Moreover, this shift is paralleled by a change in perspective in the spells, from client to scribe or ritual expert. Second, the medieval and early modern manuals contain more elements and phrases borrowed from or referencing to Christian ritual, whereas the late-antique amulets emphasize the illnesses and afflictions that the amulet should protect against. Furthermore, agency is mostly not specified in the late-antique amulets, while the medieval and early modern incantations have an intercessory structure that again compares with a Christian cosmology. We can suggest that there is a continuation in the request of the incantations, while the invocation and the *pars epica* were extended and elaborated on in response to Christian cosmology. This observation then suggests how a tradition can expand and adapt across time and space to new situations and contexts.

"Demons in Runic and Latin Amulets from Medieval Scandinavia" is the topic of the chapter written by Rudolf Simek. As opposed to popular opinion, runes never had any magical quality per se, that is to say that they would not have been used as magical symbols in any rituals or magical practices. However, the runic scripts, like all other lettering systems, could be used for any purpose including the composition of texts aimed at otherworldly powers, and that may be considered magical in a wider sense—contrary to what people usually believe. We have to distinguish between three different runic scripts in use in the first millennium AD, namely the so-called Elder Futhark, the Younger Futhark, and the Anglo-Saxon variant of the latter, the Anglo-Saxon Futhorc. It becomes obvious that although there are many amulets which neither mention the person to be protected nor the demons that are conjured up so as not to harm that person, just limiting themselves to holy texts (like the beginning of the Gospel of John) or holy names, we now do have a good impression of what demons are thought to be doing. They are quite obviously in charge of harming people through illnesses, and not just temporal temptations: in fact, the latter are never mentioned on amulets. It also seems that it was safer to address demons both by their Latin and vernacular names, and by making sure that male and female demons are both addressed. We also learn from the texts that, apart from proper exorcism formulas, also the invocation of the Trinity, the saints, and the various names of God, including Alpha and Omega, or even magic words served as protection from demons. Demons were conceived of as having proper names, as in the case of the Seven Sisters, or Gordan Gordin, and Ingordan, which allowed the apotropaic magic to take a better hold on them.

Edina Bozoky puts "Magical Letters: Unintelligible Prophylactic Formulae" in focus of her contribution. Indecipherable formulas, the meaning of which was unknown to medieval users, had to be written and worn on the body instead of being uttered. The majority of charms are intelligible formulas. They were used both in oral and written forms. These charms derive their efficacy from the meaning of the words, reinforced with sound effects when uttered, and performed with gesture and ritual. In contrast, the category of unintelligible charms is composed of strange words or cryptic series of letters. Cryptic combinations of letters, which were called *characteres*, were even more unintelligible. These combinations are—for the material in focus—compositions of Latin letters, but seem to be absolutely meaningless to a modern eye, and they are generally combined together with other kinds of charms. Medieval charms composed of magical letters were often used with other kinds of formulas: narrative charms, conjurations, and divine names Bozoky shows that the assimilation of the patient to the collective mythology and the integration of the individual in a cosmic order had a symbolic "efficacy." Conjurations addressed to the illness or to a demon were considered orders which could be immediately performed. On the other hand, Bozoky points out that formulas containing divine names and strange words had the same use as that of *characteres*. The main focus of the chapter is on the use of these wordings in the church and in some of its books. Was the church relatively tolerant with certain invocations and prayers uttered over the sick? Should unknown words, such as *characteres* and signs, be rejected only because they are "unknown"? For example, in the *Hammer of Witches* (*Malleus maleficarum*), behind these formulas one can see a pact with demons, "and the demon intervenes obscurely accomplishing the desires in order to lure into the worst."[12] The magical charms contained in medieval medical prescriptions help illustrate how medical books were used to produce amulets: a practice that made the church suspicious, as clearly shown in the *Hammer of Witches*.

Esther Fernández Medina describes and examines "The Materiality of Talismans from Early Modern Spain: Morisco (and Old-Christian) Cases." The Moriscos of early modern Spain were a minority group from both a cultural and religious point of view. As descendants of the Muslim population of *al-Andalus*, in the Iberian Peninsula, in the first quarter of the sixteenth century they were forced to convert to Christianity by Royal edicts. However, although in some areas the population still claims a Morisco origin, one can affirm that their traces have disappeared. Nevertheless, most of their cultural and religious background has been preserved in a kind of literature known as *Aljamiada*. The Moriscos kept those texts hidden from the Catholic Court since it had banned their culture, especially their form of writing. As a result of those unfortunate circumstances, many secret libraries have been discovered, preserved, and studied. Today, most of the archival collections are located in Spain, but there are also many *Aljamiado* manuscripts in other European, Maghrebian, and Middle Eastern libraries. The basis of these writings is Islamic culture, and religious texts are the most frequent among them. Other types are medical and magical ones. The most common objective in the fabrication of *herces* was the quest for health and protection, as well as for love and many other purposes. They were written using enigmatic words and symbols, and the simple act of writing and carrying them was thought to be effective or curative. The materials were adapted to the specific needs of the talisman holder by their makers and the objects were created following instructions contained in manuscripts of magical content. The writings are sometimes interwoven with medical prescriptions and/or religious formulas. The Moriscos were fond of this kind of texts and they used them profusely. The dialectic relationship between visibility and invisibility is also evident in the Morisco amulets, since they were kept hidden and contained magical symbols.

Özlem Deniz Ahlers examines "Talismans and Engravers of Talismans in the Seventeenth-Century Ottoman Society According to the Journal of Evliyā Çelebi," and observes that talismans and magical amulets are not enclosed within geographical boundaries or specific periods of art history. They appear in different forms, following the needs of a society, as a protective means to cope with the dangers of everyday life. Such is also the case in the Ottoman society, which regulated magical practices according to the teachings of Islam. Talismans with precise astrological patterns were produced to provide practical desired effects. In his monumental journal "Seyāḥatnāme," the traveler Evliyā Çelebi described a great number of talismans and their creators in the Ottoman society of the seventeenth century. Following Çelebi's observations, Ahlers illustrates where and how these talismans were used in that period.

Sarah Kiyanrad describes "Small Letters against Great Misfortunes: A Glance at Safavid Amulet Culture." The seventeenth-to-nineteenth-century Persianate amulets help to analyze the mutual relationship between materials and texts for specific purposes. Furthermore, they offer a clear idea of the production networks and of the individuals involved. Diverse media and genres—ranging from miniatures, manuals, and travelogues to remaining artifacts—reveal to us the world of Safavid amulets. Based on selected textual, visual, and material evidence, the chapter introduces a number of script-bearing amulet types commonly used in the Safavid period (1501–1722). It explores materials and textual contents and develops a profile for those people who typically produced or commissioned amulets. Furthermore, the chapter investigates the so-called *Sitz im Leben* of these objects.

Thus organized, the chapters follow both a geographical and a chronological sequence, illustrating the evolution of a tradition which originates in the ancient world from the blending of the earliest Mediterranean cultures and then progresses through changes, transformations, and selections toward Iran and Western Europe, up to the Modern period. The first chapters provide an overview of inscribed gemstone amulets in the Hellenistic and Roman Imperial periods, when the rapid increase in the epigraphic habit produced an explosion of evidence for amulets throughout the Greek-speaking world. These artifacts, produced in the multicultural environment of the Roman Empire, combine Graeco-Roman elements with Near Eastern and Egyptian ones and represent the highest phase of a centuries-long tradition which will be the main source of inspiration for later cultures. Consequently, the fourth chapter is about the reception and transformation of the ancient typologies in Early Christian Syria and their further development across Western Asia in the Middle Ages within the Syriac linguistic tradition. The chapter that follows clearly shows how the Graeco-Latin tradition, especially once transformed through Christianity, progressively embraces and replaces an older Scandinavian one. Starting from these premises, the development of a magical lore in the Middle Ages is investigated through the blending of pagan and Christian elements, as well as its relationship with the official religion of the church. The next chapter explores different patterns of change and diffusion in the Modern era. Through the study of amulets in the Morisco culture, early modern European themes and structures that had been developed by the Islamic magical tradition from late-antique ancestors are put in focus; elements that had been forgotten by Western Christianity appear again in early modern Spain. Finally, the complex evolution of inscribed amulets in modern central Asia is shown, with detailed analysis of the Persian and Ottoman contexts.

Thus structured, the chapters not only provide a diachronic analysis of the complex transformations of amulets in the diverse cultures but also offer a study on the genesis and changes of determined ritual traditions which, originating in the extremely dynamic cultural landscape of the eastern provinces of the Roman Empire, were received and adapted to the many local contexts in both the East (from Syria to China) and the West (Europe, Scandinavia, and Spain). Once transformed and adapted to the local substrates, such ritual customs eventually shaped further traditions which influenced one another through the centuries. This allows the editors to sketch, in a more general and synchronic way, where amulets appear in the landscapes and life of the diverse communities, as well as the identities of the various providers (wise men and women, herbalists, gem cutters, or scribes) who collected, manufactured, inscribed, or otherwise created these amulets, sometimes as amateurs for family and friends, but increasingly as professionals armed with handbooks and in search of profit. Such a sketch eventually shows the survival and continuity of some fundamental expressive categories which might be taken as common features of human religion.

2

Writing on Magical Gems

Reflections on Inscribed Gemstone Amulets of the Imperial Period

Paolo Vitellozzi

1. Progression in Tradition

As for textual amulets, the so-called magical gems,[1] a particular typology of gemstone amulets produced in the Imperial period, are doubtlessly one of the most intriguing sources, since they attest elaborate rituals involving a complex interaction of text, image, and medium. Unlike the majority of the intaglios of the same period, which are normally inscribed in mirror writing since they were mainly used as seals, gemstone amulets are distinctive for the presence of normal writing, thus revealing that the inscribed texts were most probably meant to be read aloud by the users. This typical feature has led the scholars to place these artifacts under a separate category labeled as "magical."[2]

However, as Christopher A. Faraone has exhaustively demonstrated,[3] despite the significant presence of text has been correctly regarded by the scholars as a distinctive feature of the so-called magical gems, this reveals an increase in the epigraphic habit in the Roman Imperial period, but it does not reflect the evolution of the use of amulets over time.

In fact, against the traditional view of a sudden increase of "magical" beliefs in this period, attributed mainly to the adoption of cults and ritual from Egypt and Near East, Faraone has shown the continuity of a long amulet-making tradition beginning at least in the classical period, explaining how these artifacts were transformed in the late Hellenistic and Roman periods, ultimately producing a plethora of evidence throughout the Greek-speaking world. This dramatic change in the shape and fashion of stone amulets, which has induced generations of scholars to keep them separate from other "ordinary" Graeco-Roman gems and cameos, consists essentially in the novel use of writing on stones those prayers, incantations, and other protective or curative speech acts that first belonged to the orally performed ritual surrounding the amulets themselves.

In fact, it is only in the Roman Imperial period that the written text takes on any importance at all, and the use of the Greek alphabet implies a Greek-speaking clientele as the main target for the gem-makers. However, as the ancient lithic tradition seems to suggest, there were probably a great number of stones and powerful images circulating independently around the Mediterranean basin long before the advent of the Roman Empire.

Although the earliest examples of gemstone amulets do not bear inscriptions, it is only when magical texts appear side by side with traditional pairings of media and images that we become aware of how these media and images were thought to have magical powers. In fact, the rise in epigraphic habits in the Graeco-Roman period and the increasing scribalization of magic makes the written versions of earlier speech acts, or, in other words of earlier rituals, finally visible to the modern observer.

Indeed, the creativity of the scribes in the Roman period lies not in their creation *ex nihilo* of the written texts that we find on gems, but rather in how they interact with the epigraphic rendition of the spoken formulas, which were thought to remain powerfully present on the papyrus or gemstone that eventually was placed on the user's body. In his work *Vanishing Acts* (2012),[4] Faraone suggests, as a heuristic model, five different levels in the evolution of inscribed amulets, with oral performance at one end and purely visual rendition at the other.

The first level is a verbal type of word-magic, in which magical names and formulas were chanted until the purpose of the ritual was achieved. In the second level these same names and phrases, now inscribed on precious stones, retain their original function alone or together with other speech acts such as prayers. But even at this level, the entire text of the amulet can still be read aloud and thus performed orally. In the third level these ritual speech acts begin to be perceived as graphic representations for the designated divine entities; in this crucial moment, the scribes begin to surround or confront the now potentially dangerous names with the words of prayers, unpronounceable symbols, and images; at this level the amulet can no longer be performed orally. In the fourth level there are crossover cases, in which the written text clearly represents the supernatural entity. In the fifth and final level, the written words are employed as pure designs, often unrelated to the specific goals of the spell in which they are used.

The perception of a written text as image is essentially a product of the Hellenic tradition of the *technopaignia*, but the notion of a linguistic nature of reality, which implies that every single grapheme has in itself an ultimate divine nature, is a gift of the Hebrew religious culture which, in this historical phase, meets the neo-platonic philosophy and the Pythagorean thought. From this point of view, magical gems can be seen as a highly representative product of the new multicultural world beginning to form in the Imperial age.[5]

As also explained by Faraone,[6] the historical evolution of written text on amulets can be seen in the examples described in the literary sources, such as the well-known Chnoubis digestive amulets.[7] Among the surviving medical recipes that mention engraved gems, Galen,[8] relying on Nechepso and followed by other authors,[9] recommends the wearing of a ἴαϲπιϲ χλωρόϲ (green jasper) with a "radiate serpent" (Chnoubis) to heal stomach diseases, while Marcellus Empiricus prescribes a *iaspis frygia aerizusa* (probably a chalcedony) bearing the well-known symbol *SSS* for his pleuritic patients.[10] Though Galen's prescription requires an image on the stone, he adds his personal experience of wearing a string of plain stones hung over the esophagus, which seems to be successful. Therefore, we have three different recipes, each from a different period: Nechepso's Hellenistic version (green jasper and radiant serpent set in a finger ring), Galen's Roman Imperial one (a string of plain jasper stones), and Marcellus' late-antique one (jasper and radiant serpent set in gold and hung around the neck). All these recipes aim at curing pains in the digestive tract by using the same gem and, in two cases, the same image, but none make any mention of inscribed text.

However, the great number of ancient gems[11] that we have bear the name *Chnoubis* or *Chnoumis* (Figure 2.1) often accompanied by the triple sigma, which is said to heal magically by itself in Marcellus' *De medicamentis*. Together with these common inscriptions, many gems bear the names or epithets used to invoke the radiant serpent Chnoubis, either with exotic formulas, such as ναaβις βιεννουθ, or with the well-known Greek vocatives γιγαντορηκτα ("breaker of giants") and βαροφιτα ("crusher of snakes"). In addition to this, there are more complex amulets adding brief prayers, commands, or even explicit references to the amulet's purpose: a British Museum moss agate[12] bears, for example, the following prayer: "Chnoubis Nabis Biennous, (give) water for thirst, bread for hunger, fire for cold,"[13] while another one once in Istanbul[14] says: "Avert from Julian, son of Nonna all (abdominal) tension, all indigestion, all stomach pain" (Trans. C. Bonner).[15]

Scholars now have some clue about the combination of Greek text and image of these stones[16] and tend to conclude that the absence of names and epithets,

Figure 2.1 Green chalcedony amulet showing Chnoubis. Perugia, Museo Archeologico Nazionale dell'Umbria (inv. no. 1249). Photo: Paolo Vitellozzi. Used with permission.

and especially prayers, in the literary sources may mean that they were probably spoken aloud directly to the image and inscribed on the gem only in a later period.

Consequently, also the divine names normally found written on the reverse of the amulets, which were thought to contain the divine essence of the represented image, were originally pronounced aloud. It seems therefore clear that the historical evolution of magical gems, starting from plain stones thought to have inner magical virtues, gradually moved on to the use of "persuasive" images[17] that could, by means of analogy, activate the energy of the stone. The next phase of this evolution was writing on the stone those words once only spoken to summon the gods represented on the amulets. Once again, the action of writing, which in the archaic period had a sacred aura, regained its original solemnity in an age of increased scribalization in society.

This progression toward inscribed texts is also theorized by Roy Kotansky,[18] who proposes a tripartite classification including unlettered amulets, made from natural substances but without any inherent literary meaning in themselves, semi-lettered amulets, whose supposed divine power is enhanced by a ritually efficacious iconography and a partial literacy of word and symbol, and finally lettered amulets, whose magical efficacy is mainly recognized in the written words preserved on them.

Such a development is clearly evident in the amulets deriving from the earliest Greek tradition, such as the Hercules phylacteries against colics[19] or the Gorgon's head restraining amulets.[20] The well-known scene of Heracles strangling the Nemean lion,[21] already widespread in archaic Greece, was thought to have curative powers in the Roman Imperial period. In his text "On the Colicky Condition" Alexander of Tralles prescribes the following treatment:

> On a Median stone engrave Heracles standing upright and throttling a lion. Set it in a gold ring and give it to the patient to wear. (Transl. C. A. Faraone)[22]

As pointed out by the scholars, this image was probably adopted because the lion's claws, placed on the naked belly of the hero, could represent the sharp abdominal pain of a colic, which, by the process of persuasive magic, is cured just as the lion is slain by Heracles. The labors of Hercules are a recurrent iconographic theme in Greek and Roman art, but this episode was probably thought to have protective powers much earlier. A carnelian scarab in the British Museum,[23] showing two *udjat* eyes behind the hero, seems to confirm this hypothesis.[24] We might even think that the *udjat* eyes in this archaic specimen had the same function of the three *kappas* that normally accompany this motif on Roman Imperial gems. The scholars have associated these *kappas* with the inscribed formula κολοκερ κολοφοσειρ which often occurs alongside the image of Hercules, but a jasper in Paris[25] (Figure 2.2) has an incantation inscribed which records the oral performance being part of the ritual: the scene is in fact surrounded by the command "Withdraw bile! The deity pursues you" (Transl. C. A. Faraone).[26]

Furthermore, Véronique Dasen has discussed an imagery that can be classified as the female counterpart of the Hercules amulets.[27] These gems, made for protecting women from a variety of diseases connected with female reproductive health, show Omphale, usually with Hercules' club in her hand, either defending herself from the asinine Seth or, on those gems where she seems to be pregnant, protecting her unborn baby: the common iambic incantation reported by these amulets says: "Stand still, womb, lest Typhon seize you!".[28]

Another popular episode is the fight between Perseus and the Gorgon. It is well known that the severed head of Medusa, probably the oldest Greek *apotropaion*, is frequent on gems since the archaic period. On magical amulets, the Gorgon's head is normally associated with Hecate: sometimes it appears as a protective emblem on uterine amulets, but more often, it serves for restraining charms (*thymokatocha*) based on the persuasive analogy between the petrifying gaze of the Gorgon and the purpose of controlling anger.[29] Most of these gems are

Figure 2.2 Red jasper amulet showing Hercules and the Nemean lion. Paris, Bibliothèque Nationale de France, Cabinet des Médailles (inv. no. 58.2220 bis). Photo: Serge Oboukhoff. Used with permission.

made of coral, which was thought to be Medusa's petrified blood, as confirmed by the *Orphei Lithica Kerygmata*.[30]

The gradual appearing of inscribed texts is even more evident in this series; in fact, while most of the amulets are not inscribed, some of them bear magical formulas or personal names, while a famous Boston gem[31] has an invocation and a prayer which probably refers to a context of personal rivalry, possibly arising from jealousy or from the need to avoid the anger of a quick-tempered master. The text reads as follows:

> Gorgon. Achilles, Valios(?), son of Tauros, Iulis. If (they) talk to Al(e)xios, let them not be believed! Chnoubis.[32]

Alongside many others, these exemplary groups of amulets demonstrate that the presence of writing on magical stone amulets, rather than a sudden exploit of magic due to an increase in superstition, must be seen as the result of a long process that went hand in hand with the spread of scribalization in society. However, the inscribed texts came soon to play a major role in the creation of magical gemstones, eventually occupying their whole surface. This phenomenon is directly linked to the use of magical formularies, which were used as models by the professional magicians whose designs were a source of inspiration for the gem-makers; indeed, as demonstrated by many scholars, the close correspondence between gems and papyri excludes the possibility of free invention and implies the existence of a centuries-old tradition that probably had a written form.[33]

2. Words Set in Stone

Over time, the act of writing, initially a direct expression of a speech act,[34] becomes a graphic phenomenon, at times employing techniques typical of drawing; this is evident not only in the disposition of the inscribed text on the small surface of the stones, which is strongly conditioned by instructions such as those in the papyri, but also in the use of the so-called *carmina figurata*, the geometric arrangements according to which magical texts are sometimes inscribed on corresponding amulets. By constructing a palindrome, *klima* ("seven-layered"), *pterygoma* ("wing"), or *plinthion* ("square") out of a magical word, a ritual expert would be able to manipulate it through its graphic components,[35] thereby increasing or decreasing the supposed power deriving from its related divine entity.[36] A meaningful example of such ritual manipulation is visible on the so-called "Thirsty Tantalus" gems (Figure 2.3), a series of hematite amulets used to control bleeding:[37] on these gems, the command "Thirsty Tantalus, drink the blood!" is originally inscribed to stop bleeding on the basis of a persuasive analogy with the mythical figure of Tantalus, but eventually the phrase, arranged in a wing-formation by the practitioners and therefore dismantled one letter at a time, is used to promote the opposite effect, since the efficacy of the inscribed command is nullified by this purely graphic operation.

The alphabetical symbols, and especially vowels, are often considered in their phonetic and iconic features on late-antique amulets, inspired either by the Orphic and Pythagorean speculation regarding *stoicheia* as utterable symbols of cosmic forces and their corresponding sounds, or by the iconic nature of ancient hieroglyphic writing: this led to the intense use of cryptography, isopsephy, and pseudo-writing and eventually to the creation of special magical symbols, conventionally known as *charaktêres*.[38]

Such artificial signs, having no apparent source in any known writing system and consisting essentially of asterisks and configurations of basic lines with small circles or lobes at each end, function as a kind of self-made "sacred" writing

Figure 2.3 Hematite inscribed amulet. London, British Museum (inv. no. GR 1928.5-20.1). Image licensed by the Trustees of the British Museum.

based on the idea of a divine, unutterable language whose mysterious symbolic qualities are able to engender charm and attraction on the users (Figure 2.4).

A cursory glance at the typology and structure of the textual parts of magical gems reveals the prevalence of divine names which are either written on the obverse, usually surrounding the engraved image, or in most cases on the reverse; this side should be considered the true core of the gem where the users place the profound essence of the ritual. This is what Lucian probably means in his account of a man who faced a Gorgon-headed Hecate and chased her away by turning his finger ring.[39] Another point that can be immediately surmised from Lucian's passage, which is confirmed both by the literary sources and by archeological evidence, is that inscriptions are always connected to the images, although in ways that are not immediately comprehensible to modern exegesis, due to the complexity, or rather to the relative obscurity of many magical formulas, which require further investigation.[40]

In many of our gems, the reverse is occupied by text, and this should warn us about the importance of written words. This is not only due to the rise of scribalization in the Imperial age but also, as previously argued, to the influence of the Hebrew tradition in the religious culture of this period; in fact, the biblical

Figure 2.4 Agate inscribed amulet. Perugia, Museo Archeologico Nazionale dell'Umbria (inv. no. 1741). Photo: Paolo Vitellozzi. Used with permission.

concept of an ultimate linguistic nature of reality, inherited by neo-platonic philosophy, eventually produced the idea, clearly expressed by Zosimus,[41] that the graphic symbols of the alphabet were a true image of the divine essence (*ousía*).

As Árpád M. Nagy has pointed out,[42] magical gems show essentially three typologies of texts. The first and most common comprises divine names mainly derived from the Semitic (and especially Hebrew) tradition, although also Egyptian and Greek theonyms are present. The second one includes formulas of non-Hellenic origin, the meaning of which often challenges the scholars since they either originate from the blending of different cultural traditions with the precise aim to elude a clear identification or are simply the product of onomatopoeic or glossolalic words. A third and far rarer type are complete and meaningful sentences, generally in Greek.

Hence the question about the content of the extant inscriptions. The large majority of magical gems, being engraved with images of gods, are inscribed with magical names or formulas (conventionally labeled as *voces magicae*), which can be normally related to theonyms or epithets which, although transliterated in

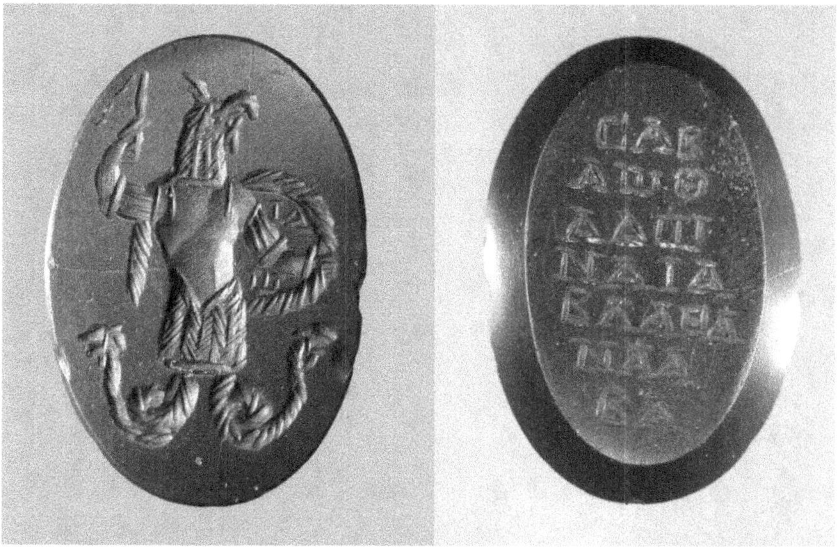

Figure 2.5 Green jasper amulet showing an anguipede. Perugia, Museo Archeologico Nazionale dell'Umbria (inv. no. 1248). Photo: Paolo Vitellozzi. Used with permission.

Greek and often misspelled, are borrowed from non-Hellenic languages and still preserve their original sound (Figure 2.5).

The idea that lies behind this use is, obviously, that the real names of the gods were those given by the ancient people who first communicated with them; therefore, the correct pronunciation (or a sufficiently convincing imitation) of those original words (Egyptian, Hebrew, Aramaic) was often thought to be the only way to summon the gods, as confirmed by the many injunctions found in the papyri to correctly utter the sacred names. Further proof of this is given by those gems bearing on the reverse the recurring formula "Great is the name of [. . .]" followed by a god's name. The writer of a gem now in Kassel explicitly states: "Give (me) charm and victory, because I pronounced your secret, real name!"[43]

The idea of an exotic nature of a god's real name is a mark of the profound change that had happened in Greek culture during the Imperial age, which is clearly visible in the papyri; foreign lore, once discredited as "barbarian," is now seen as a precious source of wisdom and therefore held in great awe.

Furthermore, we have enough elements to postulate that the magical names normally inscribed on a gemstone amulet were probably part of a longer prayer probably addressed directly to the gem, in order to summon the deity whose image was engraved on it. Proof of this is furnished by those magical *logoi* which appear identical on gems and in papyri, although in the latter they are part of

Figure 2.6 White chalcedony amulet. Perugia, Museo Archeologico Nazionale dell'Umbria (inv. no. 1771). Photo: Paolo Vitellozzi. Used with permission.

longer cletic hymns and are followed by request formulas relying on the force of the said names.[44] If uttering a god's name is the shortest form of invocation, an acclamation asserts his greatness by using a third-person sentence, either by adding a single predicate adjective[45] or by making the god the subject of a verb expressing a similar idea.[46] A white chalcedony pendant in the archeological museum of Perugia[47] (Figure 2.6) proudly proclaims that "One is the god in heaven, mortal-loving Zeo (= Zeus?), the lord for the ages!"

Although most gems are inscribed with theonyms, also expressed through long formular invocations commonly known as *logoi*,[48] the inscriptions often contain elements taken from the oral performance that surrounds the ritual. Such are essentially prayers, commands, incantations (which may include references to the amulet's purpose), and short narrative stories (which may include literary quotations).

If we attempt to categorize the speech acts found on gemstone inscriptions, it will be most useful to draw on the hermeneutic models which C. A. Faraone and A. Kropp, basing on John Searle's speech acts theory,[49] have proposed in their studies on curse tablets.[50] In fact, the starting point for the application of a pragma-linguistic approach to the study of magical texts can be found in

Christopher Faraone's *The Agonistic Context of Early Greek Binding Spells.*[51] Moving from the analytical categories formulated by E. Kagarow[52] and focusing on the performative value of verbs implying the idea of binding, Faraone identifies a new pragmatic taxonomy of archaic Greek καταδεσμοί, clearly elaborated on the basis of the illocutionary force of the sentences. He recognizes a "direct binding formula," expressed by a "performative utterance," which is exactly the concept of performative sentence as enunciated by Searle and Vanderveken.[53] He then distinguishes a "prayer formula," where "Gods or demons are urged by a second person imperative,"[54] and a "wish formula,"[55] where the victim is the subject of a third-person optative. Finally, he isolates a fourth category called "*similia similibus* formula," whose main feature is a "persuasive analogy," usually expressed by a similitude, "in which the binding is accomplished by a wish that the victim become similar to something to which he or she is manifestly dissimilar."

Faraone's taxonomy seems to be taken as a basis for the study of Roman *defixiones* provided by Amina Kropp's *Magische Sprachverwendug in vulgärlateinischen Fluchtafeln* (*defixiones*).[56] The strict application of the speech act theory to this kind of ritual texts, explicitly stated by the scholar herself, has been extremely useful in a context where the conditions of felicity, as they were outlined by Austin,[57] are fully achieved and even emphasized.

In Kropp's classification, which takes into account both the structure of the utterance and the tipology of the verbal forms, Faraone's definition of "direct formula" is extended to a more general category, called "manipulation formula."[58] This includes all utterances based on the first-person singular, in the present tense of the indicative mood, of some particular *verba defigendi*[59] implying the idea of a magical manipulation. There is then a "committal formula"[60] which is used for "offering" the victims to the gods of the underworld, either via manipulation verbs or through verbs with the sense of giving:[61] in any case, the structure of the utterance can be related to a performative sentence. The third category, called "request formula,"[62] puts together Faraone's definitions of "prayer" and "wish formula," which are clearly correlated by the presence of a request (praise, order, command) made to an agent to accomplish the magical action. Within this category, Kropp also includes the old *similia similibus* formula which is, in this view, a preliminary statement (equivalent to the poetic similitude) introducing the request. Indeed, such formulas usually do not address gods or demons and seem to be based on a persuasive analogy: they should therefore remain separated, although they can be paralleled to the genre of the *historiola*,[63] a particular kind of speech act that individuates in the past (or in the present) a normative parallel for the hoped-for future.[64]

This classification, which seems to be an evolution of Faraone's model, has the advantage of considering curse texts as pure linguistic products: the second capital element, which is even more interesting from a historical point of view, is the definition of magical formulas as speech acts with a special value (illocutionary force) given by the ritual praxis that usually surrounds the verbal action. In order to achieve further results, this model might be combined with the taxonomy formulated by Paolo Poccetti[65] in a well-known essay on the use of language in magical rituals, which is also based on the theory proposed by Austin and Searle.

Poccetti's taxonomy is focused exclusively on the structure of utterances and seems to anticipate Kropp's system: according to the scholar, if we examine the utterances of magical texts in the light of Austin's theory, we will find that they can be classified into the following main categories:

A. Performative utterances (*enunciati performativi*), consisting of the use in the first-person present tense of the indicative mood of performative verbs. Some of these verbs are not true performatives, but they act as such in a specific extra-linguistic context. This category seems to include Faraone's concept of "direct formula" as well as Kropp's "manipulation" and "committal" formulas, and even Kropp's "curse formula," which does not differ in structure from other explicit performatives.
B. Constative utterances (*enunciati constatativi*) which express the same action in the third person (i.e., X curses, binds, and nails down). This category, absent in the other taxonomies, appears to be very useful as it evidences a different communicative setting.
C. Optative-imperative utterances (*enunciati desiderativo-iussivi*) where an external agent is invoked and urged to perform the magical action. This category operates exactly like Kropp's "request formula."

Poccetti's tripartite scheme is doubtlessly helpful for its intrinsic linearity and allows to simplify the previous models, while including all kinds of contaminations which are possible, at every level, among the different types of utterance. This hermeneutic instrument, which can be applied in general to the analysis of religious formulas (prayers, oaths, etc.), can be easily extended also to the formulaic typologies (e.g., exorcistic rituals) attested in the magical papyri, which leave their echo in the text of spells written on metal phylacteries, magical gems, wooden amulets, and other magical objects. With the help of such categories, magical rituals regain their ancient pragmatic dimension, which is strongly evident in ancient terminology,[66] and they can be easily defined as the strict combination of a speech act and an extra-linguistic action that provides the conditions for the felicity of the utterance.

Further investigation on the speech acts is provided again by Faraone,[67] who proposes a refined taxonomy based on the communication setting rather than on the intrinsic nature of the main utterance: this leads the scholar to distinguish among prayers, addressing divinities, incantations, mostly addressed to a target without any cogent reference to a deity, exorcisms, aiming at commanding demons by placing them under oath or recurring to higher divine authorities, and *historiolae* ("little stories"), a sort of brief narratives providing, by persuasive analogy, a model for the magical action sought by the performer. The latter two typologies are classified as "framing speech acts"[68] since they can incorporate the former ones in complex structures involving the role of a higher superhuman power.

Indeed, if we combine these models and apply them to the corpus of our inscribed gemstones, we will see that the so-called performative utterances, or direct performatives,[69] are typical of exorcistic amulets, and this is obviously due to the nature itself of the ritual, which often implies the belief of a direct influence of the mage on the demonic entity he wishes to banish. In fact, many such amulets bear the explicit phrase ἐξορκίζω σε ("I adjure you"), while a carnelian amulet in Berlin[70] (Figure 2.7) bears the following text:

> [. . . *voces magicae*], Aba Thigaor, (I beg) forgiveness . . . [*voces*] I summon you, you that enlighten the entire world and light up all is under the motion of the Heavens . . . [*voces*], I adjure you, I, Arathor. This is the seal itself, the one that has always been inscribed.[71]

Figure 2.7 Carnelian amulet showing a series of magical symbols encircled by an *ouroborus* snake. Staatliche Museen zu Berlin, Ägyptisches Museum und Papyrussammlung (inv. no. 9871). Photo: Sandra Steiß. Used with permission.

This thirteen-line inscription, placed on the back of a small carnelian measuring only 22 × 18 × 3.5 mm, is extremely significant, since it contains the essential features of a typical exorcistic prayer: these are a complex series of non-Hellenic theonyms, followed by an invocation ending with a final command. At the end, the writer refers to the authority of an archetype, seen as a kind of guarantor of human utterance. Such recourse to a higher divine hierarchy, which in a threatening manner serves to strengthen the performer's request, is recognized by Faraone as a distinctive feature of this genre, which is able to combine the two simple speech acts of a prayer and an incantation.[72] A completely inscribed amulet from Constantinople[73] contains a more complex textual structure. The demon is first addressed in his own language through a long series of magical names: then follows an invocation to the great God, which alternates first-person performative sentences with third-person constative utterances, as well as incorporating the commands for the demon to stand apart.

> I invoke you, god, great Barbath Iēaōth Sabaōth, god seated upon the mountain of violence, god seated above the bramble, god seated on the Cherubi(m). He is the all-powerful one. He addresses you [. . .] every unfortunate encounter, Maramarauōth Iēaōth. This spell is from Sabaōth Adonai. Do not come near, because (the owner) belongs to the Lord God of Israel. Akrammachamarei Brasau Abrablain. I invoke you god, Enathiaō Phabathallon Bablaia Iaō Thalach Erou Rōsar Bōs Thouth. Do not disobey the name of god! (Transl. J. G. Gager).[74]

Although direct performatives are recurrent on exorcistic amulets, magical gems show a clear prevalence of incantations and prayers, usually expressed through request formulas, which in turn are most commonly uttered with imperatives.[75]

More frequently, gods or demons are invoked or urged for protection, cure, or the granting of benefits by a second-person imperative (Figure 2.8)—for example, βοήθ(ε)ι / help!,[76] φύλαξον *vel similia* / protect!,[77] σῷζε / save!,[78] δὸς χάριν / give charm[79]—although third-person imperatives are also attested: in fact, a gem copied in Beirut and published by Mouterde in 1930 bears the inscription κατεχέσθω πᾶς θυμὸς πρὸς ἐμὲ Κασσισιανόν ("Let all anger towards me, Cassisianus, be restrained!").[80]

Second-person commands are also present in incantations which, unlike prayers, contain little or no reference to the divine and are generally sung toward a target that requires some magical action, believing that they would work automatically in the same way of the persuasive images they accompany. It is important here to distinguish, as proposed by Faraone and Poccetti, between

Figure 2.8 Hematite inscribed amulet bearing the prayer: "Orôreiouth, s[ave] Zenobia whom Domitia bore." Perugia, Museo Archeologico Nazionale dell'Umbria (inv. no. 1746). Photo: Paolo Vitellozzi. Used with permission.

simple request formulas using imperatives and the so-called "wish formulas," where the target is the subject of a third-person optative.[81]

It is noteworthy that the direct performative sentences are mainly used in exorcistic formulaic phrases, where the receiver of the inscribed message is a demon. In all the other circumstances, commands or prayers are widely preferred, and this should warn us once again to go beyond the traditional dichotomy between magic and religion, which seems to be largely a product of our modern thought rather than a matter of fact. Indeed, several amulets are inscribed with brief prayer texts,[82] many of which show the canonical tripartite arrangement of Greek cletic hymns: *apostrophe* (or invocation), *argumentum* (or *pars epica*), and request (or *preces*).

A green jasper in the Ashmolean Museum of Oxford[83] appears to be extremely significant in this sense not only for its textual content but also for the disposition of the written words on the stone's surface. In fact, while its obverse is entirely dedicated to images, showing a complex motif centered on the mummy of a falcon-headed Osiris, its reverse is occupied by the magical palindrome αβλαναθαναλβα, often associated with solar deities and therefore perfectly representing the divine essence of the god: a short prayer is enclosed within the narrow bevel of the stone and continued on the reverse for mere reasons of space. This seems to show that prayers, once just pronounced aloud toward the image of a god, have now gained their own space as a written text, but this presence tries initially not to invade the space dedicated to the god's nature, either in form of image or symbolized in its verbal inner essence.

The prayer starts with a long sequence of magical names,[84] which, as explained by Fritz Graf,[85] can be considered as an equivalent of the classic *pars epica*, since the correct pronunciation of those words by the performer aims at obtaining the god's favor by demonstrating a perfect knowledge of his names. There follows the final request (*prex*), which also includes an extremely concise *apostrophe* in the vocative case:

> δός μοι χάριν Διονυσιάτι κύριε θεὲ ἤδη πρὸς πάντ{ε}<α>ς. "Grant me, Dionysias, favor in the sight of all. O lord God, quickly." (Transl. C. Bonner)

We are then, in front of a lettered amulet in which the written words not only enhance the persuasive power of an image but are also thought to define the power of the magical object (the engraved gemstone): in fact, while the two faces of the amulet are conceived as complementary parts of a hypothetic "One" made of visual appearance and verbal essence, the written prayer seems to orbit around this core whose power can be finally unleashed by uttering the inscribed words running around as a circle.

The idea that words are able to release the magical force of the natural medium through the activation of a persuasive image is also evident in those inscriptions which seem to be the verbal counterpart of the narrative scene engraved on the stone. In fact, it is not unfrequent to find incantations (Grk. *epôidai*) in the form of third-person sentences, with the represented god as main character, as we can see for the previously mentioned Paris jasper with Hercules strangling the Nemean lion, or a famous St. Petersburg nicolo[86] (Figure 2.9) showing a flying Perseus holding the severed head of Medusa and accompanied by the famous formula: "Flee gout, Perseus seizes you!"[87] This genre of speech acts can be included in Poccetti's classification under the definition of constative utterances and should be distinguished as they evidence a communication setting in which the magical action is said to be performed by an external agent that can even be identified as the image itself.

Some reduced forms of incantations can be found on amulets bearing mottoes, short phrases, or single words that seem to add comment on the represented motif, as if they would increase the power of the image through an incisive catchphrase that seems to be addressed to the vanquished danger symbolized by one of the figures. In this case, the speech act that serves to activate the power of the amulet is not self-referential but requires necessarily the presence of an

Figure 2.9 Sardonyx amulet showing a flying Perseus. St. Petersburg, The State Hermitage Museum, Inv. no. Ж-1517 (GR-21714). Used with permission.

image, and this is proof that the persuasive efficacy of such imageries was fully understood by the user. This is evident in a group of amulets showing a bound, naked Psyche (or Aphrodite) accompanied by the word δικαίως ("rightly!"), which clearly refers to the love attraction granted by the amulet: a green jasper in Paris, showing Aphrodite with her hands behind her back tied with a chain held by Ares explicitly reads: δικαίως δέδεσαι ("You were rightly bound!").[88] A chalcedony in the Bibliothèque Nationale of Paris shows instead the grotesque personification of envy attacked by a snake, a bird and a scorpion: the scene is accompanied by the phrase "Bad luck to you, Phthonos!"[89]

A mottled jasper formerly in the Sossidi collection[90] shows a cruel scene where a long-haired female victim is suspended by her hands from a ring, being tortured by a bow-bearing Eros, while a winged lion burns her with a torch and an eagle feeds on her liver. The inscribed reverse tells of the anger of a desperate lover devoured by his passion with the words:

> I am Blarthar Arachtha. Burn with fire the woman who is associating [with me?] as would four-fold Iaô!'[91]; (or "as Arbathairas").[92]

In all the typologies mentioned, the role of speaker is played by the performer, but in some other gems the image itself seems to play the role. On a British Museum jasper,[93] the mummy of Osiris is flanked by the words ἐγὼ ὁ ὤν ("I am the Existing One"), while two hematite amulets against sciatica in the Bibliothèque Nationale of Paris,[94] showing the old Egyptian motif of a reaper, bear on the reverse: ἐργάζομ{ε}<αι> κ{ε}<αι> οὐ πονῶ ("I work and do not toil"). In the latter case the sentence is probably imagined to be said by the reaper, but could well have been pronounced by the wearers, and maybe even used as a shorthand for customers and gem-makers to distinguish the function of the amulet.[95]

In fact, together with the scribalization of the oral performance, also the context gradually enters the small space of the amulet; therefore, many gems clearly indicate their purpose, either as a cure for diseases, or against demons and nightmares.[96] A black chalcedony from Perugia (Figure 2.10)[97] appears to be extremely interesting in this respect. In fact, the sequence of symbols engraved on its obverse is very similar to that reported in the Great Magical Papyrus of Paris[98] for a phylactery against nightmares, and the inscription on the bevel clearly indicates its function: πρóc δέμονα κέ φόβουc ("against a demon and fears"). Moreover, there is an *amen* (Grk. ἀμὴν) which is not to be imagined as spoken by the performer, but rather directly from the figure of Hermanubis in the right-hand side of the *ouroboros* circle, just like a speech bubble in modern comics. This scene is indeed quite rare and it indicates a further evolution of the

Figure 2.10 Black chalcedony amulet showing Hermanubis and the dead Osiris. Perugia, Museo Archeologico Nazionale dell'Umbria (inv. no. 1733). Photo: Paolo Vitellozzi. Used with permission.

use of writing, which does not merely improve the image, but rather becomes instrumental to the narration.

The idea of language as an action rather than a mere description of reality also serves to explain the presence of literary quotations, such as Homeric verses[99] or phrases inspired by the Gospel,[100] the sense of which was thought to change reality by providing a normative model for the expected magical action. This use of passages of poetry goes back to the Mesopotamian tradition, where short forms of popular poetry were used to embed simple prayers or charms within a narration able to provide these speech acts with a history explaining their origin. There is in fact evidence that snippets of the poem of Erra were placed in Neo-Assyrian houses as amulets against plague.[101]

This is in fact the principle of the *historiolae* ("little stories") that we read on many papyrus amulets; such short folktales, which do not address gods or demons, but rather narrate an action of one or more deities in order to provide a model for the hoped-for result, seem to operate according to the same persuasive analogy that we find in the well-known *similia similibus* formulas. Therefore, unlike the previously mentioned typologies, these spells do not explicitly expect

Figure 2.11 Jasper amulet showing a mummy surrounded by an inscription. London, British Museum, inv. no. G 241 (EA 56241). Image licensed by the Trustees of the British Museum.

the divine entities to react to the written words but are rather an equivalent of the *pars epica* of traditional prayers.

The previously mentioned British Museum jasper showing a mummy (Figure 2.11), which was probably conceived as a charm to lull to sleep an irritable child,[102] bears, for example, a long inscription[103] that correlates a present-tense *historiola* referring to the young Memnon and the amulet's user, thus demonstrating the efficacy of such correlations.

As well demonstrated by the scholars, the different speech acts employed by our gem-amulets to achieve their performative goals were not used separately by the scribes, but rather combined in multiple ways, thus creating a full repertoire of speech acts that was available on the occasion for their better paying customers.

3. Words as Images

This brief survey shows that the ritual surrounding stone amulets gradually enters the gem themselves in the form of written text as far as scribalization grows throughout society. This is also valid for those paralinguistic elements (vowel sequences, onomatopoeic words, magical hisses,[104] mouth pops, etc.) that are conceived, as exhaustively explained by Patricia Cox Miller,[105] as an attempt to destructure language in order to reach the ultimate linguistic essence of the metaphysical world. In fact, the neo-platonic philosophers, basing on what the *Cratylus*[106] says on the nature of language, argued that words contained part of the essence of things; therefore, manipulating the minimal signs of language, namely the alphabet, the makers of our amulets truly believed that they could handle the original power of creation. In this way, the alphabetical combinations of writing were thought to break the normal rules of language revealing the authentic images (*eidola*) of the gods, thus carrying forward the linguistic sensibility of the archaic shamanistic tradition on a new ground.

This ideological background leads us to explain a further step in the evolution of textual amulets, that is, when writing serves not only to fix the spoken word, but it is in itself seen as an image and object, and as such it is treated by the performers to achieve their goals.

Once again, the exorcistic amulets (see Figure 2.4), being a product of the Hebraic tradition, which poses in language rather than in images the essence of divinity, provide us with precious evidence. In fact, the design of many of these amulets, with the *ouroboros* snake that separates the symbols in the center from those near the edge, operates a metaphoric division between light and darkness, good and evil.[107]

In fact, the center of these amulets is normally occupied by the ineffable name of the supreme god, expressed with the iconic writing of magical *charaktêres*. On these magical symbols much is yet to be said, and seminal results are expected from the scholars, but we may already take as a fact that these signs, which imitate the oldest forms of pre-alphabetic writing and on which mages and astrologers made complex speculations, tentatively go back to the authentic primitive sense of writing, which was lost with the invention of the alphabet, that is expressing in one sign the inner essence of that "celestial writing" so important in the neo-platonic thought. Good evidence of this is furnished by a famous green jasper in Berlin (Figure 2.12),[108] showing on its obverse a scarab encircled by an ouroboros snake, while its reverse is inscribed with the well-known *Iarbatha*-logos:[109] this amulet seems to closely resemble that described by a Greek papyrus in Leiden,[110] where the same image must be associated with a sacred name written "in hieroglyphs, as the prophets pronounce it."

It seems also clear that not only the form and meaning of the inscribed message are important in the creation of magical gems, but also the position of the text and its graphic features are expression of a speech act that makes the amulet work. This is evident, besides the many injunctions in the papyri to write these names in the right position, in those figures inscribed with magical names in the various parts of the body, probably following the melothesic doctrines of ancient astrology.

Figure 2.12 Green jasper amulet showing a scarab encircled by an *ouroborus* snake. Staatliche Museen zu Berlin, Ägyptisches Museum und Papyrussammlung (inv. no. 9876). Photo: Sandra Steiß. Used with permission.

The manipulation of writing for magical purposes reaches its top in those visual designs that Faraone calls "vanishing acts."[111] Dwindling words arranged in triangles, or heart-shaped texts, or even palindromes are straightforward illustrations of the process of *deletio morbi* and serve to annihilate the demons that cause diseases, such as bleeding or fever. A perfect example of this is provided by an agate lentoid in the Getty Museum[112] (Figure 2.13) bearing on one side the famous *ablanathanalba* palindrome arranged in a diminishing wing-shaped calligram, while on the other side a short prayer saying: "Deliver Gaia (or Gaius?) from the fever and the shiverings and from all of her/his headaches."[113] Evidently, in this amulet, the magical palindrome is thought to be an image of the demon causing illness, and therefore dismantling this word one letter at a time, as prescribed by Q. Serenus Sammonicus,[114] means to vanquish the disease.

These techniques, which are borrowed directly from the Greeks by the late Jewish and Aramaic culture, provide significant evidence of a cross-cultural exchange in magical practices. If the examples given show a progressive transformation of a speech act into a graphic one and consequently of writing into image, the inevitable outcome can only be the transformation of the act of writing

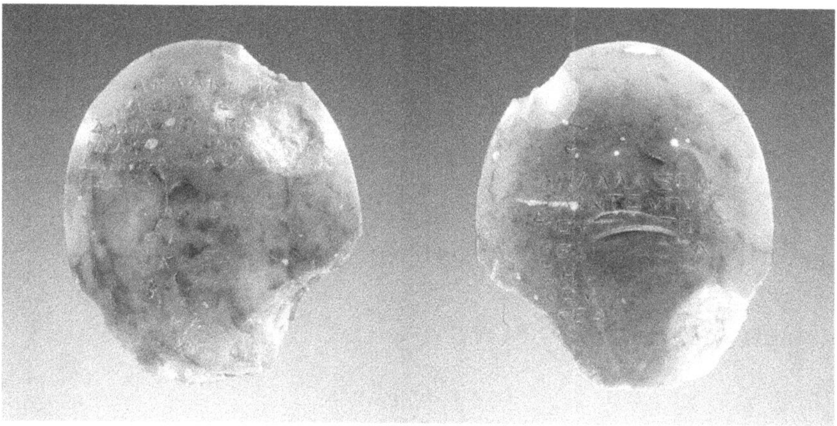

Figure 2.13 Agate inscribed amulet. Malibu, The J. Paul Getty Museum (inv. no. 73. AN.1). Image courtesy of the Getty's Open Content Program.

per se into pure symbol. As a final example, it seems appropriate to mention a British Museum gem totally engraved with pseudo-inscriptions;[115] here, the pure action of writing gains in itself a magical value, without any definite content or further operations. This is probably the ultimate step of the transformation of words into images, and also a way to mislead an illiterate customer.

4. Conclusion

In conclusion, it seems appropriate to support the prevailing theory which considers the so-called magical gems in terms of continuity with a thousand-year tradition of amuletic gemstones. The spoken words, which had always accompanied the rituals, become visible to us in the multicultural context of the Greek *poleis* in the Imperial age, where writing spread across society creating the basis for a deep change, while neo-platonic philosophy made it possible that the diverse religious cultures of the Mediterranean blended and created new concepts. At the same time, the sacred meaning that writing had for the archaic civilizations is now recovered in a new light, as mages and philosophers see the alphabetic symbols from a metaphysical point of view; this is probably another reason why inscribed gems spread across the multicultural clientele who could afford such "enhanced" precious stones.

3

Of Comprehensible and Incomprehensible Inscriptions

Remarks on Some Gems with Multi-headed Gods

Christoffer Theis

1. Introduction

The gems from late antiquity, often referred to as "magical" in literature,[1] are an important source in understanding the reciprocal influence of different cultures on each other, since they show many different Egyptian, Greek, Jewish, Mesopotamian, and/or Near Eastern elements. Based on their assumed period of origin dating between the second and fourth, or even fifth, centuries AD, these artifacts thus form a veritable treasure trove for the tradition—and therefore a *longue durée*—of motifs and symbols from different cultures. Among these gems, some of which have been known for centuries or even millennia, popular figures are displayed, such as Harpokrates,[2] Horus,[3] Chnoubis,[4] the multi-headed Bes,[5] or the goddess Hecate.[6] The number of images on gems shows that even in late antiquity, beings from different cultures enjoyed certain popularity as a motif, even though they were hardly mentioned or depicted in the sources.

Although it remains uncertain whether there are 5,000 or up to 8,000 gems in the various collections, estimates clearly show that it is doubtless a considerable number.[7] Virtually all the gems from collections and museums have been purchased and are therefore of uncertain provenance, although their generally accepted place of origin is Alexandria, the melting pot of the cultures of antiquity.[8] Also, in almost all cases, only an approximate dating can be offered and it is difficult to provide a safe classification of the gems, since hardly any can be assigned to a finding context or century. Some gems are already known from collections created during the seventeenth and eighteenth centuries AD and published in publications by Anne Claude Philippe de Caylus or Jean Chiflet.[9]

In addition to creatures with a natural number of body parts, the gems also show special creations. The focus of the contribution are some remarkable gems with representations that show beings or gods with more than one head or face. A consideration of the phenomenon of multi-headedness in antiquity is so far a desideratum of research. A few representations from the fourth and the transitional period to the third millennium, from Egypt and the Syrian region, show that animals were already depicted in this period as two-headed creatures.[10] Animals with more than one head are tangibly attested over the following millennia. Gods, to whom multiple faces are assigned as a physical characteristic, also appear in the Pyramid Texts. It must be pointed out that a designation with *ḥr.w* "faces" apparently could also be used in Egypt as a designation for multiple heads, as it can be observed, for example, with a snake in the sixth hour of the Amduat (Amd. 458).[11] The name of the reptile with five heads is called *ꜥšꜣ-ḥr.w* "The one with numerous faces," whereby the snake certainly has several faces, but the heads are not explicitly designated in the plural. With other multi-headed beings, the plural or the dual of *dp* is called "head" in Egyptian, as in a gloss to the seventeenth chapter of the Book of the Dead or at the eleventh hour of the Amduat (Amd. 759).[12] The representations of gems can be traced, as a direct parallel or in part, to earlier developments in Egypt. For some creatures, however, a new creation can also be plausible. Some of the gems with multi-headed creatures have also been inscribed and therefore the combination of image and writing can be examined together. Since gems were worn on the body or on clothing as an amulet, the inscriptions, as well as the depiction, are definitely connected with the wearer, thus posing questions about their material and meaning. Although no statement can be made about "real efficacy," the purpose and intention of the representation, that is to say what function was exercised by the god or by a being with several heads or faces in the past, can be based on tradition and/or epigraphy, thus offering a more precise classification.

As this approach can be applied to all material collections in the research of a specific corpus, a claim of completeness can never be guaranteed. There are hundreds of catalogs, collection descriptions, and similar publications that unfortunately are not accessible.[13] Hence, only a part of the ongoing research can be offered.

2. Examples of Gems with Multi-headed Beings

The gems featuring in this enquiry come from several collections and show clear ancient Egyptian influences, since the images directly match or can be traced back to an older source. Moreover, the gems should be inscribed in order to be able to provide answers to the questions mentioned earlier. It should be noted, however, that these gems bear Greek inscriptions, clearly illustrating the previously mentioned mix of cultures. This study does not include representations of the multi-headed Bes, as this being shown on dozens of gems, since these are treated in another comprehensive research work.[14] The results of this work, however, can be summarized and associated with the items discussed here. Also many well-known gems[15] with multi-headed gods from other cultures, such as Hecate, are not taken into account, since investigation should be limited to an Egyptian tradition.[16] An example is a gem at the British Museum, London, Inv. G 472 (EA 56472).[17] This medallion was made of lapis lazuli and measures 2.8 × 3 × 0.3 cm. It depicts a three-headed creature on a *tabula ansata*.

It must be said that inscriptions on gems with multi-headed creatures are not particularly meaningful when compared to those accompanying other depictions such as gods or animals. Unfortunately, modern research is trying to interpret these inscriptions into "special" meanings or to refer to a specific type of being for all members of this genus. However, it can be argued that this approach cannot be maintained for the selected examples of multi-headed beings.

2.1 Anthropomorphic Gods

A gem with a double-headed creature is Ann Arbor, Michigan, Kelsey Museum of Archaeology, 26059 (Figure 3.1).[18] The dating is uncertain as no find context is known. The gem is 2.4 × 1.9 × 0.3 cm in size, is made of hematite, and is very well preserved except for minor cracks on its sides. The figure is a two-headed deity resembling a *Dikephalos diauchenos*.[19] The body is shown frontally, the legs turned to the right. On the left shoulder is unmistakably the head of an ibis wearing the *ꜣtf*-crown. The interpretation of the head on the right is not entirely clear, it could be a bearded head of a snake wearing a red crown, or there could be depicted a second ibis head. The human torso is depicted without any special attributes. The left arm hangs parallel to the body; in the hand, the creature holds an *ꜥnḫ*-sign. The right arm is stretched out at the level of the elbow; in the hand, there is a *wꜣś*-scepter. The creature is dressed in a short apron and stands on a sun disk resting on the back of a crocodile.

A comparable depiction of a two-headed god (Amd. 892) can already be found in the twelfth hour of the Amduat (Figure 3.2), which dates back to the fifteenth century BC. This being is also represented on coffins[20] and shows two bird heads on a human body. It is named in the Amduat as *Nḥỉ* "supplicant."[21]

Figure 3.1 Ann Arbor, Michigan, Kelsey Museum of Archaeology, 26059. Drawing by Rebekka-M. Müller after Bonner 1950, 297, pl. 13 (no. 264).

Comparable representations were made during the Third Intermediate Period on coffins[22] and during the late period, as is the case with a god with two bird heads, in situ in the temple of Hibis, oasis Charga.[23] The depiction of a two-headed god on this particular gem (and in comparison to the god *Nḥỉ* in the Amduat) can be seen as the second decan of Virgo, as it was already pointed out by Joachim F. Quack.[24]

The inscription on the gem can be read as ΑΡΠΟΝΧΝΟΥΦ ΙΒΡΙ[ΝΤΑ] ΤΗΝϢΦ ΙΕΡΜΙΘΟΥΘ,[25] and with that, a variant of the αρπονχνουφι βριντατηνωφρι-formula was written.[26] This formula was once interpreted as bearing the names of the two Egyptian gods, Horus and Khnum,[27] although Dimitri Meeks was able to show that this is probably Egyptian *Ḥr pꜣ ỉwn Knm.t* "Horus, the pillar of *Knm.t*."[28] A further, longer inscription in nine lines was added on the back of the gem:

1 ΙΑΕϢΒΑΦ//
2 ΡΕΝΕΜΟΥΝ//
3 ΟΘΙΛΑΡΙΚΡΙΦ//
4 ΙΑΕΥΕΑΙΦΡΙΚ//

Figure 3.2 Amduat 892. Drawing by Rebekka-M. Müller after Hornung 1963, 192, pl. 12.

5 ΙΡΑΛΙΘΟΝΥΟΜ//
6 ΕΝΕΡΦΑΒωΕΑ//
7 ΙΦΡΙΚΙΡΑΠΕϹ//
8 ΕΠΕϹΕ Χ//
9 ΝΟΥΒΙϹ

It can be seen that until the beginning of the seventh line there is a palindrome that begins and ends with the designation Ἰάω. To this, the following ΦΡΙΚΙΡΑ is to be added in l. 7. This can be found on several other gems,[29] in which there is supposed to be an Egyptian expression, probably connected with a sun deity.[30] However, this interpretation can decidedly be rejected because of more than deviant vocalizations such as the pronunciation of the consonants. However, apart from the name of God, it remains unclear what significance lies hidden here. The following ΠΕϹΕ ΠΕϹΕ is to read as "Digest! Digest!" It concludes with the name of ΧΝΟΥΒΙϹ, before the corresponding symbol in the inscription was attached.

It turns out that the inscription is not related to the scene in any of its parts. Neither is a sun deity depicted, as it is shown with ram's heads as shown in

Figure 3. Also, it is not a representation of the god Horus, whose name appears in the αρπονχνουφι-formula. Nor it is a representation of Chnumis, which can indeed be mapped in various ways, but it is essentially a snake, which does not have multiple heads except for one document. At least the part of the inscription ⲠⲈⲤⲤⲈ ⲠⲈⲤⲤⲈ "Digest! Digest!" shows a distinct purpose. Several-headed birds are already known from the first dynasty with the testimony of Claudius Aelianus, *De natura animalium* XI, 40, since according to him at that time a bird with four heads and a crane with two heads had been born.[31]

The gem Kassel, Staatliche Kunstsammlung, 176 (Figure 3.3),[32] which could be an antique or a modern imitation,[33] measures 1.85 × 1.50 × 0.2 cm and is made from sard. A figure with two heads and four wings is shown. The heads, which are supposed to be human by design, are directed each to one side and emerge from a single neck. The body is that of a human, from whose upper body emerges a pair of double wings. Both arms are stretched out at the level of the elbows and each holds a scepter. The feet could still show traces of jackal ears, but this remains unclear due to the rough workmanship. Below the hips, the tail of a scorpion emerges. All of these attributes identify the being as related to multi-headed Bes-figures. On the left side of the creature are still ± 6 characters to recognize, but

Figure 3.3 Gem Kassel, Staatliche Kunstsammlung, 176. Drawing by Rebekka-M. Müller after Mastrocinque 2003, 240 (no. 147) and Zazoff 1970, 242, pl. 109.

Figure 3.4 Gem Cambridge, MA, 2012.1.144. Drawing by Rebekka-M. Müller after Michel 2004, 332, pl. 59, 2.

they are not readable. The inscription on the back has been inscribed in three circles: ΡΡ·ΒΔΗΥΟΝΓΡΧΜ[···]//ΝΕΛΡΧΙΡΕΙCΞΞΙΝΦ//ΛΛΝΛ//[·] Ι[·]. An interpretation cannot be given for this text.

A unique presentation is depicted on the gem Cambridge, 2012.1.144 (Figure 3.4),[34] which is made of reddish-brown jasper. Pictured is an anthropomorphic deity with seven serpents as heads. The outermost snakes sit on its shoulders and arms, as there is not enough room on the neck. The human upper body has no special attributes. The right arm is stretched forward and holds probably a poorly represented *wꜣś*-scepter; the left arm holds a flagellum. The creature is perched on a lion walking to the right. It is surrounded by two moon crescents and a star appears above the head(s). In front of the lion, two illegible symbols were added with a few lines.

1 ΒΑΙΝ//
2 ΧωωωΧ//
3 ΑΚΥΑC//
4 ΛΞΚΚΚ//
5 ΧΜΜΚ

In lines 1 and 2 we can read Βαϊνχωωωχ, while in the following ones, a barely legible Ἀβρασάξ should be recognizable.

The multi-headed snake is a graphic rendition of the most popular animal in the Ancient Near East, which was provided with several heads and has survived in this form up to the Coptic period.[35] The depiction belongs to a long tradition of anthropomorphic snake beings, such as the four snake-headed one in the 69th Scene of the Book of the Gates at the eleventh hour, already present in the New Kingdom (where the beings are referred to as *ʾInṯ.ȉw*[36]) or the three snake-headed one on the Metternichstelae, today New York, MMA, 50.85.[37] The representation on the gem reminds directly of *Pistis Sophia* 126.[38] Here, Jesus teaches Mary about the darkness, which is represented as a serpent (ⲇⲣⲁⲕⲱⲛ).[39] In this darkness are twelve penalty rooms and before each is an Ἄρχων (ⲁⲣⲭⲱⲛ). In the tenth room are several beings (ⲟⲩⲙⲏⲏϣⲉ ⲛ̄ⲁⲣⲭⲱⲛ) with the name Ⲍⲁⲣⲙⲁⲣⲱⲭ, each having seven snake heads (ⲥⲁϣϥⲉ ⲛ̄ⲁⲡⲉ ⲛ̄ⲇⲣⲁⲕⲱⲛ). In the eleventh room, the beings named Ⲣⲱⲭⲁⲣ have seven cat heads each (ⲥⲁϣϥⲉ ⲛ̄ⲁⲡⲉ ⲛ̄ϩⲁ ⲛ̄ⲉⲙⲟⲩ), while in the twelfth room, each has the name, ⲭⲣⲏⲙⲁⲱⲣ and seven dog heads (ⲥⲁϣϥⲉ ⲛ̄ⲁⲡⲉ ⲛ̄ϩⲁ ⲛ̄ⲟⲩϩⲟⲣ).

The small object London, BM, G 191 (EA 56191) is made from slightly polished hematite, measures 2.3 × 1.9 × 0.35 cm (Figure 3.5), and is dated to the third century AD;[40] however, but due to the lack of parallels, the date cannot be considered certain. The standing composite figure in frontal view has three heads on its shoulders in the order *Trikephalos triauchenos*, so each of the heads is depicted on a separate neck. In the middle there is the head of a hawk with upright feathers; on the right shoulder, the head of a jackal with two ears and on the left shoulder the head of an ibis. The body is unnaturally broad, wrapped in mummy bandages open at the neck. Both arms are bent in front of the chest. The body is wrapped in bandages down to the knees, leaving two bare human legs. From the shoulders and the thighs, a short wing emerges on each side, whereby the feathers are indicated only by a few lines. The figure pictured here is consistent with the three-headed wax figure (ἤτω δὲ τρικέφαλος) that has to be shaped according to the instructions of a protective spell in Pap. Paris, Bibl. Nat., suppl. gr. 574, Z. 3125–71.[41] The papyrus is commonly dated to the fourth century AD,[42] and can contribute to the dating of the gem. The heads are those of a sparrowhawk in the middle (ἡ μέση κεφαλὴ ἤτω ἱέρακος πελαγίου), of an ibis on the left (ἡ δὲ ἀριστερὰ ἴβεως), and of a cynocephalus on the right (ἡ δὲ δεξιὰ κυνοκεφάλου).[43] The figure should be dressed like Osiris (αὐτὸς δὲ ἔστω περιεσταλμένος ὡς Ὄσιρις). The creatures should each hold objects in their hands: the sparrowhawk a diadem of Horus (βασίλειον Ὥρου), the

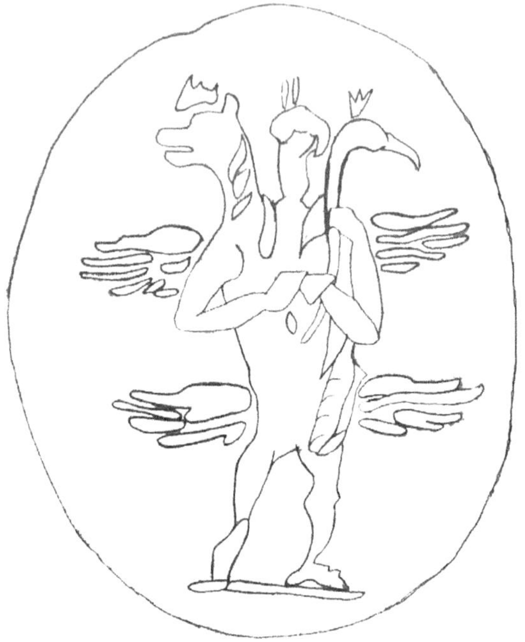

Figure 3.5 London, British Museum, G 191 (EA 56191). Drawing by Rebekka-M. Müller after Michel 2001, 110sq. (no. 173).

cynocephalus a diadem of Hermanubis (βασίλειον Ἑρμανούβιδος), and the ibis a diadem of Isis (βασίλειον Ἴσιδος), but apparently these features are not represented on the gem.

On the back of the gem, we can read the inscription **ΒΙΧⲰ// ΒΙΧⲰ ΒΕ// Υ ΒΕΥ ΧⲰΒ//Ι ΧⲰΒΙ ΒΕ//Υ ⲤΟΥΜⲀⲢΤⲀ**. The initial words **ΒΙΧⲰ ΒΙΧⲰ** can be equated with Egyptian *bỉk ꜥꜣ bỉk ꜥꜣ* "great hawk, great hawk"[44] and **ⲤΟΥΜⲀⲢΤⲀ**, as mentioned earlier in literature, with Semitic *šmr* "Protect." A translation of **ΒΕΥ** with Egyptian *bꜣ* seems rather unlikely because the word ⲃⲁⲓ is still preserved in Coptic.[45] With **ΧⲰΒΙ**, we can see *hbỉ* "Ibis," which still exists in Coptic with ϩⲓⲃⲱⲓ. To see a connection between **ΧⲰΒΙ, ΒΙΧΥΧ** "ram of darkness" and **ΧⲰΧΙ** "darkness" seems quite far-fetched. The hawk and the ibis are at least two of the three heads of the figure mentioned in papyrus; but to what extent does the head of a jackal match the papyrus description is a question that must remain open.

A comparable representation comes from the late Egyptian period on the Stele Harer Family Trust Collection, No. 111 (Figure 3.6).[46] This object, which measures 6.2 cm and is made of serpentine, shows a deity which, just like the composite figure on the gem, has three heads, each on its own neck, a human

Figure 3.6 Stelae Harer Family Trust Collection, no. 111. Drawing by Rebekka-M. Müller after Scott 1992, 160sq. (no. 111).

body, and four wings. The main head here is that of a jackal; on the right side there is the head of a bull, while the one on the left shoulder is unfortunately not visible. There are various representations of this Egyptian motif, none of which directly shows the three heads of the gems, but makes it clear that a three-headed winged creature is well known in this cultural area.

2.2 Animal Body

The god *Twtw* is well known from ancient Egyptian times and is also depicted on a gem.[47] Unfortunately, the artifact is only attested by a 1750 drawing and therefore the following description remains uncertain accordingly. It may date from the time of Emperor Hadrian (AD 117–38), but unfortunately, we cannot pinpoint where it is today. The gem seems to be relatively well preserved and is said to have been made of onyx. The 1750 publication makes it clear that these gems must have found their way to Europe very early.

Twtw was portrayed as a walking sphinx with two heads in the shape of a *Dikephalos*. The body is shown in side view; *Twtw* wears a stylized *ꜣtf*-crown on his head. The frontal head is that of a hawk, while a crocodile's head protrudes from the chest, with probably a human body hanging from it. The body is that of a lion, with its tail shaped like a snake. Under the paws there is another snake. The re-drawing shows a vowel sequence ΑΕѠΕѠ // ΗΑѠΑ. Comparable two-headed figures are found in many documents from the Pharaonic and Greek Egypt; in most of them the main face is that of a lion or of a human.[48]

Another creature with the body of an animal and multiple faces is depicted on Exeter, RAMM, Inv. 5/1946,355.[49] The gem is made of obsidian and is 1.8 × 1.35 × 0.3 cm long. In literature it is dated to the third century AD. On the back, we can see Anubis surrounded by an equally illegible inscription. A snake with two faces in the order *Diprosopos* is depicted. Around the snake, there is a short partially readable inscription of the word "ΝΕΙΚΗ," as well as following Χ, as well as different *charactêres* were attached. For the interpretation of ΝΕΙΚΗ, Sheila Hoey Middleton suggested various possibilities, such as a reading as Greek νίκη "victory" or an abbreviation for νεικαροπληζ,[50] the latter being associated with a solar aspect by Campbell Bonner.[51] Comparable representations from Egypt, for example, a snake with two faces, exist since the New Kingdom. Thus, in the fourth hour of the Amduat, *Nḥb-kꜣ.w* (Amd. 287) was depicted on top of each other with two serpent heads, which grow out of the body together.[52]

2.3 Osiris with Three Heads

The gem London, British Museum, G 525 (EA 56525) (Figure 3.7) is made of polished obsidian and measures 2.4 × 1.7 × 0.3 cm.[53] Generally, it is dated to the third century AD. The three-headed mummy Osiris is shown in frontal view and crowned with a sun disk on its head and has a human face in which the eyes, nose, and lips are only roughly indicated by notches. On each side of the head, another animal head emerges, which in both cases is that of a bird. The head also seems to be wrapped around the face like the body with mummy bandages, with a few lines on the top. The entire shape is enclosed by a neatly arranged diamond pattern, indicating the mummy bandages. The arms are hidden under the bandages and appear to be crossed on the chest, leaving the hands empty. From the shoulders and the upper body emerges a pair of double wings, the feathers are finely executed by small notches. On the right side of Osiris sits a figure wearing a wig and a crown on its head. This might be a rendition of Isis in the funeral posture.[54]

On the reverse, within an ouroboros, a winged scarab is depicted, surrounded by an inscription with the vowel sequence ΑѠΙΕΗѠΗΥΟΙΗΥ

Figure 3.7 London, British Museum, Inv. G 525 (EA 56525). Drawing by Rebekka-M. Müller after Michel 2001, 109sq. (no. 172).

ⲱⲩⲱⲏⲱⲁⲉⲏⲓⲟⲩⲱ. It seems clear that in this sequence hardly a deeper meaning may be discernible—perhaps the beginning with ⲁⲱⲓ might still be understood as an echo of the frequently mentioned Ἰάω on gems.

For a direct comparison, the statuette of a multi-headed mummy, now Baltimore, Walters Art Gallery, Inv.-No. 57.1437,[55] can be mentioned. This three-dimensional sculpture is only 4.3 × 3.4 × 1.2 cm tall and shows a standing mummy with four wings and nine heads. It is also crowned with the sun disk and has four animal protomes on each side of his head so that a total of nine heads is depicted. At the height of the *ꜣtf*-crown is a small eyelet. Overall, the parallel to the representation of the gem London, British Museum, Inv. G 525 (EA 56525) is more than conspicuous. Unfortunately, the statuette from the Walters Art Gallery does not give a precise date, but some texts show that the idea of a multi-faced Osiris goes back to the Egyptian New Kingdom. Thus, in TT 183, in the tomb of a *Nb-św-mnw* from the time of Ramses II, Osiris was already addressed with the epithet *ꜥšꜣ-ḥr.w* "(One) with numerous faces."[56] Also, the depiction of a two-headed mummy of Osiris on the Aenigmatic wall in the tomb of Ramses IX points in this direction and, at the same time, fits with the name of Osiris as *Nb ḥr.wỉ* "Lord of the Two Faces" appearing on the coffin

Cairo, Aeg. Mus., CG 6001.[57] The epithet *ꜥšꜣ-ḥr.w* for Osiris can be traced to temple texts of the Greco-Roman period, with the largest number of faces for this god in Opet I, 112, 12.[58] Here the god is referred to as the one "seven heads are on him" (*śfḫ.w ḥr.w r=f*).[59]

2.4 The Multi-headed Sun Ram

The plate Paris, Bibliothèque Nationale, 2170 is made of lapis lazuli and is 3.6 × 2.2 cm tall (Figure 3.8).[60] The dating, as well as the original context, is uncertain. A part of the left side is now missing. The representation of the two ram heads on an anthropomorphic upper body is based on the *Dikephalos monauchenos* type, where both ram heads protrude from only one neck. On the two heads is a calyx with five leaves. Especially the horns of the left head are finely modeled. Below the neck is an element that was interpreted as a sequence of seven Γ, as snakes or as streams of blood.[61] On the chest, the creature wears an amulet, which is probably a scarab according to some known parallels. Both arms are stretched forward and meet at the hands in front of the hip, where

Figure 3.8 Paris, Bibliothèque Nationale, 2170. Drawing by Rebekka-M. Müller after Delatte/Derchain 1964, 50sq. (no. 43).

it holds an *sꜣ*-sign. The figure is dressed in a skirt that reaches over the knees and it stands on a ouroboros, where three animals—a salamander, a bird, and perhaps a jackal—can be recognized. The representation of an anthropomorphic god with multiple ram heads is typical in Egypt for the sun ram. It has a long iconographic tradition and the type hardly ever changed.[62] Inscriptions referring to the sun god as a four-faced being have been attested since the Pyramid Texts, and are known up to the Greco-Roman times, as with the description of the god in a hymn from the Persian period in the temple of Hibis.[63]

On both sides, next to the ram heads, the inscription ⲤⲈⲢ//ⲪⲞⲨ//ⲐⲘⲞⲨ//ⲒⲤⲢⲰ is added. This was already read by Bonner as σερφουθ μουϊσρω on Pap. London, BM, Gr. 121 (corresponds to PGM VII, 498) from the third century AD, where this name is that of a god sitting in Pelusium.[64] Bonner, however, wants to identify him with Harpocrates. Furthermore, μουισρω appears in PGM XXXVI, 351 in a list of epithets, such as, for example, Ιάω, Σαβαώθ and Σεμεσιλαμ.[65] The inscription can be split up in three different names, ⲤⲈⲢⲪⲞⲨⲐ, ⲘⲞⲨⲒ, and ⲤⲢⲰ, which can be read as Egyptian *śrp.t mꜣꞽ sꞽw* "Lotus, lion, ram."[66] The epitheton Σεμεσιλαμ is usually explained in Hebrew as "eternal sun," which would be related to the representation, especially if one explains the being as a representation of the sun in its three forms on morning, midday, and evening.

On the back of the plate there is an inscription in eight lines:

1 ⲒⲈⲰⲀⲒⲎ//
2 ⲀⲒⲰⲀⲚⲈⲚ//
3 Ⲁ·ⲎⲀⲎⲒⲀⲒ//
4 ⲀⲒⲀⲒⲎⲞⲚⲈ//
5 ⲰⲀⲒⲒⲈⲈⲨ//
6 ⲀⲰⲘⲈⲎ·//
7 ·ⲒⲀⲰⲀⲒ//
8 ⲦⲒⲦⲞⲨⲎ//

In the inscription'Ιάω can be recognized several times in different combinations, while the rest can be interpreted as vowel sequences. Maybe ⲦⲒⲦⲞⲨⲎ in line 8 can be interpreted as Τιθοής and thus corresponding to the Egyptian *Twtw*?[67]

A depiction of the multi-headed sun ram is also found on New York City, Metropolitan Museum of Art, 41.160.642 (Figure 3.9).[68] The gem measures 1.55 × 1.4 × 0.2 cm, is made of lapis lazuli, and dates back to the third century AD. The reverse was left empty. Unfortunately, almost the entire upper half of the stone is broken off, therefore we can only deduce from parallels that originally there was a sitting figure with four heads. From these parallels, we can infer that these were ram heads protruding in pairs from an elongated neck set in the middle of the shoulders. The human torso was depicted without any special attributes. The left arm is stretched forward and holds an *ꜥnḫ*-sign in the hand. The right arm is stretched out at the level of the elbow and holds in its hand a long rod, which in parallel will be a *wꜣś*-scepter. The figure sits on a small chair. The gem also shows a vowel sequence in the still extant part. Surrounding the figure, the words "[. . .] ΑΥΟΗΩ" on the right and "[. . .] ΩΩΥΑΕ" on the left are still recognizable.

Almost identical in appearance is the depiction of a deity with four ram heads on the gem New York, American Numismatic Society, no. 25 (0000.999.35789; Figure 3.10).[69] This piece is made of hematite and measures 2.6 × 2.1 × 0.4 cm. There is neither dating nor find context in the literature. It lacks almost the entire lower and half of the left side of the back, which are broken off.[70]

The standing deity with four ram heads carries an *ꜣtf*-crown with snakes on both sides very schematically represented. The human upper body is depicted without any special attributes; from about the middle of the thighs, the gem is broken, but we can still see that the creature is clothed with a short apron. The

Figure 3.9 New York, Metropolitan Museum of Art, 41.160.642. Drawing by Rebekka-M. Müller after Bonner 1950, 297 (no. 266).

Figure 3.10 New York, American Numismatic Society, no. 25. Drawing by Rebekka-M. Müller after Bonner 1950, 297 (no. 265) and Michel 2004, pl. 31,1.

right arm is stretched forward at the level of the elbow and holds a *wꜣś*-scepter. The left arm hangs flat on the body and holds an *ʿnḫ*-sign in his hand.

Unfortunately, also in this case the inscription is only partially preserved and can be read as **ΙΑΕΩ ΒΑΦΡΕΝΕΜΟΥΝΟ** [. . .] **ΝΕΡΦΑΒ ΩΕΑΙ**, again recognizing the palindrome beginning and ending with Ἰάω, as on Ann Arbor, Michigan, Kelsey Museum of Archeology, 26059 (Figure 3.1). In this case, the assignment of this short text to the representation of a solar deity would be consistent, as postulated in earlier research.[71] The palindrome is followed by **ΔΟϹ ΜΟ** [**Ι ΧΑΡΙΝ**] "Grant m[e favor]!". This can be seen as an ancient expression of the desire for favor by the wearer. However, **ϹΘΟΜ** [. . .] written on the outer edge remains unclear in its interpretation.

There are various parallels to this type of representation, but they were not given an inscription in antiquity. This is for example the case with the gem Berlin, Aeg. Mus., 16122 (CBd-208), which dates back to the second century BCE,[72] or a gem depicted by Gabra[73] (Figure 3.11). It can be assumed that the representation alone was enough to identify the deity depicted.

The gem Paris, Bibliothèque Nationale, Fr 2896 (Figure 3.12)[74] shows an increase in the number of heads. The piece measures 2.2 × 1.7 cm and is made

Figure 3.11 Gem depicted by Gabra. Drawing by Rebekka-M. Müller after Gabra 1944, 178sq., pl. 15.

of yellow jasper. A dating is unfortunately not specified. Except for the slightly chipped rim, the piece is very well preserved. An anthropomorphic, seated deity is depicted, but in this case, it has six ram heads. These sit on a narrow line representing the neck. The human upper body has no special attributes. Both arms are crossed over on the chest; the right arm holds a *ḥqꜣ*-scepter, the left a *nḫḫ*-scourge. The torso is enveloped in a garment reaching to the thighs and no further details can be recognized. The figure sits on a *gs*-sign, with two scarabs in front of it. If we do not consider them as decorative adornments, they could be read as *tꜣ.wỉ* "both countries." On the back of the gem, the name of an archangel (Μιχαήλ) and that of the third ancestor were used with ΜΙΧΑΗΛ // ΙΑΚⲰΒ.

3. Analysis of the Inscriptions

The time of origin of the gems is to be regarded as a phase of productive handling of the material, with an ancient Egyptian concept extended to many beings. Because of their parallels, the representations of multi-headed deities discussed in this chapter have ancient Egyptian influence and may be considered, in

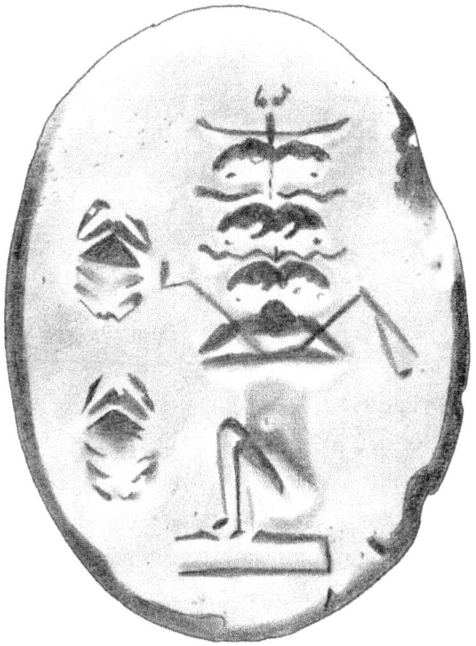

Figure 3.12 Paris, Bibliothèque Nationale, Fr 2896. Drawing by Rebekka-M. Müller after Delatte/Derchain 1964, 172sq. (no. 228) and Mastrocinque 2014, 64 (no. 151).

some cases, as a result of the pictorial rendition of their antecedents, or even be traced back to an older template. Some representations, such as the sun ram, can be traced over several millennia, but are only known from texts of the early Egyptian documents. For others, the rendering may be due to an object or a similar image; however, differences can be observed such as other animal parts. It must be pointed out, however, that today, although certainly far from all sources, multi-headed beings from Egypt are attested and in the future even more finds are to be expected in museums or in Egypt itself, where perhaps even direct parallels may come to light.

But how are the inscriptions related to ancient Egyptian motifs? By looking at the material, it has clearly been shown that the inscribed gems at least in one case contain a description of the depicted deity, but otherwise multiple faces or heads are never described. Compared to the older Egyptian material, such as texts in tombs, temples, or other inscriptions, this is a completely contradictory element, since especially from the New Kingdom and the Greco-Roman period a large number of documents are available, which explicitly mention the multiple faces or heads. The inscriptions of the gems can be sorted into several groups, most of which are also present in identical or at least comparable form in other cases.

The gem Ann Arbor, Mich., Kelsey Museum of Archeology, 26059 was inscribed with the αρπονχνουφι βρινταтηνωφρι-formula, but certainly does not show the god Horus, who is hidden in this formula. The palindrome on the back calls the deity Ἰάω, who is invoked on many gems and magical papyri.

Ἰάω is also present in the previously mentioned gem London, British Museum, G 525 (EA 56525) with a three-headed Osiris (Figure 3.7), as well as in Paris, Bibliothèque Nationale, 2170 (Figure 3.8) and New York, American Numismatic Society, No. 25 on the side of the sun ram (Figure 3.10). The figure of Cambridge, 2012.1.144 (Figure 3.4) is called Βαϊνχωωωχ—but the creature with seven serpent heads is certainly not a multi-headed Bes, whose name Βαϊνχωωωχ has often been interpreted in literature.[75] It remains unclear whether at the end of the text on the gem a prescribed Ἀβρασάξ could be seen. As for Paris, Bibliothèque Nationale, 2170, a connection between σερφουθ μουϊσρω and a god of Pelusium should be clarified, but the question remains whether it is comparable to the sun god, if one does not go through various epithets with a solar aspect in PGM XXXVI, 351. The inscription can be read as Egyptian *śrp.t mꜣỉ sỉw* "Lotus, lion, ram" and thus is clearly a reference to the sun. Paris, Bibliothèque Nationale, Fr 2896 (Figure 3.12) shows the names of the Archangel Michael and that of his ancestor Jakob with a six-headed sun ram. This clearly shows that names such as Ἰάω, Βαϊνχωωωχ, and Ἀβρασάξ do not address a specific entity, but their very frequent occurrence gives rise to a kind of "magic invocation" in general,[76] which has nothing special to do with the depicted being. Rather, it is the case that these terms were not reserved for a god or a god-being on gems as well as in magical papyri, but had many uses. This is to be proven for beings from different cultures, as for Ἰάω in the ancient Egyptian or Greek lands.[77] Likewise, Ἰάω could be written on an animal, such as a monkey.[78] The gem Skoluda, MN001 shows an Anguipedes, on which the inscription **ΙΑѠ CΑΒΑѠ ΜΙΧΑΗΛ** was attached,[79] as mentioned earlier; on Paris, Bibliothèque Nationale, Fr 2896 the name of the archangel was added to a six-headed sun ram. On the gem Den Hague, Cab. Roy., Inv.-No. 1444 representing Hecate, the word "**ΑΒΡΑCΑΞ**" was written,[80] which may also be found on Cambridge, 2012.1.144 for an anthropomorphic god with seven serpents as heads. These examples clearly show that magical names, which could well be just called *voces magicae*, are not confined to a particular type and certainly do not designate a specific being.

Many inscriptions on gems with multi-headed beings could not be interpreted, nor give any deeper meaning, as, for example, in the case of Kassel, Staatliche Kunstsammlung, 176 (Figure 3.3); elsewhere, only vocal sequences exist, such as on London, British Museum, G 525 (EA 56525), on Paris, Bibliothèque

Nationale, 2170 and on the gem bearing the depiction of *Twtw*.[81] Also on New York, Metropolitan Museum of Art, 41.160.642 a vowel sequence can be expected.

At least in one case, there seems to be some sort of inscription for an invocation or a ritual appropriate to the gem. For London, British Museum, G 191 (EA 56191), which shows a creature with the heads of a hawk, an ibis, and a jackal (Figure 3.5), the meaning of ΒΙΧΩ// ΒΙΧΩ ΒΕ//Υ ΒΕΥ ΧΩΒ//Ι ΧΩΒΙ ΒΕ//Υ ϹΟΥΜΑΡΤΑ "big hawk, big hawk, ?, ?, ibis, ibis, ?, protect!" could be an invocation matching the figure depicted. Thus, two of the three heads were directly mentioned here, of which only ΒΕΥ cannot be associated with the head of the jackal. A comparable connection between heads/faces and inscriptions is not available from the entire corpus of the magical gems.

The few certainly identifiable inscriptions are, for example, ΠΕϹϹΕ ΠΕϹϹΕ "Digest! Digest!" on Ann Arbor, Michigan, Kelsey Museum of Archeology, 26059, ΔΟϹΜΟ [Ι ΧΑΡΙΝ] "Grant m[e favour!]" on New York, American Numismatic Society, No. 25, which reflect the wholesome-beneficial direction of the gems again. This can also be said for Exeter, RAMM, Inv.-No. 5 / 1946.355 on which ΝΕΙΚΗ probably a form of Greek "victory" is present, since the piece would be considered a kind of lucky charm in an apotropaic sense as the victory is probably meant over enemies or threats. At least in these cases, the depiction of the multi-headed deities—an anthropomorphic god with two ibises on Ann Arbor, Michigan, Kelsey Museum of Archeology, 26059 and a snake with two faces on Exeter, RAMM, Inv. 5 / 1946.355—promised advantages for the wearer.

4. Resumée

Unfortunately, there is no compilation or database of all gems or at least of the publications available, so no reliable statements about distributions and frequencies are possible. It can be assumed that there are other gems with ancient Egyptian representations with several heads that could possibly be interspersed with Greek or Jewish influences. So far, no gems are known, showing a creature with several heads from Mesopotamia.[82] Although from the eastern area a variety of documents are known with images and texts of gods and goddesses with several heads this iconography seems not to have been handed down onto gems. This can also be noted for other Greek gods, which have several heads.

If one adds to the pieces analyzed in this study other objects with multi-headed creatures like Bes,[83] Hecate,[84] or those beings commonly known as Grylloi,[85] it becomes obvious that there is a total of about 250 objects. Thus, a fairly large portion of the gems were adorned with multi-headed creatures. This is in direct contrast to the situation that gods with multiple faces or heads, or the phenomenon of polycephaly in antiquity, have received so far little attention in research.

It is understandable that—as is the case with many other representations of gems—there is virtually no consensus on a name or names for multi-headed beings. All the epithets and names are confused, even the number of heads is irrelevant, as the portrayals of the sun show. Through the various names of the intercultural framework of gems, decidedly Egyptian, Jewish, and Greek influences are preserved, which go together on the gems and create new beings.

The question arises, how were the labels of the gems actually conceived and put together? Was it a decision of the stone cutter, what text did he want to write down on the gems and if so what intention can we recognize? Since, as shown, nicknames and epithets appear in the material for all beings and representations, it is decidedly clear that in various terms frequently interpreted as names in research, there is certainly no designation for a specific being, which is essential to Βαϊνχωωωχ. Or were the labels selected by the customer? Also in this case, the question of the intention must be asked. For example, what can vocal sequences say about multi-headed beings or how do they relate to the depicted god? Was it a fraud on the illiterate customer? Likewise, it could be assumed that the effectiveness was achieved by the vowels *per se*, as something "magical-looking" was written down on the apotropaic-effective gems, which in turn could provide some sort of placebo effect. Should one assume that writing was simply applied for its own sake and that it unfolded a kind of "magical" effect out of itself? According to Stanley J. Tambiah, it can be pointed out that in magical acts, no "true" or "untrue" exists,[86] but only the conviction of the actant is decisive, with which then the inscription would become effective in itself.

However, it is also interesting to direct to those things that were not written on the gems. For example, no specific threat is mentioned, which can be explained by the fact that the creatures or the gems should probably work against all sorts of threats. However, it is very noticeable that in no case a real name of the depicted figure appears. The multi-headed beings are not explicitly named, as in the case of the gods Osiris or the sun ram, but it is easy to assume that the way of representation alone makes it clear which god was depicted. It is also striking that not in one case the number of heads or a specific description of the figure is mentioned. If other objects are added, such as Hecate on the gem London, British Museum, Inv. G 1986, 5-1,111, the goddess is called by her name and thus a being who has three heads.[87]

There is no passage in the preserved books about stones or their engraving as well as in the *Papyri Graecae Magicae*[88] describing a design of a gem with an ancient Egyptian god with several heads; an exception is the ritual instruction for a drawing of a nine-headed being in Pap. Leiden, Gr. J 384, IV, 17-V, 4 (PGM XII, 121-143).[89] This instruction will be dealt with extensively elsewhere. A drawing could also be used well for the design of a gem, without this being expressed explicitly in the Greek text. As an example, in the stone book of Socrates and Dionysius, No. 36, the shape of a Chnoubis with three heads (Χνοῦβις ἔχων κεφαλὰς τρεῖς) should be cut into a dark onyx.[90] Despite the large number of preserved gems with the figure of Chnoubis,[91] there is only one gem in Cologne, Institut für Altertumskunde, no. 18, which probably shows this picture.[92] Contrary to the description in the stone book, chalcedony instead of onyx was chosen. Thus, it remains to be seen what kind of ritual was used for the design or practical application of the gems discussed here, and whether there was anything like a ritual connected to the creation or the handling of said gems. The inscription on London, British Museum, G 191 (EA 56191) could at least be interpreted as the naming of the three heads of the deity, whereby the creature was understood not as an individual but as an aggregation of three creatures.

4

Agency and Efficacy in Syriac Amulets across the Ages

Nils Hallvard Korsvoll

1. Introduction

There is still much to learn about the praxis, that is the use and circumstances, surrounding textual amulets. Certain aspects, like portability, the significance of their place and situation, and their apparent serial production, are commonly discussed, and there is a consensus on the importance of these features. At the same time there are many unanswered questions. Who made these objects, who were their clients, and how were they framed in ritual and use? This volume, building on the 2018 conference "Textual Amulets in a Transcultural Perspective," hosted by the SFB 933 "Materiale Textkulturen" at the University of Heidelberg, is a welcome contribution to these debates. My primary area of research is the late-antique Syriac amulet tradition, but here I take advantage of discoveries and publications of medieval and early modern Syriac amulets to address this volume's transcultural perspective. More specifically, I look at the self-designations and operative verbs in Syriac amulets, as these may indicate how amulets were understood to work, and then trace and discuss any changes that occur between late-antique, medieval, and early modern amulets. The available, surviving sample of Syriac amulets is admittedly too small to be representative in any way, but its limited size makes it a compact and manageable corpus. As I proceed to discuss, there are some notable changes that occur over the millennium, distinguishing the early modern from the late-antique. Indeed, some scholars argue that one can no longer speak of the same tradition. I disagree, however, and hold that there is some continuity between the different eras. Hence, by conducting a small study to compare how amulets describe and deal with agency I extrapolate some observations on the notion of apotropaic agency across the ages.

2. The Locus of Agency

Scholars have for some time debated and sought the exact location or source of efficacy in an amulet.[1] Does its power lie in the text itself, in what the text represents, in what it records, in the artifact as such, or perhaps in the material of the amulet? Starting with the last point, late-antique amulets could be made from a number of substances: papyrus, parchment, ostraca, incantation bowls, *lamellae*,[2] gems, or in the form of other jewelry—any material support that can carry writing seems to have been used.[3] At first, this variation may indicate that the material was unimportant and the locus of agency consequently elsewhere. However, at the same time gemmology was practiced across the Mediterranean,[4] and curse tablets in this area are often written out on lead, whose black color is thought to mirror the dark content of the curse.[5] Moreover, it is a recurring assertion in amulet manuals that material supports should be new and clean, perhaps mirroring traditions of ritual purity.[6] These observations then suggest that the material support of an amulet was not altogether unimportant after all.

Still, many scholars prefer to look for traces of ritual practice to explain an amulet's efficacy. J. B. Segal for instance noted that several Jewish and Mandaic incantation bowls use words that would have an onomatopoeic effect that mirrors the action or effect the spell was trying to achieve,[7] while others look at descriptions in ancient manuals or literary texts that prescribe or describe rituals to accompany the creation and activation of an amulet. For instance, one manual from the Cairo Geniza instructs the user to fill a new jar with water, recite biblical verses over it seven times, and then knead out cakes from it, using a range of ingredients like frankincense and a virgin's urine.[8] From such examples, and the primacy of spoken over written language, scholars have argued that amulets should be understood as records of a spoken ritual and that the efficacy therefore lies in the latter. Michael D. Swartz, for example, writes that an

> amulet functions not only as a physical object of power, it is a mnemonic, or script, for oral recitation. Because of this we can expect the texts to bear characteristics of those types of writing intended for oral performance.[9]

Other scholars have questioned this understanding and argued that the efficacy of a textual amulet is continually realized in the text itself. For instance, David Frankfurter argues that the late-antique Greek magical papyri combined the flexibility and vocalization of the Greek alphabet with the reverence for and efficacy of Egyptian hieroglyphs to form a flexible and user-friendly ritual or magical language. This, he continues, opened for ritually efficacious texts, and the effect of this potential is witnessed by the apparent surge of amulets in late antiquity.[10] Here, I cannot resolve this question, but I contribute to the debate with further observations on how agency is presented in Syriac amulets and how this may change or develop transculturally and/or trans-temporally.

3. Three Stages of Syriac Amulets

Syriac came to be used by the early Christian church in Mesopotamia and parts of Syria, and as Christianity spread east in the sixth and seventh centuries so did it. Syriac and Syriac Christianity have for a long time been neglected by modern scholarship, as it falls outside the disciplinary boundaries of Western academia. However, over the past decade Syriac studies have undergone something of a renaissance. More scholars are finding, presenting, and analyzing material from this religious and linguistic tradition, which spanned Asia from late antiquity until the modern era. So also when it comes to amulets, and the geographical and temporal dispersion of this one linguistic tradition presents intriguing possibilities for tracing and assessing amulets and their use from a transcultural perspective. There are, at present, three corpora of Syriac textual amulets available for study, and I compare how these express or present their agency.

The best-known corpus, which boasts a research history of over 150 years, are the so-called incantation bowls from Mesopotamia, modern-day Iraq, which are dated to the sixth and seventh centuries. They are ceramic bowls with a diameter between 15 and 20 cm, and a height of around 8 cm, and they typically have an incantation written in ink on the inside of the bowl. Most bowls have their spell written in a Jewish dialect, or in Mandaic, but there are also some bowls in Syriac, Pahlavi, and in Pseudo-scripts.[11] There are currently about 2,000 known examples held in various museums and collections around the world, with something close to a third of these published.[12] When found in controlled excavations, the bowls have been discovered upside down under homes.[13] Many specimens, however, have no known findspot or provenance, and there have been several controversies over allegedly illegal or illicit incantation bowls.[14] In response to the growing awareness of the illegal export and trafficking in antiquities and ancient manuscripts, several professional organizations direct their members to only publish artifacts that were acquired or belonged to a recognized collection before April 24, 1972, which is when the 1970 UNESCO Convention on the Means of Prohibiting and Preventing the Illicit Import, Export and Transfer of Ownership of Cultural Property came into force.[15] Although criticized for being an arbitrary and insufficient boundary, it is a commonly recognized demarcation and I adhere to it in this enquiry.

Next, there is a number of early modern amulets and manuals with instructions for making them, coming from Kurdistan or Northern Iraq. They are made of paper and found in single sheets or in codices of varying sizes and extents. They are often small, suggesting they were meant for everyday use and possibly to be transported (which in turn can suggest that they were used by itinerant ritual experts).[16] The scribal hands vary, from fairly finished to rather rough. These manuscripts and amulets have also been known to scholars for some time, and they have occasionally been discussed in connection with the incantation bowls. The first and best-known example is Herman Gollancz' translation of three such codices, which he called the *Book of Protection* (1912). Several so-called magical manuscripts were acquired by European missionaries north of Mosul and around Lake Urmia at the end of the nineteenth century, and since then they have been presented and discussed sporadically.[17]

Finally, the perhaps most exciting corpus for this triangulation of Syriac apotropaic practice come from the so-called German Turfan Expedition, where several sites at Turfan in western China were excavated in four campaigns from 1902 to 1914. Tens of thousands of manuscripts were discovered and brought to museums and libraries in Germany, reflecting the richness and diversity of this Silk Road oasis in the Middle Ages.[18] Long acknowledged for its importance for Manichaean studies,[19] Erica C. D. Hunter and Mark Dickens more recently began mining this treasure trove for manuscripts or fragments written in or using the Syriac script.[20] Finding over a thousand specimens, these mainly stem from the site of a large monastic complex at Shuïpang, near Bulayïq, which was excavated during the second season (1904/5). Here, what appears to have been a large monastic library included a broad range of liturgical and other ecclesiastical literature belonging to the East Syrian tradition, but of special interest to me are "a small number of prayer-amulets whose physical size indicates that they came from pickct-sizcd handbooks."[21] The study and publication of manuscripts and fragments from Turfan is far from complete, but Hunter's efforts so far provide a basis and certain important observations that are pertinent to my questions here.

4. Agency and Self-presentation in Late-Antique Amulets

Starting with the late-antique amulets in Syriac, there are very few references either to someone having made the amulet or to a preceding ritual. There are some instances where the incantation refers to itself as spoken,[22] and a few others where it refers to the process of writing.[23] Yet in general the incantations are without references to their own production or composition.[24] One notable exception are five bowls that contain the so-called Joshua bar Perahiya-*historiola*, which refers to itself as a writ of divorce and is presented as the work of the Talmudic sage Joshua bar Perahiya.[25] However, this is a *historiola*, a widespread apotropaic device that does most likely not reflect the actual amulet's production, but rather places it within the story of a hallowed sage. *Historiolae* were used already in ancient Egypt and Babylon, being mythic stories employed "as exemplar of the handling of the situation" addressed in the amulet or spell.[26] Indeed, the typical formula "just as . . ., so also . . ." introduces *historiolae* already in early Hittite rituals.[27] Hence, I cannot glean much information about their sense of agency and its locus from the late-antique amulets, neither in how they present themselves nor in how they cast their agency. It remains unclear whether they rely on preceding rituals or on the authority of their makers for efficacy. Or, indeed, on something else.

Occasionally, there is an unidentified and unspecified agent in the spells, revealed by lines or invocations written in the first-person active:

(13) . . . *ʾnʾ ktbty ʾlhʾ nʾsʾ mn hš wlʿlm ʾyn wʾmyn ʾmyn ʾmyn slḥ*[28]

(13) ". . . I wrote, God heals, from now and forever."[29]

This may point to an unidentified maker or scribe, but the most common format or tense for expressing agency in Syriac incantation bowls and amulets, as Hunter has already noted,[30] is the passive. For instance, the incantation bowl CBS 9008 starts with:

(1) *mzmn hnʾ kʾsʾ l[ḥ]tmtʾ* (2) *dbyth dhnʾ dʾdb[y]h b[r] ʾsmndwkt* (3) *dtyzh mnh wmn byth m[b]k[l]tʾ* (4) *wlwṭtʾ wḥyl̈mʾ byš̈ʾ byš̈ʾ ʾsyryn [mzrzy]n wmšrryn*

(1) "Prepared is this bowl for the sealing (2) of the house of this *dʾdbyh* son of *ʾsmndwkt* (3) that may depart from him and from his house the *mevakkalta* (4) and the curse and the very evil dreams. Bound, armed and made strong."[31]

Another one, AO 207964-O, starts with:

(1) *l[q]yṭyn ʾsyryn zryzyn ḥlyṣ̈yn qmyṭyn wḥtymyn ḥršʾ̈ dʾš̈tyn ḥrštʾ̈ wt[m]nʾ* (2) *dtkyn [t]wknʾ drṭ[n]n ryṭnʾ wʿšpn ʿšpʾ̈ lylyʾ wymʾmʾ.*

(1) "Gathered, bound, armed, tied, held and sealed are the sorcery of sixty witches and the eight ones, (2) who cause harm, who mumble a mumbling and charm charms by night and by day."[32]

Indeed, this example not only points out the predilection for the passive tense or voice in this corpus. It also demonstrates another common feature, namely that the incantations are far more concerned with the demons, ills, and afflictions they are to protect against than with the agents or powers that ensure this protection. To use Fritz Graf's terms, the incantations consist mostly of an extensive *request*, while the invocation and *pars epica* are quite short.[33] It seems that it is the actions and nature of the problems that require precision and accurate description, while the agency that effects the protection against these ills remains unspecific.

Despite this lack of clues in the texts, and the absence of any description of incantation bowls in historical sources, their special format and placement under thresholds or in the corners of homes suggests that the physical object is somehow important for the agency of these artifacts.[34] For instance, in the bowl CBS 9010 the threshold is mentioned in a caption on the outside of the bowl, which is thought to indicate where it was meant to be deposited.[35] Moreover, most bowls are found buried upside down, something many argue connects with their frequent use of the verb *kbš*, "pressing" or "pressing down"—suggesting that they were meant to trap demons under them.[36] Indeed, Frankfurter draws parallels between the bowls and Mishnaic references to the practice of trapping scorpions under bowls.[37] Another theory, pointing instead to the frequent use of the verb *hpk*, "to overturn," is that the bowls function by so-called sympathetic magic—that the demons shall be overturned just like the bowls are overturned.[38]

However, in his recent introduction to incantation bowls, Shaul Shaked observes that the incantations rarely refer to their material support: only in a few cases are the bowls referred to as *kʾsʾ*, "bowl"; the more common terms for self-presentation are the generic *ḥtmʾ*, "seal"; *ʿbd*, "act"; *rʾzʾ*, "mystery"; or *ʾsrʾ*, "binding."[39] Indeed, Christa Müller-Kessler has found several examples of incantation bowls and *lamellae* using the same incantations, which further downplays the importance of the material support.[40] Some scholars have suggested that the bowls represent a magic circle, but others instead see them as

> the culmination of a heritage which harks back to the protective rituals of the Neo-Assyrian and Babylonian periods when apotropaic figurines were buried at various points in both private and public buildings.[41]

This interpretation emphasizes the texts and drawings of the incantations, placing their agency with the written and drawn representations on the artifact and not with the artifact itself. Indeed, this compares with Shaked's observation above on what the amulets call themselves: not only are the terms pointing to the artifacts themselves oblique, but they also most often occur only once—in the introduction of the incantation—if at all.

A final aspect here is the assumption that the bowls were made in some sort of serial production.[42] Again, this is not described in historical sources, but deduced from the considerable number of duplicate or parallel bowls: "On occasion a single, standard text is found in multiple copies, used by different practitioners,"[43] and there are several cases where one hand has written several bowls.[44] Some scholars argue that the bowls were made by itinerant experts traveling between sites and communities in Mesopotamia, possibly carrying a manual or working from *Vorlagen* to produce the large number of duplicates.[45] At the same time, these are rarely exact parallels or duplicates, so the individual maker or scribe appears to have had a degree of creative freedom.[46] In other cases, the spelling of the incantations varies according to features of spoken Aramaic, so scholars continue to debate whether the incantations were transmitted orally or in written form.[47] These features then further complicate the picture, as the deliberate use of standard texts and phrases places an emphasis on the text over the scribe or ritual expert, while the evidence of variation and adjustment in turn detracts from the importance of the text. Evidently, the amulets are effective even if the text or rite is not reproduced correctly.

5. Agency and Self-presentation in Medieval Amulets from Turfan

As I mentioned, we still await the complete publication of all the material found at Turfan in western China, but Hunter has made some initial studies and publications.[48] The extent and detail of these sources are far from equal to the previous corpus in either scale or detail, but it is a start. First, there is, again, nothing in the incantations themselves to identify the clients or the scribes who wrote or copied them.[49] Indeed, the examples from Turfan are mainly fragments from codices containing recipes, that is, instruction manuals for making amulets, and are therefore not produced for or linked to a specific client.[50] Neither are there any traces of a named or identified agent behind the amulet or recipe. However, the site that the fragments come from is a monastic complex, and these instruction manuals seem to have been part of its library, filled also with liturgical works and theological treatises.[51] Marco Moriggi recently opened a discussion on the propensity of early Syriac clergy to dabble in magic and amulet production,[52] and such practices are well known in other regions at the time.[53]

Hunter herself has furthermore pointed out parallels between the incantations from Turfan and the early modern manuscripts from Urmia,[54] in which some of the scribes, as I discuss later, identify themselves as priests.[55] Hence, it seems reasonable to consider the Turfan-amulets monastic.

Indeed, in form and language they do appear more *christianized*, with quotes from scripture and invocations of holy figures. The incantations retain the passive voice from the late-antique corpus, leaving the agent or speaker of the text itself unidentified, as seen in the excerpt from the fragment Syr HT 99 (Recto):

> (5) . . . *n' 'w mwr'n', wntdkr* (6) . . . *' dḥršwt' ṣlwt' hd'* (7) . . . *wn' d't 'hd wbmrḥmnwt'* . . .,
>
> (5) ". . . And may it be commemorated (6) . . . of sorceries, this prayer (7) . . . that is recalled by mercy/alms . . . ."[56]

Yet they differ in their concern for the powers by which their aims are brought into effect. They invoke God, Christ, and saints to protect them and to act on their behalf, placing the agency of the incantation squarely with them:

> (1) . . . *bryšyt 'yt[why] h[w'] mlt'. hw mlt' 'yt[why]* (2) *[wbl'd]why 'pl' ḥd' hwt mdm dhw' bh [ḥy']* (3) *bṣlwth dmry tmsys sh[d']*
>
> (1) ". . . In the beginning was the Word and the Word was (2) and without Him there was not even one thing in which there was life (3) [. . .] by the prayer of Mar Tamsis the martyr."[57]

The ills and afflictions that dominated in the late-antique examples are not forgotten, but they share space and importance with the benevolent powers that execute the wishes in the incantations. Moreover, there is a change in the terms of self-reference in these incantations that reflects this shift: Instead of *ḥtm'*, "seal" or *r'z'*, "mystery," the incantations refer to themselves as a *ṣlwt'*, "prayer"—paralleling Christian terminology. Overall, the incantations take up a more intercessory tone, and the apotropaic agency lies with the powers they invoke.[58] However, where and at what time the act of intercession takes place, be it at the moment of writing the incantation, at the initiation of it, at the repetition of it, or in its constant presence in written form, remains unclear.

6. Agency and Self-presentation in Early Modern Amulets

The early modern examples of Syriac amulets come, as I have mentioned, from codices listing recipes for how to make them. The incantations are dotted with liturgical phrases, biblical references, and invocations of biblical figures and saints. For instance, spell #35 in Gollancz' codex A opens with:

> *bšm ʾbʾ wbrʾ wrwḥʾ dqw: ṣlwth wbʿwth wtkšpth wtḥnnth dmry dnyʾyl nbyʾ dnḥt lgwbʾ dʾ̈rywtʾ lʾ ḥblwhy . . .*
>
> "In the name of the Father, the Son, and the Holy Ghost. The prayer, request, petition, and supplication of Mar Daniel the prophet, when he went down into the den of hungry lions, and they did him no harm . . . ."[59]

In fact, each recipe is ascribed to a saint, in some cases a biblical figure or the Virgin, linking it expressly to their intercessory powers: *ḥrmʾ dmrty mrym ṭwbnytʾ dḥšḥ mṭl kʾ̈ryhʾ*, "The anathema of my Lady, the blessed Mary, which is of avail for sick persons."[60] In some cases, the title also includes the problem or illness that the incantation is meant to work against, and it appears that some saints are specialized in healing certain types of sickness.[61] Yet Hunter also notes that while the more conventional prayers in the prologues of the codices are called *ṣlwtʾ*, "prayers," the titles of the more prosaic recipes in the manuscripts use the common, apotropaic *ʾsyrʾ*, "bindings," or, less commonly, the more liturgical *ḥrmʾ*, "bans" (*anathemae*).[62] Still, these incantations also include supplicatory terminology comparable to the Turfan examples; *ṣlwtʾ*, "prayer"; *tkšptʾ*, "petition"; *bʿwtʾ*, "request"; and/or *tḥnntʾ*, "supplication." As in spell #35, these are often combined in lists to stress the action and attitude of the appeal.[63]

The vocabulary in these amulets suggests a closer proximity to Christian rites and practices than the two previous corpora, and as I mentioned earlier some of the scribes even identify themselves as priests in the colophons.[64] The making and administration of amulets by local priests was noted by Western missionaries at the end of the nineteenth century.[65] Syriac codices are typically blessed with extensive colophons, postscripts added by the scribe with information on the production, date, and ownership of the codex. This is also the case for the magic manuals, where the colophons situate them in villages across Lake Urmia and in north-eastern Iraq.[66] Indeed, again in Gollancz' codex A, the manuscript ends with a long entry detailing procedures for diagnosis and treatment of various ills, which includes detailing which monastery one should go to for the cure.[67] For example, if you are troubled by anxiety:

> *ʿwmrʾ mry gywrgys ktybtʾ ddḥltʾ wzwʿtʾ*
>
> "[In] the monastery of Mar George [you will find] the prescription for fear and trembling."[68]

Finally, concerning use, several spells in this corpus refer to themselves as something to be written and then hung upon a client or user.[69] This, again, is a common practice in many other apotropaic traditions.

In this corpus, then, locating the agency is a small task. The requests are explicitly placed in the mouth of saints or deities, either in a descriptive third-person singular or sometimes quoted as direct speech.[70] An example of the former is

wʾmr mrn lmrym hʾ ʾsrnʾ skr ʾnʾ lhwn b̈ššly dprzlʾ wb̈kʾpʾdnḥ̈šʾ

"... and our Lord said unto Mary: See, I bind and stop them with chains of iron and stones of brass ...."[71]

while the latter may look like this appeal from Saint George: *mryʾ ʾlhʾ ḥyltnʾ hbly šʾltʾ hdʾ*, "O Lord, God of Hosts, grant me this request!"[72] The recipes all use similar, formulaic phrases like *dṣly wbʿʾ*, "he prayed and besought," or *kšp*, "he entreated," then followed by lists of powers, *historiolae* or biblical references.[73] Something that further stresses the intercessory regime of these amulets is that there is a recipient to these entreaties, either *mryʾ ʾlhʾ ḥyltnʾ*, "lord God Almighty," or *mrn yšwʿ mšyḥʾ*, "our lord Jesus Christ."[74] This leaves no question as to where the agency is located. Furthermore, the saint's entreaty is commonly presented in a past tense, placing the action outside and before the formulation of the incantation. In many cases, the incantation even specifies that the request was given at the time of the saint's martyrdom. Referencing their martyrdom, for maximum power if you will, of course makes sense, but this also gives a further hint that the agency was thought to lie outside the amulet and its immediate use. Hunter, in line with this, hypothesizes that the incantations "function as a mnemonic device."[75]

This sense of recording and rendering agency, rather than effectuating it, also echoes in the persistent self-references in the amulets that describe themselves as written. Indeed, it is repeated in a common formula found in almost all these manuscripts, referring to *ṭʿyn ÿwdʾ hlyn*, "the bearer of these writs," which is such a well-established phrase that it regularly occurs in a standard abbreviation *ṭ : yw : h*.[76] An interesting aside, which also points toward the appreciation of these amulets as something written, is the Syriac word for *writ*, which is *yûde*, from the letter *yûd*. This is the smallest of the Syriac (and Semitic) letters, often represented with a simple dot, and Gollancz comments that a "magical scrap of writing or talisman is called *yûde*"[77]—commonly used as a diminutive term for brief, small texts. Finally, I must add that there are some examples where the agency is connected with the act of writing and therefore immediate to the amulet. For example, spell #20 in Gollancz' codex C closes with *ktwb ʿl ʿyn ʾ ʾmyn*, "Write upon the eyes, Amen!"[78] Here, then, the agency lies not in the commemoration of or appeal to earlier events, but in the current action. Hence, although the former examples are by far the most common, the latter show that the corpus is not unison.

7. Traces of Ritual Expansion

Indeed, Hunter has made some further observations that suggest the understanding of agency in these amulets is more complex. In a study of the structure and composition of the incantations, she identifies different sections or units.[79] Among these, Hunter describes one type of unit that differs notably from the others.[80] Usually found towards the end of the spell, these so-called prohibition units drop the invocations and intercessory tone found earlier in the spell, and instead emphasize the ills that are to be protected against. In the anathema of Saint George in Gollancz' codex A, for instance, one example reads:

> *ntbṭl ʾwlṣnʾ ʿpypʾ mn ʿʿnh wmn qnÿnh wmn byth dṭ : yw : h : twb ʾsyryn šḥnʾ wmwtnʾ wqws kwrhnʾ mwṣlyʾ . . .*
>
> "May the twofold danger be annulled from off the flocks, from the cattle, and from the house of him who beareth these writs. Furthermore, may there be bound the inflammation, the pestilence, and jaundice, the sickness of Mosul . . . ."[81]

Taking up Graf's terminology again, these are the requests, whose tone and format differ from the invocation and *pars epica* (1991).

There is "no mention of the saint, or of God,"[82] and the text shifts to the perspective of the client.[83] Hunter continues to observe that,

> apart from its intrinsic interest, the list of evils is of minimal value to the anathema's function. Rather it is a static element, being merely the object of the saint's actions and descriptive of the amulet's scope.[84]

In other words, the prohibition units bear many of the traits found in the late-antique amulets and incantation bowls; a passive voice, emphasis on the dangers or evils to protect against, and an agency expressed from the perspective of the client. Hunter also notes that there are parallels to the incantation bowls and how this "ancient inheritance can be witnessed in the 'agency' that has been selected," and that it stands somewhat in contrast to the other units in the spell with their "Christian tenor."[85]

Now, a premise in ritual and liturgical studies is that brief or basic ritual patterns or units with time are expanded and elaborated upon.[86] Indeed, Hunter suggests that the incantations consist of different units or components that would have been combined according to circumstance or the taste of the scribe.[87] Also studies on late-antique incantations argue that they consist of units that were combined in different settings on different artifacts.[88] Adopting this premise, I propose that these prohibition units, found toward the end of the early modern incantations, are remnants of the late-antique incantations and formulas. The invocation and *pars epica*, however, developed and expanded "within a Christian culture-religious context."[89] And looking at the amulets from Turfan, it appears that this expansion had happened already by the Middle Ages. Over the centuries, which saw the cementation of Christianity and the Syriac language's primacy within it, the apotropaic formulas were added to and expanded by intercessory phrases and elements borrowed from liturgy and Christian prayer. Thus they acquired an overall emphasis on intercession, thereby seeing agency as something external to the amulets, while the features more dominant in the late-antique amulets, with their concern for problems and the perspective of the client, remained in the prohibition units.

8. Conclusion

Despite the many benefits of using Syriac amulets to study textual amulets from a transcultural perspective—their restricted number and their temporal and spatial distribution—issues of survival and representation, which plague all historical inquiry, remain a challenge. For a fuller picture we await further publications both from Turfan and from the early modern period. Still, my examination shows that while it is difficult to pinpoint a specific locus of agency, there are certain trends and tendencies in and across these Syriac corpora. First, there is a shift from the domestic context in the late-antique corpus, to a clerical or monastic context in the medieval and early modern corpora. Moreover, this shift is paralleled by a change in perspective in the spells, from client to scribe or ritual expert. Second, the medieval and early modern manuals contain more elements and phrases borrowed from or referencing Christian ritual, whereas the late-antique amulets emphasize the ills and afflictions that the amulet should protect against. Furthermore, agency is mostly not specified in the late-antique amulets, while the medieval and early modern incantations have an intercessory structure that again compares with a Christian cosmology.

These shifts are in some ways considerable, and as I noted at the beginning one may ask whether the three corpora can, in the end, be considered part of the same tradition. However, my examination, building heavily on observations already made by Hunter and others, finds features in the medieval and early modern amulets that compare with the late-antique ones. I therefore propose that there is a continuation in the request of the incantations, while the invocation and the *pars epica* were extended and elaborated on in response to Christian cosmology. This observation suggests how a tradition can expand and adapt across time and space to new situations and contexts. In some respects, it may change so much that it borders on becoming a new tradition, while in others it continues to hold remnants of the initial one. Such dynamics play into debates on cultural memory, transmission, and other fields of theoretical discussion,[90] but these will have to be addressed on another occasion.

5

Demons in Runic and Latin Amulets from Medieval Scandinavia

Rudolf Simek

As opposed to popular opinion, runes never had any magical quality per se, that is to say that runes would have been used as magical signs in any ritual or magical practice. However, the runic scripts, like all other lettering systems, could be used for any purpose including the composition of texts aimed at otherworldly powers, and that may be considered magical in a wider sense.

In any case, we have to distinguish between three different runic scripts in use in the first millennium AD, namely the so-called Elder Futhark, the Younger Futhark, and the Anglo-Saxon variant of the latter, the Anglo-Saxon Futhorc. The Elder Futhark seems to have developed some time in the first or early second centuries AD and the first inscriptions turn up more or less simultaneously from Southern Alpine regions to Denmark and Norway. The inscriptions preserved over the next 700 years number only 200, and if we deduct those on bracteates (the fifth- to sixth-century Germanic imitations of Roman medallions), we have an even much smaller number of under 100 runic inscriptions. However, it is those bracteates in particular that give us an impression of the wide use of runes including some interesting self-description of the "rune master" as well as a number of "magic" words such as *alu* and *ota*, *salu* and *laukar*. Of the five types of bracteates (called M, A, B, C, and D respectively) the M bracteates bear inscriptions, but only in one single case proper runes can be identified while eleven others bear senseless texts imitating Roman lettering. Of the A-bracteates, showing a male head, forty-seven out of eighty-five pieces carry some sort of inscription, ranging from Roman lettering to mixed texts to runic words. The B-bracteates, showing one or more humans standing or sitting, thirty-nine out of eighty-three pieces carry inscriptions of all the types mentioned. The most popular group, however, were the C-bracteates, showing a male head over a four-legged animal, 116 of which carry runic inscriptions.[1]

Many inscriptions in the older Futhark contain only a single word, a name, or short inscriptions naming producers or dedicators of objects. A notable exception is the fibula from Nordendorf I in the Alamanic area, which names not only dedicator and receiver but also three mythological names, of which we may identify *wodan* and *wigiþonar* as the south Germanic form of Odin and Thor, but the third name, *logaþore*, remains cryptic, although it could be assumed that this too could denote a god, unless it is a derogatory term for the two previous deities.

Late in the eighth century, in Scandinavia, the runic script was simplified to only sixteen signs, resulting in the so-called Younger Fuþark, but contrary to that in Anglo-Saxon England two more runes were added to the twenty-four letter Elder Futhark and the result is called the Anglo Saxon-Futhorc. The Younger Futhark was especially developed into an everyday script for use in the vernacular languages of Scandinavia, covering a wide variety of uses and running to currently over 6,000 inscriptions. This ranges from memorial inscriptions, including some 2,000 Swedish grave stones dating mainly to the eleventh century, to the more economic use of runes in the shape of letters, tags, and documents, of which several thousands are known from eleventh- to thirteenth-century Norway. In the same medieval period, all over Scandinavia runes were also used for copying prayers and other Christian formulas onto wooden or metal objects. Small wooden or metal crosses bearing runic inscriptions with the Latin standard prayers like the Our Father or the Ave Maria may be mainly interpreted as objects of personal worship and/or grave goods. Invocations, conjurations, benedictions, and exorcisms in runic Latin inscriptions, on the other hand, were mainly inscribed in small lead, and occasionally copper, sheets, but there are also wooden amulet sticks, like two obstetric amulets. The younger one is dated to around 1350 and comes from Bergen Bryggen (Søre Engelgården; N631).[2] It reads as follows:

A: **maria : peperit : cristum : elisabet : peperit : iohannem : baptistam : in : illarum**
B: **ueneracione : sis : absoluta : æcsi : inkalue : dominuste : uacat : ad : lu**

A: *Maria peperit Christum, Elisabeth peperit Iohannem Baptistam. In illarum*
B: *veneratione sis absoluta! Exi, incolae! Dominus te vocat ad lu[cem!]*
A: "Mary gave birth to Christ, Elisabeth gave birth to John the Baptist. In their
B: veneration be perfect! Come out, bald one! The Lord calls you to light!"

Another octagonal stick from Schleswig, now fragmentary and later used as a knife handle, is much older and dated to the mid-eleventh century and shows that such charms were used throughout the Christian Middle Ages.[3] In manuscripts the formula is found also in manuscripts of the same period.[4]

These medieval amulets differ substantially from the few we have in the Elder Futhark, like the Ribe Skull Fragment, dated to *c.* 720–30, which reads:

> A: **ulfuRAukuþinAukHutiuR. ʽHIAlbburiisuiþR**
> B: **þAIMAuiArkiAuktuirkuniṇ.** [hole] **buur**
>
> A: *Ulfr auk Ōðinn auk Hō-***tiur**. *Hjalp* **buri** *es viðr*
> B: *þæima værki. Auk dverg unninn. Bōurr.*
> "A: UlfR (= the wolf) and Odin and high-*tiur* (= Týr?). *buri* is help against
> B: this pain. And the dwarf (is) overcome, Bóurr." (The second part of the inscription may also have to be translated as: "Buri is help against the pain and against the dwarf. Bóurr is overcome.")[5]

As is immediately obvious from these few examples, the main differences in amulet use after Christianization is the use of Latin and the dependence on standard Christian conjuration formulas which are also found in medieval manuscripts.

What they do have in common are the references to the respective mythological world, be it the gods and beings (not all known to us) of the polytheistic Germanic world, or the various saints of the Christian world. Both are called upon to be of assistance against those evil powers, seen as the source of all adversities, especially the source of all illnesses.

We do not really know which beings, in heathen times such as the pre-Viking period in which the Ribe amulet was made, were considered to be the most dangerous for human health: was it the *þursar* or the *tröll*, or was it *álfar* or even the *dvergar*, as the Ribe amulet seems to insinuate? Or even the *wolf*, mentioned on the Ribe amulet as well as on an eleventh-century copper amulet from Sigtuna, which is even more enigmatic than the one from Ribe?[6] What we should not ignore is the possibility that different ailments (as well as, possibly, other adversities) were associated with different otherworldly beings. A typical cause of illness was obviously something called the worm, as both Old English and Middle High German charms testify to, where it is at times called Nessia or similar. This may have been considered to be the source and cause of internal inflammations, ranging from toothache to cancer.[7] However, we have no example of such a charm referring to a worm-caused illness in our old Scandinavian amulets. Nor do amulets tell us anything about the rôle of *thursar* and *tröll*, although we might gain a glimpse from much later literary texts.

The advantage of amulets as a source for the history of religion and mentality is the directness with which they speak to us. The material we have at our disposal today for the study of amulets is bound to be only a very small section of what was in circulation in the Middle Ages; nevertheless they offer us a direct insight into the fears and beliefs of people a millennium ago. Since most amulets from the eleventh century onward are actually written in Latin, even though they are executed in runes, and the formulas which were used also partly recur in manuscripts, it is the variants on our copies on metal that give us the greatest insights.

One of the best known of these amulets, and at the same time the longest runic inscription found in Denmark to date, is the Blæsinge lead tablet. It can only be roughly dated to the twelfth to fifteenth century, but the slightly fragmentary text may be considered typical for medieval lead amulets, even though it is more detailed than many others

×coniurouos :sæptæ̣ṃ : sororæsọṭ??ọr???????ṣ : ræṣ. . .

æ̣ḷffrica : affricẹasoriaaffoca : affricala : coniurouosætcon : tæstor: pærpatræm :

ætfiliumætspiritum ⁝ sanctum ⁝ ụṭnọn : nocæatis : stamfamulum : dæi : næquæ

ịn×hoculis : næquæinmæmpris : næquæinmædullis : næcinullocomp

inemæmbrorumæius : utinhabitæt : inteuirtuscristi : alṭissị

mị : eccæcrruụçæm : donmini : fukitị : partæs : aduæṛsæ : ụiçịṭḷæọ : dætrịbụịụ

daradi × : dauit : innominæpatrisætfilii :ætspiritussanctiamæn××

cristus : uincit : cristus : ræknit : cristus impæræt : cristus : lipærat +

cristustæbænædicat : aboomi : malo : ḍæfændat : a : k : l : a : batær : nostær : × :

Coniuro vos, septem sorores . . .

Elffrica (?), Affricea, Soria, Affoca, Affricala. Coniuro vos et contestor per Patrem

et Filium et Spiritum Sanctum, ut non noceatis [i]stam famulum Dei, neque

in oculis, neque in membris, neque in medullis, nec in ullo comp

ine membrorum eius, ut inhabitat in te virtus Christi altissimi. Ecce crucem Domini, fugite partes adversae, . . .

"I conjure you seven sisters /. . . Elffrica, Affricea, Soria, Affoca, Affricala / I conjure and admonish you through the Father / and the Son and the Holy Spirit that you don't harm this servant of Christ, neither / in the eyes, nor in the members, nor in the marrow nor in any of the joints of his members / so that the virtue of Christ the Highest may inhabit you. / See the Cross of the Lord, flee you hostile forces!"

Here, Seven Sisters are named, and although two of the names are lost, it is clear that the conjuration is aimed at the same Seven Sisters which are—under somewhat variant names—well known from medieval manuscripts and which stand for demons believed to cause various types of recurrent fevers such as malaria.[8]

The Seven Sisters are by no means a Nordic phenomenon, but their invocation in conjurations of them is attested in manuscripts found in Munich, in the British Library and the Vatican Library, among others, and the origins of these fever demons may well lie in the Near East rather than in Europe.[9]

However, it is not common that such detail and names are applied to the conjuration of demons on lead amulets, although the standard formulas are found on a great number of lead amulets, namely the conjuration of demons, the invocation of divine, or saintly help, a description of what sort of help is sought, and, finally, the exorcism formula which is given in a somewhat abridged form on the Blæsinge runic lead tablet, but can be found in a fuller version on other lead amulets, such as the cross-shaped runic one found in Madla church in Rogaland, Norway, and which is dated to *c.* 1300 (NIyR 248), the line A (originally probably intended as the last line) of which reads:[10]

A: + **esse krucem tomini fugite pa͡rtes atue͡rse : uicit leo. detribuiuta ratiks ta͡uit**

A: *Ecce crucem Domini, fugite partes adverse, vicit leo de tribu Juda, radix David*

A: "See the Cross of the Lord, flee, hostile powers! The lion of Judah's tribe has triumphed, the root of David"

This answers directly to the medieval exorcism formula, which found its way finally into the printed *Rituale Romanum* of 1614 and is still preserved in nineteenth- and twentieth-century ritual handbooks of the Roman Catholic Church, as part of the official exorcism formula, introducing the actual exorcism by showing the cross:

V. Ecce Crucem Domini, fugite, partes adversae.
R. Vicit Leo de tribu Juda, radix David.
V. Fiat misericordia tua, Domine, super nos.
R. Quemadmodum speravimus in te.
Exorciamus te, omnis immunde spiritus, omnis satanica potestas, omnis incursio infernalis adversarii, omnis legio, omnis congregatio et secta diabolica . . .
"See the Cross of Christ! Flee, you hostile forces! The lion of Judah's tribe has triumphed, the root of David. Let your mercy rest on us, Lord, In whatever way we have trusted in you. We exorcise you, all you unclean spirits, you powers of Satan, all temptation of the hellish adversary, all of the devilish legion, community and sect."[11]

Here this text is expressly listed under the chapter *De exorcizandis obsessis a Daemonio* "For the Exorcism of One Possessed by a Demon." which makes it clear that the amulets did use an official church formula of exorcism, rather than trying to repel demons of illness in any odd way, even though that formula could appear in abridged versions.[12] This is hardly surprising given the very small size of some of the lead amulets: a relatively new find from Randers in Jutland measures only 2.9 by 2.8 by 0.8 cm in its folded up state,

But demons are invoked not only through formulas or under the coded names of the Seven Sisters but also quite directly. However, only a relatively small number of all lead amulets, especially the Danish ones, have been unfolded and thus been made legible; among those, the longest ones are the lead amulets from Blæsinge (Zealand, Sj 50) and Schleswig, the lead amulets from Romdrup (Northern Jutland) and Bregninge (on Ærø), and a comparable piece from Halberstadt; to this we may add the two very fragmentary parts from the lead amulet from Viborg (Jutland, MJy 32, dated vaguely to 1050–1300[13]) and the one from Lille Myregård from Bornholm.[14] Compared with the total number of lead amulets found—Imer[15] lists 30 amulets with text for Norway, 20 for Sweden and over a 100 for Denmark—these long and readable pieces are only a small number, to be sure. But among those yet to be unfolded there will also be a number which only contain pseudo-runes, like the lead amulets from Æbelholt (Sj 11), Vokslev (NJy 57), and Køge (Sj 14).[16]

Even though Danish runologists are, for obvious professional reasons, mainly interested in those amulets executed in runic script, it cannot be stressed enough that there is no substantial difference between amulets written in runes and those written in Latin script: they are throughout composed in the Latin language, they use texts and phrases from the Bible or Christian liturgy, and they invoke the help of the Christian god, his angels, and saints. Whether the Trinity, the mother of god, angels, and archangels are invoked, these amulets all serve as protection against the various sources of illnesses, namely demons.

It is interesting to see that Scandinavian scholars only just recently have begun to talk not only about the illnesses mentioned on the amulets but also about the demons which were, throughout the Middle Ages, considered to be source of those illnesses although Klaus Düwel pointed out long ago that amulets, like other magical inscriptions, are aimed at demons and thus must be in a language understood by them.[17] At any rate, the amulets are a document of medieval folk religion and therefore we have to view the texts and their uses within the High Medieval mental framework, despite the modern reluctance to talk about something as obviously medieval as the belief in demons and their master, the devil.

How deep an insight into the medieval fear of demons, and their concept, the amulets can give us, can be shown by a few examples from Denmark and Germany where the demons are not only explicitly conjured up to be banned but where they are also identified with beings from folk tradition dating back to heathen times.

The most explicit of those is the lead amulet from Schleswig (eleventh to twelfth century), which is also among the largest amulets found to date, measuring around 144 mm by 54/59 mm. When folded up into a tiny parcel it only measured around 40 x 30 mm. The inside, which contains the actual conjuration in Latin script in eight lines, reads as follows:

> +Initiu(m) s(an)c(t)i eu(an)g(e)lii s(e)c(un)d(u)m Ioh(anne)m. In pricipio erat v(er)bu(m) et hoc
>
> v(er)b(u)m initio caret e(t) sine fine manet. I(n) no(m)i(n)e d(omi)ni n(ost)ri Iesu Chr(ist)i
>
> c(on)iuro vos demones sive albes ac om(ne)s pestes om(n)iu(m) infirmitatu(m) ac
>
> om(ne)s int(er)iectiones in unicum d(eu)m patre(m) om(n)ip(otente)m ac Ie(su)m Chr(istu)m filiu(m) eius
>
> ac sp(iritu)m s(an)c(tu)m, ut n(on) noceatis famulo d(e)i neq(ue) in die nec i(n) nocte
>
> nec (i)n ullis horis. Ecce cruce(m) + d(omi)ni, fugite partes adv(er)s(ae), vic(it) leo
>
> (de t)ribu Iuda, radix D(av)id, am(en). Cru(x) † benedicat me n(omen) am(en)
>
> Crux + Chr(is)ti p(ro)tegat, crux Chr(ist)i erua(t) me n(omen) a diabolo ac om(n)ib(us) mal(i)s am(en).
>
> "The beginning of the Holy Gospel according to John. In the beginning was the Word and this / Word has no beginning and remains without end. In the name of our Lord Jesus Christ / I conjure you, demons and elves, and all the infections of all illnesses, and / all obstructions, by the one God, the almighty Father and his Son Jesus Christ / and the Holy Spirit, that you may not harm this [male] servant of God by day or by night, / nor at any hours. See the Cross + of Christ! Flee, you hostile forces! The lion / of Judah's tribe has triumphed, the root of David. Amen. / May the Cross bless me, N., Amen. / May Christ's + cross protect, may Christ's cross deliver me, N., from the devil and from all evils, Amen."

In the first two lines we find a quotation from the beginning of the Gospel according to John which is more fully found on the amulet from Bregninge Church on Ærø. This Bible text was considered to be particularly powerful against all evil, probably because of the reference to the divine word. But the fascinating thing about this text is the conjuration of *demones sive albes ac omnes pestes omnium infirmitatum*: this was obviously meant to take care of all possible demons which were a source of illness. By calling them by their vernacular name, *albes*, the writer would have wanted to make sure he was understood by all demons, whether they understood Latin or not!

A notable omission on this particular amulet is the omission of the name of its bearer, that is, the one to be protected by this Christian magical charm. The writer must have copied the text from another amulet or more likely from a text on parchment, but had only a minor grasp of Latin and probably did not realize that the bearer's name should be inserted in the place of N. ("nomen") in the last line of the charm. This does not greatly matter for our understanding of Christian magic.

Another amulet reverting, for safety's sake, also to the Latin and vernacular terms for demons, was found in Romdrup Church in Northern Jutland near the Limfjord, which dates to the period just before 1200;[18] the inscription of six lines is again on the inside of a parceled-up lead sheet, which has also some crosses and the names of god on the outside:

† In nomine patris † et filii † et spiritus sancti amen † adiuro uos eluos uel

eluas aut demones per patrem et filium et spiritum sanctum ut non noceatis huic famu-

lo dei nicholao in oculis nec in capite neque in ulla compagine membrorum set in

habitat in eis uirtus christi altissimi amen † christus uincit † christus regnat † christus imperat

† christus hos oculos cum capite et ceteris membris benedicat † in nomine patris †

et filii † et spiritus sancti amen ††† †a†g†l†a†

In English translation this reads as:

"† In the name of the Father † and the Son † and the Holy Spirit, Amen. † I conjure you, elves [masc.] or elves [fem.] and demons by the Father and the Son and the Holy Spirit, that you may not harm this [male] servant of God Nicholas in the eyes nor in the head nor in his members, but rather that the power of Christ may inhabit him. Amen. † Christ conquers † Christ rules † Christ reigns † Christ bless these eyes together with the head and other members † In the name of the Father † and the Son † and the Holy Spirit, Amen †a†g†l†a†"

The magic word *agla* and its distinct apotropaic function in Christian benedictions, exorcisms, and conjurations have been discussed in detail elsewhere[19] and can also be found—without explicit reference to demons—on the runic lead amulet from Lille Myregård in Bornholm, which on one side contains the Ave Maria, and on the reverse an invocation to God followed by a triple agla, but here in a more varied form: **gala akla a?lala**.[20]

The most distinctive feature of the Romdrup amulet is the explicit distinction between male and female *elves* and their unquestionable identification with demons, furthermore with demons which could harm the person in question with a number of different illnesses.

A very close resemblance to the Romdrup formula has recently been found in Svendborg on Fyn, where the text also talks about *elvos vel elvas & omnes demones.*[21]

Despite the relative vicinity of the Schleswig and the Romdrup amulets, albeit on different ends of the Jutland Peninsula, the demons which obviously were called by the Old Norse term *álfar* appear in different spellings: whether *elphos*/*elphas* is an attempt at Latinizing the word "*álfar*" is hard to say, but the Schleswig text apparently uses a more Germanized version in the word *albes*; this collective noun is answered by yet another lead amulet from even further south, from Halberstadt in East Germany, dated to 1142, where only a single "*elf*" by the name of Alber (the Med. Saxon equivalent to ON *álfar*) is called upon, who is identified as "Devil and Satan." The first part of the inscription, meant to preserve a certain Tado from illnesses, reads as follows:[22]

> In nomine patris et filii et spiritus
> sancti et in nomine nostri iesu christi. Adiuro te
> alber, qui uocaberis diabolus vel satanas, per patrem
> et filium et spiritu sanctum et per omnes angelos et arcangelos . . .
> "In the name of the Father and Son and the Holy Spirit / and in the name of our (lord) Jesus Christ, I conjure you, Alber / who is also called devil (and) Satan, through the Father and the Son and the Holy Spirit / and through all angels and archangels, . . ."

Whereupon it goes on to describe the illnesses that this Alber might (and should not) cause.[23] Calling the demons of illness ON *álfar*, ODan *elphos/elphas* or in Latinized OHG *albes* points to a common Northern European concept of the *álfar* in the High Middle Ages, which is confirmed by some occurrences of *álfar* in OIcl saga texts, where it is clear that the *álfar* mentioned refer not to a heathen concept of *álfar*—which we can no longer fully grasp—but of a Christianized

Northern European medieval concept, in which the term had become a synonym for demons.

That these *álfar* were indeed seen as demons of illness, and emanations of the devils, is shown by a number of new finds of other such lead amulets also in East Germany, where the phrase *eluos uel eluas aut demones* is replaced by similar invocations that were obviously considered synonymous: the explicit phrase *coniuro uos demones et uos Filiis diabolis* on a lead tablet from Seelschen/Ummendorf in Sachsen-Anhalt,[24] the sentence *coniuro vos veh. demone* on a lead tabet from Salhausen near Wolmirstedt,[25] and also the fragmentary—*et diaboli* on an amulet from Klein-Dreileben in Sachsen-Anhalt[26] are all included in conjurations very similar to those tests mentioning the *álfar*.

Another possibility of invoking demons was apparently by calling them by their traditional, but non-Germanic names, as we have seen in the case of the Seven Sisters. But yet one more type of invocation starts by calling them by some magic formula, often reading *Gordan Gordin Ingordan*, as on the abovementioned lead amulet from Bregninge.[27] That phrase is known from several Danish amulets,[28] and we find it also in medieval manuscripts, the best known of which is certainly the Carmina Burana, where they are mentioned in a stanza about the conjuration of demons:[29]

> *Omnis creatura fantasmatum*
> *que corroboratis principatum*
> *serpentis tortuosi, uenenosi,*
> *qui* traxit *per superbiam*
> *stellarum partem terciam,*
> *Gordan, Ingordin et Ingordan,*
> *per sigillum Salomonis*
> *et per magos Pharaonis,*
> *omnes uos coniuro, omnes exorcizo,*
> *per tres magos Caspar, Melchior et Balthasar,*
> *per regem Dauid, qui Saul sedauit,*
> *cum iubilauit uosque fugauit.*[30]

> "Every phantasmal creature who strengthens the lordship of the twisting and venomous serpent who through pride seduced away a third of the stars, Gordan, Ingordin and Ingordan, by the seal of Solomon and by Pharaoh's magicians I conjure you all, I exorcise you all, by the three wise men, Caspar, Melchior and Balthasar, by King David, who placated Saul when he made music [cf. 1 Sam. 16:23] and put you to flight."

The question is whether the three names actually represent a conjuration formula or the names of demons, but the context in the Carmina Burana makes the latter more likely.[31]

The latest addition to amulets bearing these three names is the abovementioned newly found Svendborg amulet, which mentions (in Latin script, with Greek letters[32] in between)+ *Gordan A & ω + Gordin A & ω + Ingordan A & ω* +,[33] and where it is less likely that the names were conceived as names of demons.

To sum up, it can be said that although there are of course many amulets which neither mention the person to be protected personally nor the demons that are conjured up so as not to harm that person, and just limit themselves to holy texts (like the beginning of the Gospel according or John) or holy names, we now do have a good impression of what demons were thought to be doing. They are quite obviously in charge of harming people through illnesses, and not just temporal temptations: in fact, the latter are never mentioned to my knowledge on amulets. It also seems that it was safer to address demons both by their Latin and vernacular terms, and by making sure that male and female demons were both addressed. We also learn from the texts, that apart from proper exorcism formulas also the invocation of the Trinity, of saints, and of various names of god, including Alpha and Omega,[34] magic words like *agla* also served as protection from demons. And we finally hear that demons were conceived of as having proper names, as in the case of the Seven Sisters, or possibly even under the names Gordan, Gordin and Ingordan, which allowed the apotropaic magic to take a better hold on them.

6

Magic Letters

Unintelligible Prophylactic Formulas

Edina Bozoky

Most charms are intelligible formulas used both in oral and written forms. These charms derive their efficacy from the meaning of the words used, reinforced with sound effects when uttered and performed with gesture and ritual. In contrast, the category of unintelligible charms is composed of strange words or of cryptic series of letters. Ancient magical words such as *abrasax* or *abracadabra* were derived from ancient foreign languages (Hebrew, Greek), so medieval users would not have known their original meaning. Cryptic combinations of letters, called *characteres* or *caracteres*, were even more unintelligible. They are composed of letters of the Latin alphabet but seem to be absolutely meaningless to the modern eye. They occur in medieval medical recipe books and also in individual text amulets. They are generally combined together with other kinds of charms.

1. The Usage of Letter Charms

In the *Lacnunga*, a curious charm ensures protection against a dwarf. The formula had to be inscribed on the arms and was combined with the medical instruction to drink a concoction made of rubbing celandine (*Chelidonium majus* or *Ficaria verna*) mixed with ale. In this case, the meaning of the letters could be resolved: *t* may stand for Trinity, *p* for pater, *N* for *nomen*, *UI* for *Victoricus*, and *M* for *Macutus*.

> "Write this along the arms against a dwarf":
>
> + *t* + *ω A*
>
> "And rub celandine into ale."

Sanctus Macutus, Sancte Victorici.
"Write this along the arms against a dwarf":
+t+p+N+ω+t+UI+M+ωA
"And rub celandine into ale."
Sanctus Macutus, Sancte Victorici.[1]

Another formula recommends wearing on oneself an inscribed sheet of parchment to obtain favors from a lord, or the king, or another man. The formula begins with a series of letters:

> "If you want to go to your lord, or the king, or to another man, or to a meeting, then you must wear these letters; each of them will be gracious and friendly to you":
> *XX. h. d. e. o. e. o. o. e. e.e. laf. d. R.U. fi. d. f. P. A. x. Box. Nux. In nomine patris Rex. M. p. x.xix. xcs. xhi. ih. Deo. eo. Deo. deeo. lafdruel. bepax. box. nux. bu. In nomine patris rex marie. ihs. xpc. dominus meus. ihc.*[2]

Against theft, one must write in silence a formula containing letters and put it under the heel of one's left shoe.

> "When somebody steals anything from you, write this in silence and put it in your left shoe under your heel, then you will soon find out about it."[3]

Several charms composed of letters were used to stop bleeding. In a recipe book of the fourteenth century which copied more ancient recipes—right after providing a narrative charm in English for the same use—an instruction in Latin recommends a series of letters to write on something and put it on one's navel.

> *For to staunche blode of hors.*
> *Pone ista signa ad umbilicum scripta super aliquid. Fac pe.n.m.x.a.s.z.i.ii.iii.*[4]

A charm in a manuscript of the twelfth century contains a mixed formula with letters:

> *Ad restringendum sanguinis de venariaris effluentis*
> *In nomine patris et filli et spiritu sancti. Sta. sta. stagnum. fluxus sanguinis, sicut stetit iordan in quo iohannes ihesum christum baptizauit. Kyrieleison. amen. Pater noster. Ecce crucem. d. f. p. a. u. l. d. t. i. r. d. in nomine domini. Ad instruum sanguinis. Scribat in folio et detur patienti hec. Sicut uere credimus quod beata uirgo maria peperit dominum infantem uerum et hominem sic tu uena retine tuum sanguinem in nomine patris. Stomen. Kaloc. Stomen. Meta Fonn.*[5]

In the same manuscript, another composite charm was used against fevers. Its first part consists of unintelligible words, followed by the names of God and an instruction which orders to write the charm on a lead cross and to attach it around the neck of the patient. In the end of the charm there are verbs and a series of letters.

> *Contra febres*
> *Hon. con. ton. ron. yon. zon. at. Heli ihesus. on. ihesus. christus. ihesus. Grama. ihesus. ton. ihesus. christus. ihesus. sat. ihesus. christus. ihesus. Scribatur istud in cruce plumbea et suspendatur in collo patientis. Ardeo. sentio. fugio. Dextera. d. f. y. d. d. e. m. d. d. fy.*[6]

In an Anglo-Norman manuscript of the *Letters of Hippocrates*, the instruction specifies the manner of writing a charm composed of letters and proves its efficacy:

> "Write these letters on two places of a parchment and attach it on both thighs. If you don't believe in it, write these letters on a knife and kill a pig with it: not a single drop of blood will come from it."
>
> *Item escrivez icestes lettres en parchemin en deus lius, si li liez sur ambesdeus les quisses. Si vus nel creez, escrivez les lettres en un cutel, si en ociez un porc; ja gute de sanc ne li charra. Cestes sunt les lettres p.g.c.p.e.v.o.x.a.g.z.*[7]
>
> "Bleedinge to stanch, wryte these words in parchment & bynde them vpon both thy thighes.—p.n.b.t.C.e.v.exoq. & yf you will not beleeue yt, wryte these letters on a knyfe & kyll a hogge ther wth & he will not bleede."[8]

A similar charm *Par sainc est che* with proof is recommended in the *Médecinaire liégeois*. The charm begins with an invocation to Mary and a conjuration addressed to the vein to retain the blood, and ends with a formula containing *caracteres* (*karaktes*):

> *Max.pax.nax.y.II.debet.anevba.aut nevba. Ces karaktes escris en un brief. & mes sur le pie u loie des sa maint, si cesserat. & se tu de chu doites, escris ces lettres en un maince de cutheal & oci ent un porke, n'en isterat sainc.*[9]

The same evidence is suggested in a Provençal version of the *Letters of Hippocrates*:

> *Flum de sanc.*
> *A femna q(ue) aga flum de sanc, fay li portar escrit en parguames verges el col aquestas paraulas ho caractas : p.x.33.c.p.o.q.x.a.33.a. E se no vols creyre q(ue) aysso no sia vertat, escryeu aquestas caractas en cotel quant volras ausire (un) porc, q(ue) non salira sanc jamays.*[10]

In the same manuscript, letters are recommended against infertility. The charm must be written on a virgin parchment without either the husband or the wife knowing. The formula can be proved:

"If you don't want to believe in it, write these words on a tree which can't keep its flowers, and it will do so immediately."

Per aver e(n)fant. A femna q(ue) non pot aver enfant, fassa escrieure aquestas paraulas en parguames verges de guiza e de manieyra q(ue) lo marit ni la molher non sapia deguna caussa, portant sobre sy : o.dd.u.d.o.d.r.p.s. Se no vols aysso creyr'e vols ho proar, pausa aquestas paraulas escrichas en cal(que) loc de (un) albre q(ue) non puescha retenir sas flors, aqui messeys las retenra.[11]

To facilitate childbirth, a Provençal recipe recommends two solutions: a ritual and an inscription. According to the ritual, one must take some earth and, facing the door, put it under the woman's head. If it doesn't work, one must write letters and tie them on her thigh:

P(er) e(n)trav(i)same(n)t d'e(n)[fant]. Per femena a cui es entrav(i)satz l'enfant el cors prenes la t(er)ra on se torneia la porta; si la metes sus lo cap de la femna en cors, e tantost lo gitara. E si per aventura tot no(n) lo gieta escrives aquestas letras e lias las li a la cueissa: r.m.?.?.o.t.r.o.x.a.b.l.q.q.f.m.q.r.[12]

Series of letters were often used against epilepsy. For example, a charm recommends to write letters on a brass ring and to wear it on the middle finger: "you will not fall." And "take the ring and pour three drops of holy water through it on the sick."

a.g.j.a.b.j.C. A. e. s. q. s. l'[13]

Collections of the fourteenth and fifteenth centuries contain often non-medical charms: for example, protection against enemies:

"The person who wants to keep away from his enemies harm, must wear on himself written letters":

Enemicz. Persona q(ue) velha q(ue) sois enemicz no li fasso degun mal, porte aquestas en escritz sobre sy : e.et.o.q.t.q.g.ooo.12.1.o.n.o.n.q.q.99.f.p.e.d.n.h.o.v. xxv.[14]

The *Médecinaire liégeois* contains also a charm of letters against enemies:

"A l'anemis chachier del maison, escris al paroit: *ppp.o.e.y.e.p.p.b.p.d.c.*"[15]

Another charm recommends wearing letters written on a virgin parchment to avoid wrongful imprisonment:

"Prionier. A perssona q(ue) sia mes a tort en presson, porte ho aga aquestas letras escrichas en parguames verges : rr.ii.x.b.q.e.b.a.e.nq.q(ue)..p.i. +"[16]

To know the whereabouts of stolen objects, one must write *caracteres* on a virgin sheet and put it under the head: in this manner, one will learn the truth in dreams.

> "A truovar i furti : Se vuoi sapere di cierta cosa furata, scrive in carta virgine questi caratteri e poni sotto il capo quando vai a dormire, et sentirai in sonnio la verità : *b, F,L, c, d, be, tra, L, per, x, h, ce ij, h, h, qz, i, h, s, +h, x, s, per, x, e.*"[17]

In the same way, to know if a sick person will be cured or die, one must write letters on an egg.

> "Perrét un eof ke seit puns meime le jor k'il ad maladie, si escrivét su sette lettres *i.so.s.p.q.x.s.y.x.s.9.o*. Pus metét cel of là ors de[suz] le cel en saf liu e pus l'endemein depescét cel of. Si sanc en ist, si murrat; si n'i ad nul signe de sanc, si garrat. Esprové chose est."
>
> *Ad probandum si eger possit evadere necne. Recipe ovum quod sit a gallina positum eadem die quo cepit egrotare et scribe super cum incausto has litteras + ygo. s. ff. x. g. y. x. g. 9. Postea pone ovum per noctem foras sub libero aere. Et postea in mane frange caute ovum; si sanguis inde exit, morietur; si nulla est ibi macula sanguinis, procul dubio evadet.*"[18]

2. Letter Charms in Individual Textual Amulets

In individual textual amulets we can find a great variety of formulas. The Canterbury cathedral amulet,[19] dated from the mid-thirteenth century, is an actual anthology of apotropaic charms. It is the first text amulet which combines ancient and new magic formulas.

Proportionally divine names occur most often: nine times. There are also "classic" formulas: the *Letter of Abgar*, mentions of the *Letter of Charlemagne*, the *Letter of Columba*, and the charm of the *Seven Sleepers of Ephesus*. All kinds of blood-staunching charms are assembled.

Series of letters occur several times. In the first column, it is recommended to look at "Greek signs"—but in fact these are Latin letters—in order to obtain favors from everybody; later, a series of letters and unintelligible words must be kept on oneself in order to be loved and esteemed by everybody and to be protected against all disturbances; then another series of letters ensures the victory to the honest bearer and that nobody could damage him; finally, a list of divine names must be tied on oneself. In the second column, a series of letters is inserted into a list of divine names and a liturgical invocation to the Lord, asking him to protect the supplicant from the spirit of fornication. In the fourth column, a series of letters is preceded again by a list of divine names. The instruction says: the person who would carry these letters will be unvanquished. In the fifth column, there is also a small series of letters following divine names: one must utter these names against the tempest. Later on, an instruction specifies that

> Pope Leo sent these letters to Charlemagne who made haste to wage war, letters brought by an angel of the Lord to saint Gregory, and all Christians must carry them on themselves.

In the sixth column, a series of letters is inserted in a formula to stop bleeding. One must write it on a *bref* and hang it on their breast: bleeding will immediately stop. Skeptics are suggested to carry out the same "experiment" with a pig as mentioned before.

In another individual textual amulet called the "*Sachet accoucheur*" (birthing amulet), the apotropaic formulas are mixed with magical letters. Unfortunately we do not know the whereabouts of the object studied by Alphonse Aymar in 1926.[20] Several parchment pieces were kept together in a small rectangular linen purse. Parchment n° 3 was a complex folded amulet written at the beginning of the fourteenth century, containing an actual anthology of magical formulas, series of letters, and magic seals. In the first square of the verso, according to the reference, a series of letters offered by St. Leo to Charlemagne protects whoever keeps it on himself against enemies, sword, drowning, poisons, snakes, demons, plagues, and all kinds of harm. And whoever carries it on himself and looks at it every day will not be killed by any weapon. Letters are interspersed with divine names and end with the liturgical formula *Christus vincit + Christus regnat + Christus imperat*.

In the second square an instruction orders to write on a lead leaf a series of letters and keep it under the right foot. Two other squares bear several series of letters. A series instructing to write on a virgin parchment was used against epilepsy. Two series also written on a virgin parchment and kept on oneself could make the bearer loved by all men and women, and a last series of letters grants even the love of his enemy.

3. Diffusion and Efficacy of Letter Charms

Letter charms were often written on individual amulets (*brevi*). Few pieces have been preserved, but they were incredibly widespread. Some physicians, such as John Ardene (1307–77), even recommended them[21] against nosebleed and wounds:

> *p.x.b.c.p.o.p.x.a. b.q.a.*[22]

So did Thomas Fayreford (active between 1420 and 1460):

> *G.k.B.x.k.2.l.o.x.a.o.l.R.o.l.*[23]

According to some mentions, *brevi* were often written on strips of vellum and sold for 5–8 florins or in equal sums. In 1298, the Statutes of the *Università della Lana* of Siena prohibited its members to make vellum, because it could be used to write *brevi*.[24] In 1458, Ser Luca di Feo, a priest of the territory of Siena was punished for making *brevi* on which this formula was written:

> *x.b.r.q.d.a.e.p. et mentem sanctam spontaneam honorem Deo et patrie liberationem. Guaspar, Baldaxar et Menchior, Christo è nato, Christo è morto. Christo è resuscitato. Yhesus auctem transiens per medium illorum ibat.*[25]

Formulas of *brevi* could also be copied out of recipe collection books which served as exemplars.

Some documents evoke *brevi* with magical letters and signs, without transcribing them. When a plot against Pope Benedictus XIII (1406–7) was discovered, magister John of Athene had on himself, in a little box, several *brevi* written on parchment and on paper, a wax apple containing a little *petacium* with several writings and *terribiles* and unintelligible *caracteres* with signs and names; a little scroll containing St. John's Gospel and unintelligible *caracteres*; and on an image of the crucifix and on that of a child were also *caracteres*. In this case it was claimed that they were not used for personal protection but to harm someone.[26]

The formulas composed by series of letters were used only in written form. The instructions specify that they should not be uttered but had to be written on a parchment, on another support, or even on the body. They had to be in contact with the user's body. In general, "the mere fact of their presence was sufficient, and there was no need for them to be seen."[27] According to Reginald Scot's *Discoverie of Witchcraft* (1584), the formula composed of letters against thieves must never be uttered, but carried on oneself:

> A popish periapt or charme, which must never be said, but carried about one, against theeves.[28]

> I doo go, and I doo come unto you with the love of God, with the humilitie of Christ, with the holines of our blessed ladie, with the faith of Abraham, with the justice of Isaac, with the vertue of David, with the might of Peter, with the constancie of Paule, with the word of God, with the authoritie of Gregorie, with the praier of Clement, with the floud of Jordan, *p p p c g e g a q q est p t 1 ka b g l k 2 a x t g t b am g 2 4 2 1 q; p x c g k q a 99 p o q q r*. Oh onlie Father + oh onlie lord + And Jesus + passing through the middest of them + went + In the name of the Father + and of the Sonne + and of the Holie-ghost +.

The instructions concerning charms of magical letters rarely specify the ritual which could have accompanied their use, but the action of binding is often evoked. "The act of binding is perpetuated as an enduring source of protection in the case of magic knots, mostly adorned with magic characters, that were worn round the neck."[29] In intelligible charms, the meaning is essential. In the conjurations, a direct order is addressed to a supernatural power or to the sickness. In narrative charms, the healing power is expressed by the *historiola*'s protagonist.[30] In unintelligible charms, the meaning of the letters does not play any part in their efficacy. On the contrary, the lack of an apparent meaning, the incomprehensibility of the formulas, suggests their belonging to a secret language with a hidden meaning.

4. Comparison with Letter Charms of Antiquity

Modern scholars call unintelligible words or series of letters "Ephesia grammata" or "voces magicae." Originally, the term "Ephesia grammata" designated six words engraved on Artemis' statue at Ephesus. One could wear these words as amulets against demons, bad luck, and to obtain a supernatural help. Just like strange or distorted words, unintelligible series of letters have been thought to possess specific power,[31] a mysterious language, understood only by the supernatural powers.

In the ancient magical formulas there are often series of vowels or letters and signs. In particular, there are Greek vowels: but they were associated with the seven planets and also with the angels, and thus they had their own meaning. "But in many places in the magical papyri the seven Greek vowels appear in a form which suggests that special significance has been attributed to their visual representation";[32] they were inscribed in a triangular arrangement, as in a charm of the magical papyrus (*PGM*) XCVIII, asking Sarapis to heal Artemidora:[33]

A	Victorious in everything is
EE	the nourisher of
EEE	the whole inhabited
IIII	world, lord Sarapis,
OOOOO	deliver
YYYYYY	Artemidora.
OOOOOOO	

In *PGM* I, instructions depict how to obtain an assistant demon. After a long ritual preparation, one had to write the Greek vowels in two triangles. After the sacrifice of a falcon, the performer had to utter a spell beginning with the pronunciation of the seven vowels.[34]

In another spell (*PGM* XIII), the uttering of the heptagram is a part of a ritual performance:

> Speaking to the rising sun, stretching out your right hand to the left and your left hand likewise to the left, say "A." To the north, putting forward only your right fist, say "E." Then to the west, extending both hands in front [of you], say "E." To the south, [holding] both on your stomach, say "I." To the earth, bending over, touching the ends of your toes, say "O." Looking into the air, having your hand on your heart, say "Y." Looking into the sky, having both hands on your head, say "O."[35]

In the same formula, the performer calls on the ruler of all, by the voice of the male and female gods pronouncing the seven vowels in different combinations. And the seven vowels had to be written also on a gold lamella in the shape of "wings"—writing the vowels in successive lines, in each line dropping one letter from the same end until only one is left.[36]

5. Conclusion

Medieval charms composed of magical letters were used with other kinds of formulas: narrative charms, conjurations, divine names, and the like. Most of these letter charms were used for permanent protection or long-lasting use, apart from the blood-staunching formulas (but these formulas were very often combined with narrative charms and conjurations) and the ones used to facilitate childbirth. It would seem that for an immediate effect, narrative charms and conjurations were considered the most pertinent. Narrative charms created a correspondence between the "mythical" and the actual situation of a sick person.

The assimilation of the patient to the collective mythology and the integration of the individual in a cosmic order had a "symbolic efficacy." Conjurations addressed to the illness (or to the demons of illness) were considered as orders which could be immediately performant. On the other hand, formulas containing divine names and strange words had the same use as that of *caracteres*. If the church was relatively tolerant with certain invocations and prayers on the sick, formulas consisting of unknown words, *caracteres*, and signs had to be rejected.

The *Hammer of Witches* (*Malleus maleficarum*) suspected a pact with demons behind these formulas: "because of the unknown words and the written *caracteres*, there is a tacit pact with the demon, and the demon intervenes obscurely accomplishing the desires in order to lure into the worst."[37]

Unintelligible formulas are a category of text amulets which are composed of strange words or of cryptic series of letters. Some of them derive from words, names, or formulas in another language, for example, the ancient magical words "*abrasax*," "*abracadabra*," or "*AGLA*" and "*ANANIZAPTA*." Medieval users could not know their original meaning. Meaningless combinations of letters, called *characteres*, were even more unintelligible.

These formulas were used exclusively in written form, inscribed on parchment, on jewels and other objects and applied even on the body. They offered healing, protection, or acquisition of wealth.

According to a mention, they must never be uttered, but carried on oneself. The charms of medieval medical recipe books and that of individual amulets are often combined together with other—intelligible—prophylactic formulas.

The church was suspicious of unintelligible formulas because of the unknown words and *characteres* which they contained. The *Hammer of Witches* (*Malleus maleficarum*) suspected a pact with demons behind these formulas.

7

The Materiality of Talismans from Early Modern Spain

Morisco (and Old-Christian) Cases

Esther Fernández Medina

1. Introduction

The Moriscos of early modern Spain were a minority group from the point of view of culture and also on religious grounds.[1] As descendants of the Muslim population of al-Andalus, in the Iberian Peninsula, they were obliged to convert to Christianity by means of Royal edicts in the first quarter of the sixteenth century. After being expelled in 1609–10 from the Spanish Monarchy, they spread around the Mediterranean, settling in the Magreb, Italy, Turkey, and, even, America. Even though, in some areas the population still claim their Morisco origins, we can affirm that their traces have completely disappeared.[2]

Nevertheless, most of their cultural and religious backgrounds have been preserved in a kind of literature known as Aljamiada (from "aljamía," *al-a'jamīa*, i.e., the others' language) due to the peculiarity of the Romance language written in Arabic.[3] The Moriscos used to hide those scripts because of the Catholic Monarchy's prohibition of their cultural features, especially with regard to writing. As a result of those unfortunate circumstances, many secret libraries have been discovered, preserved, and studied. While most archival collections are located in Spain, it is also possible to find volumes of Aljamiado manuscript in other European, Magribian, and Middle East libraries. Aljamiado scholars have shown that these writings lay their basis on the Islamic culture since religious texts are the most frequent among them, with medical and magical issues in the second place of importance.[4]

2. Means and Aims of Morisco Textual Amulets

As religion, medicine, and magic were frequently intermingled areas, we must consider them in an inclusive approach regarding the study of Aljamiado manuscripts. Textual amulets, or talismans, contained symbols, letters, or prayers that acted as remedies for any kind of pain or trouble. They were directed to ease the illnesses of humans and beasts, as well as to achieve many other benefits and objectives as, for instance, treasure hunting. We also find talismans to avoid calamities, providing safety before attacks, shipwrecks, storms, or, even, the Inquisition trials.[5] In that fashion, magic was present in any kind of manuscript, even of juridical or religious matters, where specialists were offering instructions for the creation of talismans. They reveal that magical beliefs were ever-present in the Morisco daily routine.

Quoting from the classical study concerning magic in the western Islam by Edmond Doutté, *Magie et religion dans l'Afrique du Nord*:

> The most commonly used talismans were those easily carried around, for instance, those consisting in graphic characters and signs. These written talismans are without any doubt the most generalized and they are called by the Arabs with the name of *herz*, term derived from "ḥrz" signifying "to preserve." The talismans still called *ḥerz*, *ḥeŷāb*, *maʿāda*, *nūfra*, are also carried around for a particular purpose, or, in general, to ward off bad luck.[6]

The term *hirz* (حرز i.e., protection) was largely used by the Moriscos. Many examples of worn talismans are described in inquisitorial trials. In that way, the Christian authorities also called "herce," "hirce," "alherce," or "alhirce" those written artifacts in their Romance transcriptions. The notion of the paper material on which the talismans were commonly written could be added to the previous definition. Easily acquired, paper or linen material was preferred over parchment or metal, due to their low cost, in order to store everyday recipes, prayers, or *herces*.[7] Differently from the Islamic period of al-Andalus, the Moriscos did not elaborate their *herces* on metal support,[8] even though they persisted in wearing them over the body, hidden between the garments, hung around the neck or inside pouches.[9]

This sort of portable talismans was an ancient practice already existing in the oldest civilizations. And, in such a fashion, our description of Morisco textual magical artifacts would fit with that of Jacco Dieleman's from Egyptian studies, just replacing the papyrus material with paper:

> A talisman or "textual amulet" is an apotropaic text written on a separate strip or sheet of linen, papyrus, or metal, which, when folded or rolled and tied, was

> worn as a personal form of protection on the body, usually a string around the neck.[10]

Relating to their content, Morisco talismans combined simultaneously religious formulas, such as Koranic verses and divine names, enigmatic language and magical symbols.[11] Although not many original examples of separated talismans have been preserved, the uninterrupted chain of magical works, and the Morisco fondness in talismanic developments, leads us to acknowledge an early use of textual talismans in al-Andalus. Thus, the practice of writing magical formulas on paper with Koranic verses and some other elements taken from the Islamic esotericism can be traced from East to West, in a continuum, until they merge into the practices of the Moriscos of early modern Spain.[12]

3. Written Talismans for Health Purposes

Numerous instructions to make talismans are found in manuscripts, but there is still no single corpus for all Andalusian and Morisco examples. It is even worse for the separated talismans on paper, which eventually disappeared from the archives, as it is the case of many of them recorded alongside the inquisitorial trials. The Tribunal of the Inquisition prosecuted the magical practices as a form of heresy, thus leaving a good number of testimonial documents to study the materiality of talismans in early modern Spain.[13]

A recent edition of inquisitorial documents made by Ana Labarta lists and describes two papers with instructions to make talismans from the trial of Jaime Bolaix, in 1585.[14] It was in Valencia, a region where the Arabic language and culture was still alive as far as in the last quarter of the sixteenth century. The instructions were assembled with a recipe to clean metals and another one to make soap, as a small booklet of common recipes. The first magical text gives instructions on how to make a talisman to bring down a fever. It reads as follows:

> Take a blue linen and write on it these names: *Qaš.našin ʿz.tadyšin Dah.lš ʿn.d Qarqašin*. After writing the names on the linen, roll a chicken egg in it and toast it on the fire without letting the linen burn. Give the egg to the person suffering from fever. With the shell of the egg, roll it inside the linen, and hang it around the neck of the person. He will be free [of the fever] God willing, and he won't suffer it again.[15]

Surprisingly, the author added the source of the talismanic remedy:

> I found this [instruction] written in the first volume of al-Burzulī's book, owned by *al-ḥubs* [i.e., the guardian of goods] of the *maqṣūra* [i.e., the site of someone important] of the Zaytūna mosque in Tunis.—May God keep It and make Its memory endure. The cited book tells that the names are taken from the "alfaquí" [*al-faqīh*, i.e., jurisconsult] Ibn ʿArafa—Have God, exalted Be, mercy on him!

And, interestingly enough, the inquisitorial qualifier adds in the margins of the document:

> There is a "herce" written as a way of Moorish rituals and witchcraft.[16]

As we said, unfortunately, this piece has now disappeared.

The individuals who had the knowledge or skills to elaborate talismans were usually versed in religious prayers. They had access to textual sources and were called "alfaquíes" (الفقيه, *al-faqīh*, i.e., jurisconsult, lawman). Their role in the Morisco communities was not only guiding people in their religious practices and legal cases but also providing means to healing.[17]

Our second magical recipe explains the way to elaborate a magical square (وفق, *wafq*), known as *budūḥ* (بدوح), a very popular seal (خطم, *khatim*) to ease childbirth. This symbol was also used as a form of protection against calamities, to ward off inquisitorial or civil authorities, as well as to preserve health. This popular artifact found in Arabic, as well as Latin and Hebrew manuscripts, was named after the acronym made up of the letters in its corners.[18] We find an instruction to elaborate the popular *budūḥ* in an Aljamiado manuscript preserved in Madrid. This manuscript is part of the set found in Almonacid de la Sierra (Zaragoza) at the beginning of the twentieth century and edited also by Labarta in 1992.[19]

It also includes the recipe to make the popular talisman for childbirth, which reads as follows:

> *Alḥerce* for the woman. When she couldn't give birth, hang it on her left leg and she will give birth, with God willing. And this is it: *Wa-hiyya alf allā Manāfaṭīš Laṭīš khala' wa-law tāmyam wa-l-ta'īs khala' ḥamala bi-qu(ra)wa Allāh al-Ḥayy al-Qayyūm*. [Magic square] Finished.[20]

In the case of Islamic studies, Emile Savage Smith has pointed out the difficulty to assess the actual use by talisman makers of the instructions given in the magical treatises. But, while other artifacts as magical bowls or magic shirts deviated from texts in the Islamic tradition, in early modern Spain we can trace some continuity between the inquisitorial cases and the Aljamiado manuscripts. Even though magical treatises contained an important mythical background that the sociopolitical constraints censured, Morisco "herces" seemed more alike their manuscript sources.[21]

4. Prophylactic Talismans for Various Purposes

We can learn of the strength of Islamic culture, also with respect to magical artifacts, from further examples in the Inquisition of Valencia, a region where Muslims remained tied to their cultural roots. In 1597, Leonés Benali was found in possession of a talisman protecting from iron, meaning swords or knives, as well as against evil or misfortune. Leonés was a merchant and a cartwright, and we can therefore deduce that the talisman was aimed to protect him in the long journeys along the Spanish roads from possible assaults. The singularity of this talisman resides in the combination of Koranic verses and esoteric elements. The trial goes on to describe the paper talisman as including on one side the verse 255 of the second chapter of the Qur'an, known as *Sūrat al-Baqarah* (سورة البقرة), the most common verse for protection within the Koranic text, as well as a magic square, on the other.[22]

The preservation of Islamic culture or heritage on behalf of the Moriscos had to do with the sacred meaning of Arabic script since the Qur'an was revealed in this language. This endowed its letters with protective and healing potential. Arabic script acquired apotropaic meaning, as well as portions or pages of the Qur'an had talismanic value. Likewise, Moriscos used to hide them under their clothes. For those reasons, inquisitorial authorities prosecuted any Muslim manifestation, thus identifying Arabic script with Islamic faith.[23]

Leonés was well aware of the prohibition of the Arabic script. He had the paper hidden inside his garments, on his chest. He had tried to throw it into a nearby stream just moments before facing the officials, at the gates of the city of Valencia. But, unfortunately for him, he was discovered. The Inquisition account describes the violence shown by the officials the moment of the discovery.[24]

The Moriscos made great use of this kind of artifacts containing Koranic writing, enigmatic language, and magical symbols, as numerous cases of the Inquisition show. To this regard, we can quote the trial of Leonor de Mendoza, from Granada:

> In the first audition she said she guessed she had been held because of those papers that had been found in her house.[25]

Namely, some papers written in Arabic and a seal with Arabic letters. Those papers were later qualified by the experts of the Holy Office (i.e., the Inquisition) as referring to the law of Mahoma (i.e., Islam). To defend herself, she told the inquisitors, that:

> Those papers had been offered to her by a Morisco when she was sick, and he told her that only having them in her power they would provide health, that they were good for everything and for treasure hunting. And since she had the papers in her power she felt cured from the heart pain she suffered. Then, she thought the papers and the things they included were good. Also, the Morisco told her that in those papers there were good Koranic prayers, but he did not tell her to recite them.[26]

The following document could be a faithful example of this sort of talismans that were hidden and carried around. It is a loose paper located in the Real Academia de la Historia, in Madrid, containing a verse from the Qur'an followed by a short prayer composed by what seems to be Beautiful Names, and some enigmatic or magical words (see Figure 7.1):

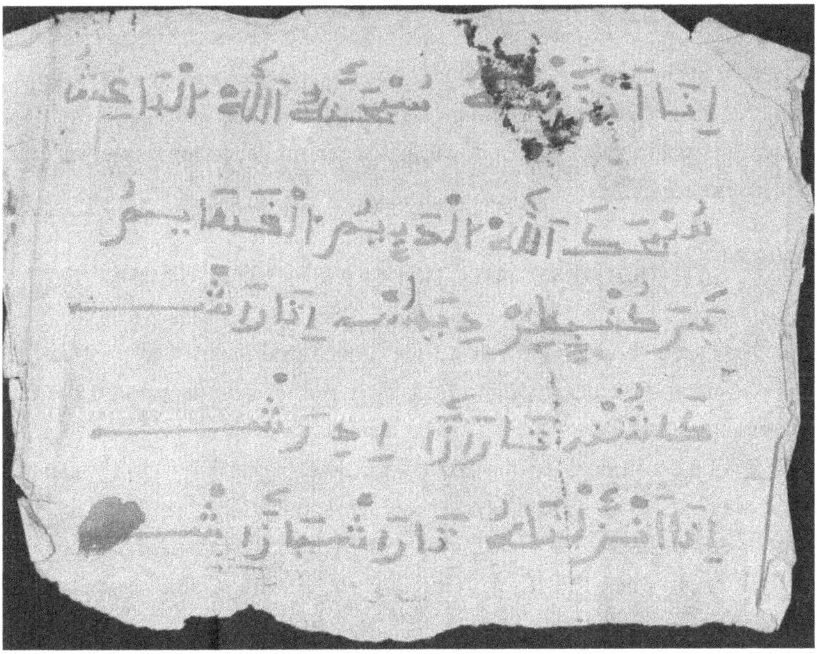

Figure 7.1 "Herce," sixteenth century?, Ms. V25 (II/9416, caja n° 25) BRAH, loose paper. © Real Academia de la Historia. Spain.

> *Innā 'anzalnāhu. Subḥanahu-llāh al-Bāgiṯu*. Subḥaka-llāh al-Dā'imu* al-Qahāimu*. Barakunbilir dīallāh Itārāš Kāšun Tārāzā Idiraš. Innā 'anzalnāhu Tārāšbāzāš.*
>
> "We send It down [i.e., the Holy Quran] [Sūrat al-Qadr, 97:1]. Glorified be God, the Resurrector. Glorified be the Permanent, the Persistent. *Barakunbilir dīallāh Itārāš Kāšun Tārāzā Idiraš*. We send it down. *Tārāšbāzāš*."[27]

As for the ink, the *alfaquíes* preferred using saffron to write their *herces*, which hinders deciphering those parts faded by time. Sometimes, the act of writing was not enough, and the script was dissolved into water and drunk in order to recover the lost health. They would write them with this kind of ink, or even with rose water, which would easily dissolve in plain water. References to these practices are also found in the inquisitorial archives. Given that the prophylactic use of the verses of the Qur'an was accredited in the "Medicine of the Prophet," it was a very popular practice in the Islamic world. Using an outsider approach, we could say that the medicinal, the magical, and the religious found a perfect communion in this kind of practices.[28]

The Islamic belief was frequently linked to the Moriscos' magical practices for healing purposes. We saw it in the previous examples, as also in that of Rafaela Mayor, from Xátiva. This last one was found in possession of two *herçes* that were offered by a doctor (probably an alfaqui) to cure a *seca* (i.e., a sickness in the nodes) in the neck and the groin. She also confessed to have been living as a *mora* (i.e., Muslim) for twelve years. According to the description of the talisman maker, the doctor was a Morisco who had been punished for unknown crime, since his nose had been cut off.[29]

5. Written Talismans for Love and Other Purposes

As we have seen, the Morisco *herces* were carried in the same way people would their prayers and recipes, hidden under their clothes or hung around the neck. Furthermore, they were stitched inside their clothes. As in the case of another Morisca who sent her skirt to a tailor, who then found in a hem the talisman aimed to create harmony between her and her spouse. She simply had forgotten about it. Her name was Isabel de Lopo, from Malón, in Aragón, in the year 1595. Her trial starts when the tailor found this paper with Arabic characters. She justifies herself in this way:

> She confessed that three years ago a certain new convert [i.e., a Morisco], as he saw that she was always fighting with her spouse, gave her a paper. He put

> it inside the hem of her skirt, advising her not to tell anyone and she would find peace. She had worn the paper until she took the skirt to a tailor and she supposed that he had taken it. But she never knew what the paper contained, since the Morisco never told her.[30]

The inquisitorial term for talisman, *herce*, would also be replaced by *nómina* or *cédula*, or even simply *papel* (i.e., paper), if its content was not specified. Although Isabel claimed not to be aware of its contents, and even to have forgotten about it, the written paper was a talisman aimed to channel her psychological distress. She considered its effectiveness real and maybe also did the inquisitors.

Another good example of a love talisman is one from the Escuela de Estudios Árabes in Granada, which combines geometrical and scriptural patterns with a kind of cuneiform script (i.e., an ancient Koranic calligraphy). We find numerous examples of such instructions for love purposes in the Aljamiado manuscripts, thus showing their extensive use (see Figure 7.2).

A large number of magical characters and symbols appearing in the Arabic and Aljamiado manuscripts became part of the array of the European ritual magic. For its users, it permeated the magical practices of the Old Christians.

Figure 7.2 مجموعة مؤلفات في الأمداح النبوية [Maŷmū'at mu'allafāt fī l-amdāḥ al-nabawiyya], Ms. nineteenth century? Arabic (GR-EEA ms4), Biblioteca Escuela Estudios Árabes, f. 87v.

This is clear in the case of Diego de Vargas, who, seeking help from a healer or *santiguador* in order to cure a herpes, was eventually convinced of the efficacy of those enigmatic signs for love purposes. First, the *santiguador* blessed or prayed on the sickness:

> Diego de Vargas, butcher and inhabitant of Ronda was testified in the city of Marbella by a witness that 8 or 9 years ago when feeling sick, having come to his notice that the prisoner prayed [santiguaba] the herpes [maldita], and cut it and healed other infirmities, he had called for him in order to cure his sick leg. And he cured him by praying upon [santinguándole] him.[31]

Immediately, after this first description, we find our love procedure:

> And talking about a certain woman in whose house he used to enter, and whom he kissed her, and whom he held without getting more from her, the prisoner told him that he would give him something to get whatever he wanted from her. He told him to write on the palm of his hand five or six words. He did, as the prisoner told him, and they were not in Latin nor Romance, nor in any other language the witness could understand. Having them written, he should go to bed without talking to anyone or reciting any prayer.[32]

The last procedure of writing on the body of the client seemed to be still in use in many rural areas around Andalucía, until the last century, thus in a traditional Christian context. The words were, as the witness claims, neither Latin, Romance, nor any other language he knew, so probably he had had some kind of enigmatic, maybe even Arabic shaped letters written on his hand. The use of enigmatic letters or symbols could fulfill a rhetoric function rather than having a specific meaning to be decrypted or forming a logical sequence.

Further possible purposes could be material or economic, as well as proper treasure hunt. The next inquisitorial example showing notions of ritual magic is that of Antonio de Piedrahita, a Morisco from Arévalo. He was found in possession of a written paper, most probably in enigmatic letters, inside a pouch. A Morisca had offered it to him without saying what was written on it, only that just by wearing it he would have good luck in selling his stock. Then, the authorities searched for confirmation:

> When they showed the paper that was written with saffron to some of the Moriscos who were imprisoned [. . .] all of them said that it was not Moorish writing. In the expertise of Jerónimo Espinel, he said they were superstitious characters many of which are in the *Clavicula of Solomon*. And the contents of this paper serve to demonic submission in order to have good luck and success

> in anything asked and intended. It was for having good luck in selling stock, as it appears in the role of the Sun sign which prevails over gold and finances.[33]

The Old-Christian population considered the Moriscos as having a special charm for magical issues. There is a good number of references in the inquisitorial archives that show their active roles in ritual magic enterprises, and even their collaboration with Protestant individuals with regard to treasure hunting. In this type of rituals, the knowledge of the Solomonic letters and other magical symbols was greatly appreciated. In Europe, astral and magical treatises, or *grimoires*, went back to Arabic sources as in the case of the *Clavicula Salomonis*.[34] The seals there contained would function as a mystical means for authority, since they represented the Seal of Solomon, the biblical king and Islamic prophet who had power over demons, and many other forces. And the Moriscos seemed to have a direct link to that written language.[35]

6. Conclusion

As I have already hinted, the most common objective in the fabrication of *herces* was the quest not only for health and protection but also for love and many other issues. They were written using enigmatic words and symbols, and the simple act of writing and carrying them was thought to be effective or curative. The materials were adapted to the specific needs of the talisman holder by their makers, usually law men. Their elaborations would follow the guides contained in the manuscripts of magical content, sometimes intertwined with medicinal recipes, and mostly with religious formulas. The Moriscos were fond of this kind of elaborations and they used them profusely. Their *herces* gave them, maybe, the reassurance of divine or mystical protection in times where their lives were at stake.

8

Talismans and Engravers of Talismans in the Seventeenth-Century Ottoman Society According to the Journal of Evliyā Çelebi

Özlem Deniz Ahlers

1. Introduction

This chapter is based on a paper presented at the interdisciplinary conference "Textual Amulets in a Transcultural Perspective" at the University of Heidelberg on April 10, 2018. In this chapter I will characterize several aspects which I portrayed at the conference more in detail. With the help of dictionaries, encyclopedias, and especially literary descriptions of talismans new definitions of the word will be developed. The literary descriptions which establish the basis of this chapter were composed by Evliyā Çelebi[1] (born in 1611 in Istanbul, died in 1683? in Cairo). His descriptions, which he allegedly observed, noted, and written down during his 51-year-long voyage (1630–81), are a rich source of cultural studies.

The travel journal with his 4,000 pages is the most extensive of the Orient. It was written down most likely in Cairo, Egypt, by Evliyā Çelebi in the seventeenth century where he had retired to.

The principal object of this chapter will be to emphasize the relevance of his descriptions regarding the research on the nature of talismans and Ottoman amulets. Talismans and magical amulets are not confinable to territorial boundaries or a certain period of art history. They manifest themselves in different forms, following the needs of a society, as a protective means to cope with the dangers of everyday life. This counts as well for the Ottoman society which regulated magical practices according to the teachings of Islam. The word "talisman" or "Turkish *ṭılsım*" (*adj. ṭılsımlı, muṭalsam*) is used in context with certain purposes. For specific effects talismans with exact astrological constellations were produced.

In his monumental journal *Seyāḥatnāme* the traveler Evliyā Çelebi described a multitude of talismans and their producers in the Ottoman society of the seventeenth century. Following Çelebi's observations the chapter attempts to show where and how these talismans were put in practice during that period.

In section 2.1 one can find the words for amulets and talismans used in Turkish language area while in sections 2.2 and 2.3 one can find literary transmissions from the West and the East with examples from modern works. In section 3 talismans from the *Seyāḥatnāme*[2] will be presented in detail. In section 3.1 one can find descriptions of "enchanted fish that swim in Van Lake."[3] In section 3.2 there will be descriptions of city talismans in Cairo as they are found in the *Seyāḥatnāme*. Sources and translations are also to be found in section 3.

2. Definitions of Talisman

This section aims to describe the diversity in the character of talismans in the Ottoman period which affects the modern days, to frame them according to the most frequently used shapes, to hint under which categories they can be searched for and which sources are relevant for the study of Ottoman society. This will be done with the help of dictionaries and encyclopedias.

Ṭılsım in modern-day Turkish is like the word "*Talisman*" in European languages and derives from the same root of the Greek verb "τελέω" meaning "to finalize, to come true."[4] It was borrowed from Τέλεσμα deriving from the Arabic ṭılasm which was in turn adopted by Ottoman Turkish.[5]

Enzyklopädie des Islams (EI) defines the word as follows:

> Talismane sind eine mit astrologischen und anderen magischen Zeichen versehene Inschrift oder mit solchen Inschriften bedeckter Gegenstand, insbesondere auch die Nachbildung von Tierkreis und Planetenbildern oder Tierfiguren, die als Abwehr oder Schutzzauber dienen. Als der Vater der Talismane gilt der weise Balinas,[6] der nach der Überlieferung in zahlreichen Städten Abwehrzauber gegen Stürme, Schlangen, Skorpione usw. hinterlassen hat.[7]

In the article ṭılsım of the İslam Ansiklopedisi (IA) the following definition is given:

> Talisman is defined as the influence which active celestial forces exert on passive earth forces at specific times.[8]

Furthermore, the differences between the words *amulet* and *talisman* are mentioned in the article. Amulets are consecrated objects described with various words in Turkish. Talismans on the other hand are tools used to activate certain powers. In Turkish the term ṭılsımlık is used, meaning "to be provided with a talisman."

In the Ottoman-English dictionary by Redhouse the word is translated as *magical spell*.[9] In another well-known Ottoman-Latin dictionary by Devellioğlu talisman is defined as a magical object or person. As a second definition *çare* (resort, way out) is given. A third definition gives *sihir* and *büyü* (magic and spell). These entries in the common dictionaries reflect the connection between magic, talismans, and amulets.

The entry on talisman in the historical dictionary by Pakalın[10] provides a distinction between the generic magic *sihir* and talisman *tılsım*. While magic can be performed without any object, talismans are created with the help of constellations and the ultimate nature of the object.

It is remarkable that many sources describe a connection between talismans and astrology or other magical images. For example, in the Ottoman-Latin dictionary by Meninsky from the seventeenth century, talismans are described as magical images engraved under the right constellation.[11] The reason for this lies in the two most important attributive characteristics of talismans: they must have a purpose and they must be prepared at the right time. By doing so the talisman becomes unique.

Another important work dealing with the history of talismans was written by Manfred Ullmann. In his work "Die Natur- und Geheimwissenschaften im Islam" (Natural science and hermetism in Islam) he portrays the development of talisman tradition, starting with Hellenistic knowledge of Aristotle and Plato available to Al-Būnī:[12]

> Genauso, wie es bei der Alchemie der Fall ist, so sind auch bei der Magie die Überlieferungswege, auf denen das griechische Material zu den Arabern gelangt ist, nicht genau bekannt, und wie bei der Alchemie, so bilden auch hier die Pseudepigrapha einen breiten Unterbau für die spätere Literatur, für die großen arabischen Kompendien.[13]

In Ullmann's work one can find yet another definition for talisman, given by an Ottoman scholar Ṭaşköprüzāde. Ullmann cites him as follows:

> Das Wort Talisman (*ṭılasm*) bedeutet unauflösbarer Knoten; andere meinen, es sei ein Anagramm für *musalliṭ* (Macht verleihend), weil es zu den Substanzen der Macht und Herrschaft gehöre. Diese Wissenschaft untersucht die Art der Vermischung der aktiven himmlischen Kräfte mit den passiven irdischen Kräften zu geeigneten Zeiten im Hinblick auf die durch sie erstrebten

> Tätigkeiten und Einwirkungen, mit Hilfe von Ihnen zugeordneten Kräfte verleihenden Räucherungen, die die Spiritualität jenes Talismans herabziehen, damit aufgrund dieser Dinge seltsame Wirkungen in der Welt des Entstehens und Vergehens eintreten. Taşköprüzâde (died 1030/1621 Mevżūātü l- ulūm).

We have learned so far that a talisman can only be completed at the right point in time. Therefore, a ritual is conducted which is supposed to determine the appropriate time for the process and the purpose of the talisman. The exact point of time is thus determined by the purpose and the target.

In the Turkish language these practices are summarized under the term *havas ilmi* (science of Ḫavāṣ). Even in modern times many books about this topic are still being published. This "science" deals with properties and characteristics of inanimate objects. The word itself is derived from the Arabic plural form of characteristics *ḫāṣṣa*.

2.1 Written Transmissions of Talismans

2.1.1 Literary Transmissions

Literary transmissions of talisman can be found in world literature. There are manyfold examples of talisman being used as a metaphor—and they are surprisingly similar.

In the German-speaking language the theater play *Der Talisman* by Johann Nestroy gives a very good example for the usage of the word "talisman" as a metaphor. The red-haired protagonist Titus receives a present as a talisman that is supposed to change his life. The talisman is a jet-black wig by which he can hide his red hair and thus escape from poverty.[14]

Yoko Tawada also named one of her books "Talisman." In this compendium of literary essays she presents talismans used as protection against all sorts of problems caused by other people or entities.[15]

In the literary transmission of the Islamic culture area, talismans are a very common theme. Called Ḳıṣaṣü l-anbiyāʿ or Ḳıṣaṣ-i anbiyāʿ "tales of the Prophet" they are a widespread category of literature that delivers a kind of interpretation of the Qur'an parallel to the theological exegesis. Through this category, the tales of the Prophet have been commented on continuously. Not only tales about the prophets but also tales about pious men, saints, and heroes play a prominent role. And because Islam is based on Judaism and Christianity, stories from the Old Testament were integrated with Islamic transmission. Through these stories moral values and miracle tales were passed on in Arabic, Persian, and Turkic-speaking language areas. Descriptions of miraculous artifacts, namely talismans, that were dedicated to certain prophets hold their place in literary transmission. The Turkic people who adopted Islam mainly via the Persian culture also adopted many folk tales and sufistic traditions. Thus, many prophets and Israelite kings were passed on as messengers of God:[16] for example, Adam, Idrīs, Noah, Hūd, Abraham, Joseph, Lot, Job, Moses, David, Solomon, Jesus, and Muḥammad. One can also find saints such as Ḫıżır, the wise Loḳmān and Alexander Ẕū l-Ḳarnain (Alexander the Great), the Seven Sleepers, or Samson in the collective memory of Islamic religion.

2.1.2 The Seal of Muḥammad

The Seal of Muḥammad is his most known talisman. It is a birthmark occurring between his shoulder blades. It says that Muḥammad will be the last prophet and it is found in the Qur'an in surah 33:40:

> Muḥammad is not the father of any one of your men, but the Messenger of God, and the Seal of the Prophets; God has knowledge of everything.[17]

Many Hadiths draw a connection between the Seal and a talisman, for example, by Muslim (5218, Book 24):[18]

> Anas reported that when Allah's Apostle decided to write to the Kisra (the King of Persia), Caesar (Emperor of Rome), and the Negus (the Emperor of Abyssinia), it was said to him that they would not accept the letter without the seal over it; so, Allah's Messenger got a seal made, the ring of which was made of silver and there was engraved on it: "Muhammad, the Messenger of Allah."

Also linked together in the same way are, according to the prophet's tales, the robe of Joseph and Samson's hair; and also, according to the novel of Alexander, the construction of talismans in the cities he conquered and according to Apollonius of Tyana the construction of talismans in the city of Medain (Ctesiphon) in the Sassanid era.

2.1.3 The Seal of Solomon (the Seven Seals)

The Seal of Solomon is especially present in Moḥammedan magic art. Winkler describes in his work "Siegel und Charaktere in der muhammedanischen Zauberei" (Seals and Characters in Mohammedan Magic) the following seal with his symbols in detail:[19]

> Thanks to Winkler we know of many formulas that occur in Moḥammedan magic. The hexagram was combined in Islamic transmissions with the Arabic

and celestial alphabet thus becoming the Seal of Solomon.[20] The type face itself was an instrument to pass on secret messages and the celestial alphabet played a dominant role in this kind of magic.

2.2 Words for Amulets and Talismans in Modern-day Turkish

The Turkish language knows several words for amulets and talismans. One of them is *nazarlık*. Another one is *uğurluk* which was used for horseshoes, elephants, and depictions of pomegranate, the Hand of Fatima and ẕülfikār, a sword with two blades which belongs to ʿAlī ibn Abi Tālib. These lucky charms get their luck from the shape of the artifact.

An exact distinction between amulet and talisman is not found in any source. Gruber gives a good summary about this.[21] But it is possible to differentiate them along their level of personalization. Simple amulets are an unpersonal mass product while talismans must be produced in a ritualistic manner that integrates their purpose as well as the specific point of time depending on a specific person. It is worth pointing out that a simple amulet can be enchanted with a personalized intention and become a talisman, for example, when handed over while reciting a prayer.

2.2.1 Nazarlık

The word is used as a superordinate concept for objects that are supposed to ward off the evil eye. The blue eye *mavi boncuk* (blue pearl) is known as *nazarlık*. The word *nazar* derives from the Arabic and means "gaze" while *-lIk* is a nominal noun suffix that is used in Turkish to create new nouns. As a defense or protection these objects are worn on the body or garment and are frequently hung on doors and walls in homes and shops.

2.2.2 Maşallah

Maşallah is an expression to ward off the evil eye and translates to "what God wants." It is very commonly used in daily life. Hammer-Purgstall describes the meaning as follows:

> Den Neid, wenn er nicht von ganz besonders bösartiger teuflischer Natur, muss der Gedanke entwaffnen, daß wenn es Gottes Wille war, so viel Reichtum oder Schönheit zu gewähren, der Mensch, der den damit Betheilten beneidet, wider den Willen Gottes sich auflehnt.[22]

2.2.3 Muska, Cevşen, Hamayil, Vefk, and Hırz

While *nazarlık* is considered more as a lucky charm, *muska*[23] is a well-known talisman in Turkey. It is written on a piece of paper and incorporates prayers or surahs from the Qur'an, the Hadiths, or magic squares. The piece of paper is folded and placed in a protective layer of waxed cloth. Finally the cloth is wrapped seven times. There are many ways to fold the cloth but most commonly it is folded in a triangular shape. The Muska is worn like an amulet on a chain or pinned to the clothes.[24] The word "Muska" derives from the Arabic *nusḫa* and translates as "handwritten example." In old Turkish there is the word *tomar* that hints at type faces and is used as a talisman.

If placed in a silver shell of any shape it can also be called *cevşen. Cevşen* is a protective prayer commonly known as Cevşen-i Kebīr and Cevşen-i Sagīr. In Ottoman texts the used word derives from the Persian word for armor. In the Ottoman language the word used is *hamayil* which means "a waistband." It is plain to see that *cevşen* and *hamayil* were meant to be worn on the body.

Additionally, the word *vefḳ* is used in relation to magic squares and engraved on the artifacts. Last, but not least, the word ḥırz is often used in Ottoman poems as a talisman in the form of ḥırz-ı emāni, meaning: "where wishes are kept."[25]

2.3 Exemplary Motifs and Signs

2.3.1 The Hand of Fatima

Another popular amulet that is commonly worn in Turkish society as jewelry while also being documented historically in miniatures and paintings is the Hand of Fatima. *Fatma'nın eli* is a noun compound in modern Turkish, while during the Ottoman era the Arabic word for "5" (Hamse-i ʿĀl-i Aba) and the Persian Pençe were combined to *Pençe- i ʿĀl-i Aba*. The hand symbolizes five persons as a whole, each finger representing one: the prophet Muḥammad, Fatima (his daughter), Ali (his cousin and son-in-law), Hasan, and Hüseyin (the sons of Fatima and Ali).[26] A depiction of the Hand of Fatima was drawn in a book of oracles written in Ottoman language. A name is written on every finger.[27]

2.3.2 Ẕülfikār*—The Sword of* ʿAlī

In Alevi Islamic tradition wearing the double-bladed sword of ʿAlī ibn Abi Tālib is documented without interruption throughout history. The sword is used as a motif in calligraphy, on tombstones and other works of art from the Bektashi Order.[28] On a Talisman shirt from the Topkapı Palace (Istanbul) from the nineteenth century we find two double-bladed swords at shoulder height. Also depicted on the shirt is the Seal of Solomon and several magic squares. The length of the shirt is 98 cm.

The appearance of magic squares on artifacts is very common. A detailed view of talisman shirts from the sultans is given by Hülya Tezcan in her book *Talisman Shirts in the Topkapı Palace*.[29]

2.3.3 Bedūh

When it comes to seals and rings, the Halûk Perk Museum presents a diverse collection of which a few mentionable objects will be given as an example (see Figure 8.1):

> The Seal of Bedūh ist practically a 3 x 3 square, also called Saturn square. In this square every row horizontally, diagonally and vertically adds up to 15. In the corner of the square one can always find the numbers 2, 4, 6 and 8. These are the numeric values of the word Bedūh after the *ebced* calculation. The arabic letters are ح و د ب and the numeric value in arabic numbers is ٢ ٤ ٦ ٨. These straight numbers build a unity with 1, 3, 5, 7 and 9 thus creating the magic square. The alphabetic characters were written on letters to make sure they were reaching their destination in time. They are also used in magical practices for birth assistance and generally considered as protection against diseases and sickness. This is why they are found on many bowls and cups for daily use as well.[30]

According to Hammer-Purgstall seals and talismans can be differentiated by the direction the text (the names of God or proverbs from the Qur'an) was engraved. Talismans would be using the usual direction while the inscriptions on seals would always be anticlockwise.

Figure 8.2 shows a seal ring that is mirror inverted and yet was used as a talisman. The ring is shown again inverted in this chapter to make it more readable. The numbers are more comprehensible this way. The seal ring belonged to a person named ʿAlī Riżā. On one side of the ring is his name, on the other

٤	٩	٢
٣	٥	٧
٨	١	٦

4	9	2
3	5	7
8	1	6

Figure 8.1 Seal of Bedūh with numeric values. Halûk Perk Müzesi.

Figure 8.2 Three sides of the seal ring of ʿAlī Rıża. Halûk Perk Müzesi.

side the depicted magic square, and on the third side the names of the Seven Sleepers.[31]

3. Talismans in the Seyāḥatnāme

As mentioned in the introduction, EÇ has described a multitude of talismans in his oeuvre Seyāḥatnāme. His descriptions offer information about talismans and their usage in the Ottoman society of the seventeenth century. They have not yet been translated completely into German. All the following citations are translated into English.

Evliyā Çelebis travel log is divided into ten volumes in a systematic manner. Every city is described in paragraphs with the same categories. The headings are marked in red. One can find these headings especially in vol. 1, where he describes Istanbul, and in vol. 10, where he describes Cairo.

Within Evliyā Çelebis travel log one can find then unexplained natural phenomena that in the seventeenth century were considered miracles. Another good portion of the travel log consists of examples of architecture and buildings of the Antique and Byzantine era like the Pyramids of Gizeh, the Tower of the Winds, and the Parthenon in Athens, as well as the Columns of Theodosius, of Arcadius, and of Constantine; the Tekfur Palace (Porphyrogennetos Palace); the Mosque of Zeyrek (Pantokrator Monastery); and, of course, the Hagia Sophia in Istanbul. An example from the latter building would be the "sweaty column." Evliyā Çelebi described more buildings and examples of architecture such as the Al-Aqsa Mosque in Jerusalem that had been built, like many other buildings at that time, using spolia. Furthermore, he describes technical structures such as the Noria of Hama, the Nilometer in Cairo, and many other sculptures.

The usage of the word "talisman," though, is not restricted to Evliyā Çelebi but is found throughout many other geographical works from the Islamic tradition. Researchers have found out that the name "Tilasm" was used sporadically to describe special locations, sculptures, and pre-Islamic buildings.[32] In doing so some authors sought to give these talismans an Islamic tradition.

It is remarkable that Evliyā Çelebi did not try to impose an Islamic tradition on what he described, which sets him apart from other authors. He offers a special and subjective point of view on talismans as protection for the people, for cities, and the environment. The following examples seek to clarify his point of view and are direct translations from his travel journal.

3.1 Description of Lake Van[33]

According to the historian Şeref Ḫan, the Venerable Sultan Bend-i Māhī was a scholar of Alexander the Great. Since he very much liked the water and air of Bārgīrī, he settled there. He made a talisman, to obtain nourishment for himself and for the people and buried it in this place. Due to the effect of this talisman once a year fish come to this talisman and visit the sacred site Sultan Bend-i Māhī, where they are caught on their return. This is an extraordinary miracle.

3.2 Translations of the Talismans in the Citadel of Cairo[34]

> [80r1] . . . I have not seen such an inscription in any other country, only on a non-flowing fountain in the tinker quarter in Belgrade, along the moat of the castle on the Danube. There I saw this inscription, which resembles one above the picture of a bird, but I have not deciphered it. The well educated people of Cairo believe that, depending on the bird calls that came out from the picture, this species of birds does not come to Egypt. [5] In fact in Egypt there are absolutely no storks, magpies, owls, eagles, buzzards and starlings. An extraordinary wonder.
>
> *Scorpion Talisman* [80r6] In the upper citadel there are scorpions, but when they sting people, nothing happens, and if they do sting, the pain goes away after a couple of hours. The talisman is in the divan hall, which was erected by Sultan Kalavan on 44 pillars. There are similar ones in Isvān.[35] The scorpion is on the top of the pillar, which is to the right of the large vault, towards the Tatar quarter. On the top of this pillar, there is an encircling round iron and on top of this the scorpion talisman hanging from its tail, that can be seen.
>
> *Snake Talisman* [80r12] Opposite this pillar with the scorpion talisman, there is another one with the depiction of a striped snake. On this pillar there are also two lines of inscription, a talisman inscription, serving as a talisman against snakes. [15] There are not so many snakes in the town of the serpent king[36] nor

in the citadel of Cairo. God willing they do not harm anyone, yet they are still the most feared animals.

Centipede talisman [80r16] On a pillar there is an iron centipede talisman with two lines of magical inscription. Thanks to this talisman there is still no harm from the centipedes in Cairo.

Fever talisman [80r17] Thank God there is neither quartan fever nor malaria in the citadel. If a person with malaria from another country stays in the citadel for three nights, God willing he will be cured, since there is a three-line inscription on a pillar at the Ḥelvacı-Muḥammed-Aġa gate.

Talisman against colic [80r21] On another pillar there is a talisman against colic.

Plague talisman [80r21] There is also a pillar with a talisman against the plague on it. It is said to be ascribed to Ebū ʿAlī Sinā.[37] It is a blessing in the citadel of Cairo, that nowhere else can be found. Nevertheless, they die from various diseases, such as diarrhoea, pleurisy, facial paralysis and buboes. Thank God all the talismans described are still effective. [25] Each of these inscribed pillars was individually provided with magic squares by a master of natural sciences to show its artistic beauty and power.

[80v1] First of all, the yellow pillar was provided with a talisman, by which the slaves would not escape from the fortress, another by which thieves would not break into the house, an[other] by which slaves and servants would not betray their masters, and if they betrayed them, their hands would be broken, and another pillar against the infidelity of women. There is yet another one, by which no damaging fire burns in Cairo, and thank God this talisman still exists.

3.3 Descriptions of the Professional Guild of Seal and Talisman Engravers in Istanbul[38]

This description of Istanbul is from 1635. This is the year Murad IV advanced on Baghdad and was accompanied by a cavalcade of professionals. Evliyā Çelebi's description is the only one of this event and he lists 1,109 professional guilds, categorized into 57 main groups.[39] Relevant for this chapter is the fact that one of these groups was the guild of seal and talisman engravers. In the following paragraph the complete translation is given as it was written down by Evliyā Çelebi:

Professional Guild of the Silver Seal-Engravers and Amulets [heykel], or Silver Seal and Talisman [ṭılısmāt] Engravers: Another guild of artisans: they cannot engrave Yemenite agate. [188a] Among them there are masters who are able to inscribe seals and talismans with taʿlīḳ, nesḫī, rıḳʿa, and reyḥānī writing, as if they were a Koranic verse taken from Allah's Koran verses. Their workshops: 15, Servants: 40, their master the venerable ʿ*Ukkāşe* saw the seal of the prophets on the back of the venerable Prophet and, for infant and senile illnesses, began to entirely write this effective protection prayer "Eʿ ūzü bi-kelimātillāhi t-tāmmāt" and to engrave it on yellow copper. At the behest of our Prophet, he wrote down the İsm-i aʿ ẓam - prayer and engraved it on steel. İsm-i aʿ ẓam: "Bismillāh, yā aẓīme l-ḫaḍar, yā serīʿa z-zafer, yā maʿ rūfe l-eṡer." He wrote the entirety of this protection.

The venerable Prophet himself put his belt on him and the venerable *Ukkāşe* kissed the seal of the Prophet on his back. His tomb is near a leisure spot in Maraş. These silver engravers paraded on their carts and adorned their shops with various seals, statues, magic squares, and Emāni- amulets and with other talismans.

4. Summary

The preceding descriptions from sections 2 and 3 referring to talismans could prove the existence of talismans and their use in Ottoman society. Although magic is officially forbidden in Islamic context, this prohibition seems to be irrelevant when it comes to talismans. All around the globe where protection and defensive mechanisms were needed, talismans seem to exist. The artifacts mentioned in this chapter have been used as protection as well as for luck.

In the chapter where Evliyā Çelebi describes the professional guilds of engravers (section 3.3) he lists the words *mühür*, *heykel*, *vefḳ*, ḥırz- ı emānī, and muṭalsam (adj. of talisman) in a row. We can find these words in modern-day Turkish. Talismans have been used as auxiliary means to accomplish a certain purpose. They can take forms of inscription or magical squares and are clearly provable in EÇ's travel log. In his Seyāḥatnāme one can find historical facts alongside fantastic tales. The exact difference between these two necessitates further research. Finally, Evliyā Çelebi is presenting posterity and researchers manifold descriptions of talismans, buildings, sculptures, and natural phenomena.

9

Small Letters against Great Misfortunes

A Glance at Safavid Amulet Culture

Sarah Kiyanrad

1. Introduction

"Why heed the waves when Noah is piloting our Ship of State"—this hemistich from Saʿdī's *Gulistān* is found on an illustration (folio 18 verso) from the famous early-sixteenth-century *Shāhnāma* of Shah Ṭahmāsb (*r.* 1524–76). The image depicts Firdausī's "Parable of the Ship of Shiism" (Figure 9.1a).[1] It appears here that not all passengers feel their belief in the abilities of the two depicted oarsmen, or their "spiritual guide" Noah, is sufficient. Taking a closer look at the image, we notice a young seaman on the upper left, who is sitting on the ship's mast, the sleeves of his shirt and the trouser legs rolled up. Around each of his upper arms, he wears a gold-colored amulet (a kind of *bāzūband*) attached with what appears to be a simple string. The object on his left arm is a cylindrical amulet box; the amulet on his right arm is triangular in shape, the tip pointing upwards (Figure 9.1b). The observer is tempted to assume that these amulets were meant to ensure a safe voyage.[2]

Sheila R. Canby convincingly demonstrated that the objects depicted in this special *Shāhnāma* mirror the material reality of early Safavid Iran (1501–1722);[3] it follows from this observation that the illustrated amulet shapes were common in the early sixteenth century, as was the depicted way of attaching them to the upper arm. Recent studies have in fact increased our knowledge of remaining Safavid amulets, especially high-value specimens made from paper.[4] Safavid amulet culture does not, in many ways, differ much from the amulet culture of the previous centuries in content, form, or reason for application.[5] Having said that, after the Twelver had been established as the official doctrine a gradual transformation of textual and iconographic contents took place, which

Figure 9.1a *Firdausī's Parable of the Ship of Shi'ism*, Folio 18v from the Shāhnāma of Shah Ṭahmāsb; painting attributed to Mīrzā ʿAlī (active *c.* 1525–75); Tabriz, *c.* 1530–5. Metropolitan Museum of Art; Accession Number: 1970.301.1.

was to unfold in the decades and centuries to come.[6] This already indicates that those who made use of amulets did apparently not consider these objects to be inconsistent with their creed.[7]

In this chapter, I would like to outline some observations on Safavid amulets as reflected in a range of remaining visual, material, and textual sources. Rather than focusing extensively on knowledge necessary to the composition of amulets and normative texts, I will approach the material with more practical aspects in mind—and with the aim of providing a rough overview of amulet use in Safavid Iran. Admittedly, the evidence examined was predominantly produced in (or focused on) larger cities and thus provides information mainly on amulet culture in (mostly Western Iranian) metropolises, and seldomly discusses religious minorities; hence, the information available does not show the whole picture. Local amulet cultures were certainly diverse, but, for lack of sources, cannot be dealt with here.[8] Unfortunately, space does not allow us to discuss here seal amulets and generally amulets made from stones extensively; it shall have to suffice to make some references. Last but not least, the focus will be on script-bearing artifacts.[9]

Figure 9.1b *Firdausī's Parable of the Ship of Shi'ism*, Folio 18v from the Shāhnāma of Shah Ṭahmāsb; painting attributed to Mīrzā ʿAlī (active *c.* 1525–75); Tabriz, *c.* 1530–5. Metropolitan Museum of Art; Accession Number: 1970.301.1.

2. Materials and Contents

The Persian language has a large variety of names that designate amulets; frequent terms in the Safavid era were *ṭilsam/ṭilism*, *taʿvīẕ*, and *duʿā*.[10] Most Safavid paper amulets and seal amulets feature verses and surahs of the Qur'an (or the whole Qur'an),[11] parts of the hadiths, a number or the whole of the so-called ninety-nine beautiful names of God, *charakteres*, *vafq*s (usually translated as "magic squares") and pseudo-script, and occasionally floral and geometric decoration.[12] The same goes for amulets made from metal (inter alia, silver, iron, and alloys such as brass).[13] These last elements bear witness to the close link between amulets and so-called magic bowls/incantation bowls, and talismanic shirts.[14] A seventeenth-century talismanic shirt from Iran has, for instance, the signs of the zodiac, *vafq*s, verses of the Qur'an (Q), the ninety-nine "beautiful names of God," and the names of the four archangels on it.[15] Another talismanic shirt dating from the Safavid era is inscribed all over with verses of the Qur'an.[16] Still another Safavid shirt has, next to the aforementioned elements, also the prayer *Nādi ʿAlīyan*.[17]

Gems inscribed with religious phrases are often made from chalcedony,[18] and jade, too, was a material of choice in the Safavid era. A dated (1085/1674–5), 7×7.2 cm large amulet from nephrite jade in the *Khalili Collection* (TLS 1855) has the famous Throne Verse (Q II: 255) on the one side, and a prayer for the "Fourteen Infallibles" (*chahārdah maʿṣūm*; Muḥammad, Fāṭima, and the twelve imams) on the other side (both inscribed in positive).[19] Another jade stone (2.2×2.5 cm), reused and mounted in the Qajar era (1796–1925), had been inscribed with the Throne Verse in the Safavid period (*Khalili Collection*; TLS 3141).[20] The Throne Verse may also be found on a heart-shaped seventeenth-century chalcedony amulet (5.8×4.6 cm; *British Museum*; SL.9), on which are likewise inscribed the surah *al-ikhlāṣ* (Q CXII) and the *shahāda*.[21] The old idea that gems were endowed with specific characteristics and powers, as for instance prominently elaborated on in al-Bīrūnī's lapidary *Kitāb al-Jamāhir fī maʿrifat al-javāhir* (*The sum of knowledge about precious stones*; eleventh century),[22] certainly still prevailed in the Safavid era.

It is, however, quite difficult to tell in retrospective whether a surviving gem or seal had been used as a mere decorative/adorning object, for sealing, or as an amuletic device (or whether it combined all these functions). Researchers have traditionally considered seals inscribed in positive to be amulets, since they could not, in contrast to seals inscribed in reverse, have been used for sealing. But even in that case a decorative function may be within the realm of possibility; moreover, the strict distinction between amuletic and non-amuletic seals has in the meantime been questioned.[23] We generally know, based on the literary and material evidence available, which forms and materials would have commonly been used as amulets. When it comes to remaining artifacts, we are, however, only able to suggest a possible amuletic purpose which was either realized—or not. For example, it is hard to tell whether or not amuletic power was ascribed by their wearers to two remaining seventeenth- to eighteenth-century steel *bāzūbands* without inscription (5.8×17.9 cm) in the *Tanavoli Collection*.[24] Or were they yet to be inscribed with verses, *charakteres*, and images?

Some contemporary observers mention that for religious reasons, animal skin was not appreciated; having said that, manuals often urge one to write on parchment, especially gazelle parchment.[25] Scroll amulets written on gazelle parchment have indeed survived (Figures 9.2a, b, c).[26] Paper (apparently from cotton fiber)[27] was commonly used for amulets. There were three main types of paper amulets in the Safavid era: single sheet-amulets, scroll amulets/amulet scrolls, and so-called miniature Qur'ans[28] (Figure 9.3). All three types were usually inscribed in ink, the ingredients of which possibly contributed to the

Figure 9.2a Silver amulet case and scroll from gazelle skin, Iran, eighteenth or nineteenth century (?); 70.5 × 4.4 cm. Bayerische Staatsbibliothek; Cod. arab. 2616.

amulet's efficacy. According to popular tradition, every writer had his own secret recipe for ink production; and it was believed that the perfect ink had to "rest" some time after its ingredients had been mixed. The best results were expected from ink that rested while being bound to a camel traveling to Mecca.[29] A fifteenth-century writer calls the "peacock ink," an ink refined with

> a little henna water, myrtle-leaf water, woad-indigo (*wasma*) water, a bit of rose water and narcissus liquor, saffron water and powdered aloe, crystalline salt, a little pulverized pearl and coral, musk and whitish ambergris, gold and silver, copper and bronze gilt, cinnabar, and lapis lazuli.

the "very best."[30]

"Miniature Qur'ans" are here defined by their codex format. When using the term, we should be aware that several of those small manuscripts are actually compendia of different texts, such as (parts of) the Qur'an, hadiths, and prayers. In some instances they even contain a divinatory instruction, a so-called *fālnāma*, at the end;[31] the sheets (and respective covers/boxes) come in different forms, such as circular or octagonal shapes.[32] An octagonal amulet box designed for a miniature Qur'an (G.6; 4.4 × 1.6 cm) from circa 1700, which is currently in

Figure 9.2b Silver amulet case and scroll from gazelle skin, Iran, eighteenth or nineteenth century (?); 70.5 × 4.4 cm. Bayerische Staatsbibliothek; Cod. arab. 2616.

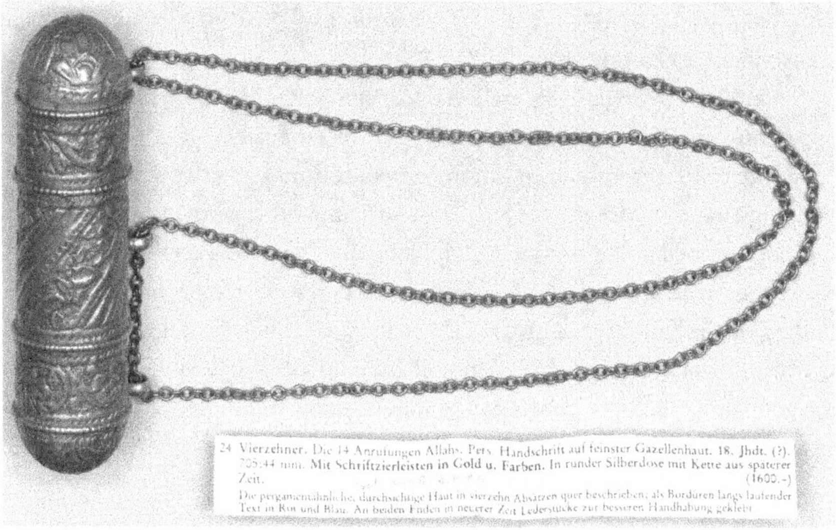

Figure 9.2c Silver amulet case and scroll from gazelle skin, Iran, eighteenth or nineteenth century (?); 70.5 × 4.4 cm. Bayerische Staatsbibliothek; Cod. arab. 2616.

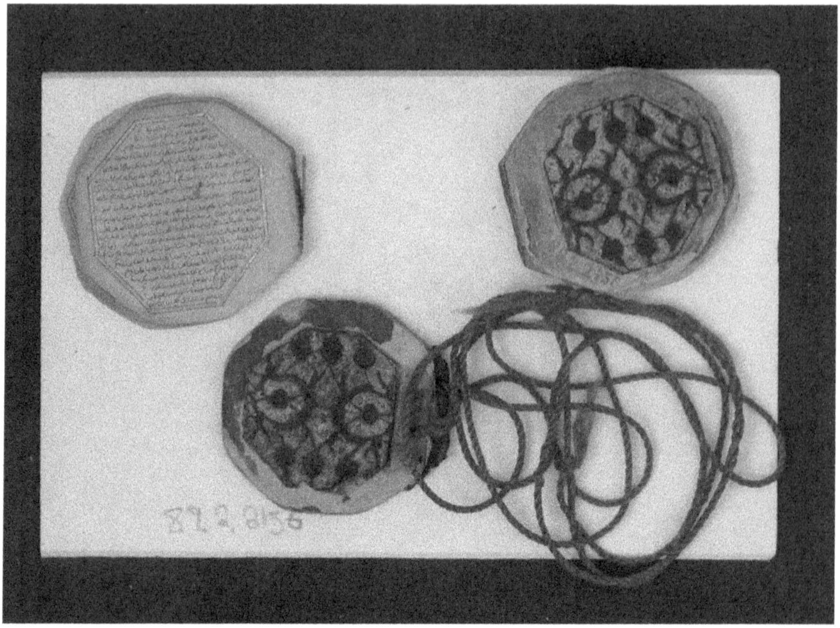

Figure 9.3 Miniature Qur'an, Iran or Turkey, seventeenth century; 3.2 × 3.2 cm. Metropolitan Museum of Art; Accession Number: 89.2.2156.

the *Tanavoli Collection*, has a *Basmala* on its top; on another amulet box in the same collection (G.8; d. 4.1 cm), likewise from circa 1700 but octagonal in shape, is inscribed a quotation from Q LXV: 3.[33]

Since the rectangle was believed to symbolize divine perfection, they apparently avoided producing papers in rectangular shape.[34] Indeed, the "majority of extant miniature Koran codices feature a regular octagon as their defining shape."[35] Miniature Qur'ans—and many other amulets as well—were typically penned in a diminutive script known as *ghubārī*, literally "dust script," a tiny hand with letters 1–2 mm in length. Certain scribes apparently specialized in the *ghubārī* hand, as the nisba of the following scribe who copied a miniature Qur'an indicates: Muḥammad Amīn al-Kātib al-Ghubārī (Muḥammad Amīn, the ghubārī scribe).[36] According to Heather Coffey, what followed from the use of this script was what she calls "textual intimacy":

> This I define as a pious urge to keep close to the text out of devotion to it, facilitated by a drastic reduction in scale, which offered the owner the twin advantages of portability and proximity.[37]

Indeed, script mattered. Although easily readable texts are found on amulets, they can also contain Pseudo-scripts, single letters, and *charakteres*, intertwined, hardly decipherable characters and, quite often, Kufi.[38] Engelbert Kaempfer, an observer of late Safavid Iran (1684–5), reports that ʿAlī was (as is commonly believed) considered to be the inventor of Kufi,[39] an aspect which probably bestowed this script with a special efficacy in the eye of the beholder. Furthermore, as a drawing by Muʿīn Muṣavvir demonstrates (dated 1663), some amulets consisted of "magic squares" (*vafqs*) only.[40] Encryption and the deliberate creation of obstacles in legibility and understandability are transcultural, timeless characteristics of amulets; strange elements are considered effective, maybe because their application requires expert knowledge and thus establishes or reinforces power constellations. Moreover, these restrictions in readability show that the text's efficacy is not dependent upon its being *read*: "The very presence and detailed inscription of Qurʾānic verses conveys protective power regardless, or perhaps because of, its illegibility."[41] It, however, appears that (apart from Pseudo-scripts) the *theoretical possibility of the text being read* remained quite important; in contrast to the early modern Christian environment, we do not, to my knowledge, have book-shaped pendants in Safavid Iran, that is, pendants that merely "refer to the book as a *symbolic form* by condensing conceptions of the book as a medium for salvation and memory."[42]

Another common amulet type was the so-called amulet (or talismanic) scroll. Generally only a few centimeters in width, these handwritten[43] scrolls could reach a length of several meters, and many remaining examples exceed 10 m in length. Early modern amulet scrolls from Iran normally measure 10 cm in width and 6–8 m in length.[44] They are inscribed in ink in different colors, most often black/brown, but parts of the inscriptions (or titles) can also be rendered in red, green, or blue, to name just a few. The remarkable length was achieved by gluing several paper strips together. For instance, a Safavid scroll bearing the date 957 (1550) consists of nineteen, and another scroll, dated 986 (1578), of fourteen strips.[45] Once rolled up, the scroll could still be worn in a comparatively small amulet case on the body. Tobias Nünlist distinguishes Qurʾanic scrolls ("items that contain a copy of the entire or nearly entire text of the Qur'an") from prayer scrolls ("scrolls that contain chosen verses from the Qur'an together with additional elements such as prayers, squares, representations of different objects, and so on").[46] One cannot help but draw a parallel to the content of the aforementioned miniature Qur'ans. Nünlist furthermore differentiates between Arabic, Persian, and Ottoman-Turkic scrolls; among the characteristics of early modern Persian scrolls he counts stylistic elements taken from Timurid and Turkman art and architecture.[47] Also, the use and arrangement of *ghubārī* in such a way that many lines of the diminutive script together form another, large and readable "meta-text" makes up one of the Persian scrolls' characteristics.[48]

Safavid amulet scrolls often invoke ʿAlī and the Twelver imams, a fact that distinguishes them from scrolls coming from a Sunni context (however, ʿAlī and the imams were, as noted earlier, venerated in milieus outside the Twelver/Shia context as well); for instance, in one case, the names of the "Fourteen Infallibles" are attested,[49] as is also observable on a seventeenth-century Safavid amulet case.[50] The names of "The Five" (Muḥammad, ʿAlī, Fāṭima, Ḥasan and Ḥusayn) are extant also on other "effective" objects; they are stamped on each single link of a Safavid mail shirt, endowing the shirt with protective power (Figures 9.4a and b). Another striking element of Safavid amulet scrolls—but also of miniature Qur'ans—(a characteristic which may, however, be already observed in previous times) is the occasional use of Persian.[51]

On both miniature Qur'ans and amulet scrolls the date of copying (or other important dates concerning the artifact's biography) is sometimes recorded. Suffice it here to mention a few examples: a Safavid scroll from the *Fondation Martin Bodmer*, Cologny (Genève; Mus.no. CB 542), has the year 957 (1550).[52] Another Safavid amulet scroll in the colophon reveals that it was written in 986

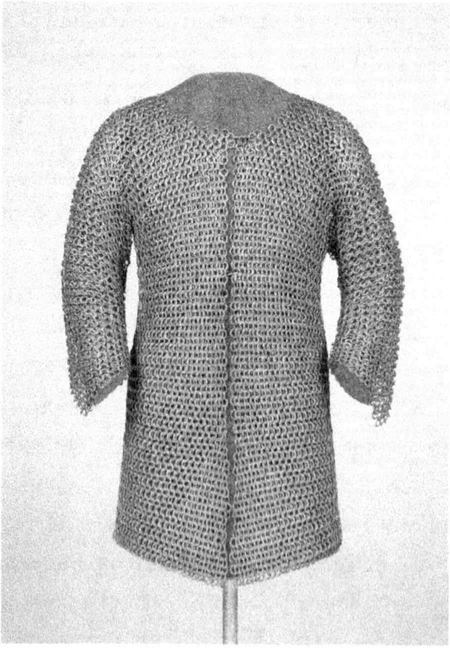

Figure 9.4a Mail shirt, Iran, *c.* 1500–1600. Metropolitan Museum of Art; Accession Number: 2014.198.

Figure 9.4b Mail shirt, Iran, *c.* 1500–1600. Metropolitan Museum of Art; Accession Number: 2014.198.

(1578).[53] A Safavid miniature Qur'an (*Ghassan I. Shaker Collection*) shows the date 1024 (1615/1616).[54] An impressive number of further extant miniature Qur'ans with copying date—ranging from 944/1537–38 to 1081/1671—demonstrate that these objects were produced throughout the whole Safavid era, though hitherto examples dating to the second half of the sixteenth to seventeenth centuries prevail.[55]

Last but not least, literary texts disclose (see below) that there must have been small paper sheet amulets for the use of less wealthy people. In contrast to the amulet types discussed earlier, virtually none of these amulets has remained. However, their production is well attested in travelogues; the already mentioned drawing by Muʿīn Muṣavvir displays the approximate size and possible content of this kind of amulet.

3. Producers

Amulet scrolls were sometimes produced in what has been called "milieus with heterodox learnings."[56] A specimen written in 986 (1578) (*Chester Beatty*

Library, Dublin; Inv.no. IS 1623) gives the name of the scribe, a certain Muẓaffar b. ʿAbdallāh al-Ḥasanī al-Māzandarānī, who might have had ties with the Ẕahabī Sufi milieu in Shiraz.[57] It is furthermore known that dervishes used to wander around with large amulets in their hands.[58] While it is highly plausible that Sufi shaykhs were, due to their supposed *baraka*, in a sense ideal amulet makers (some talismanic shirts, too, bear the name of a Sufi shaykh),[59] we will see that amulet production was by no means exclusive to them. Amulets were so widespread, it appears, that we cannot suppose their production was limited to a certain milieu; for example, renowned religious scholars of the Safavid era serving at court adopted and adapted sophisticated ideas on the art of writing amulets/talismans (*līmiyā*), as the case of the manual *Asrār-i Qāsimī* (*Qasimian Secrets*) (or rather its interpolation) demonstrates.[60] Furthermore, amulets make part of the "most commonly anthologized materials that connect households in Isfahan."[61] In her study on Safavid anthologies (*majmūʿa*s), Kathryn Babayan writes:

> talismans infuse these collections with formulaic prayers, magic numbers, and squares. Sometimes talismans took the form of inscriptions to guard households from theft, recipes to shield loved ones from fever, or stopgaps to prevent men from having "corrupt thoughts and lustful dreams."[62]

An amulet scroll kept in Berlin (*Staatsbibliothek zu Berlin*, Ms. Or. Oct. 146) had once been given away by Mīrzā Makhdūm al-Ḥusaynī al-Sharīfī al-Jurjānī, a religious scholar who was appointed *ṣadr* in the short reign of Ismāʿīl II (*r*. 1576–77) and later fled to the Ottoman Empire.[63] A lavishly decorated Safavid miniature Qur'an was copied by the aforementioned Muḥammad Amīn al-Kātib al-Ghubārī.[64] Cornelius Berthold provides, based on extant objects, the names of at least eighteen *ghubārī*-scribes who copied "pocket" and miniature Qur'ans or amulet scrolls in the Safavid era: ʿAlī b. Muḥammad b. Ibrāhīm al-Ḥāfiẓ Sabzivārī ('Azhdar'); Ghubārī b. ʿAbd al-Karīm al-Sabzivārī; Ḥasan b. Muḥammad al-Hāshimī; Ibn Bahāʾ al-Dīn ʿAlī Nūr al-Dīn Aḥmad; ʿImrān Asad Allāh Shaykh al-Simnānī; Muḥammad Sharīf; Muḥammad Aṣghar b. Muḥammad b. Muḥammad b. ʿAlī b. Ḥaṭīb al-Sabzivārī; Niẓām b. ʿImād al-Dīn Najjār; Karīm b. Ibrāhīm; Ibn al-Ḥājj Qāsim Muḥammad Ṭāhir; Aḥmad b. ʿAbdallāh; 'Kalb-i Āstān-i ʿAlī' ʿUmrānī Asad Allāh Shaykhū Simnānī; Shaykh Najab b. Shaykh Faraj b. Shaykh Manṣūr; Ḥusayn b. Ḥusayn al-Ḥasan al-Ḥusaynī; Ḥājjī Shaykh Ḥasan b. Shaykh Amīn al-Dīn; ʿImād al-Dīn Ḥasan b. Ibrāhīm; Ibrāhīm b. Mihr b. Manṣūr; and Ibrāhīm b. Ḥājjī ʿAbd al-Jalīl Shirvānī.[65]

In general, amulets commissioned by members of the court, let alone the shah, tend to be high-value objects of sublime craftsmanship made from and decorated with expensive materials (such as gold leaf)[66] and were doubtless manufactured by the most renowned amulet-writers. Those were skillful calligraphers and sometimes also religious protagonists. The Capuchin priest Raphaël du Mans, who lived in Isfahan from 1647 until his death in 1696, reports that even common people purchased amulets from *mullās*; they wrote passages of the Qur'an on paper, which were then suspended from the body.[67] This may be confirmed by the fact that we find, inter alia, the text for an amulet (*duʿā*) meant to heal a feverish child in a Safavid anthology belonging to Kāẓim, a religious judge.[68]

It is interesting that it was believed in later centuries that in the Safavid era the Twelver scholar Shaykh Bahāʾī (*d.* 1621 or 1622) had engraved a powerful inscription or symbol on two stones and buried them in the vicinity of Shiraz and Isfahan so that these two cities' inhabitants were spared from the plague.[69] In fact, the idea of *ṭilism* was not, as was the case in earlier centuries, restricted to small, portable objects, but could likewise refer to (purportedly powerful) ancient statues and buildings, particularly when script-bearing. The famous Ottoman traveler Evliyâ Çelebi recorded in 1647 during his first sojourn in Iran that:

> In Ardabil, outside the city, there is a round and black stone that is heavier than iron. [. . .] Ancient priests and sages have written inscriptions in Hebrew characters on the black stone. [. . .] When there is no rain in Ardabil, the notables, the high and the low and everyone roll this rock in the city. By the grace of God, it rained for three days and nights in Ardabil and all the fields, villages and towns were showered with God's merciful rain. Then they roll the stone again to its place, and the rain stops.[70]

Çelebi continues to report that some people in Ardabil believed this "talisman" had been created by the forefather of the Safavids, Shaykh Ṣafī al-Dīn (*d.* 1334).[71] These are thus two examples of how people attributed the creation of talismans to dazzling Safavid religious figures.

Thomas Herbert, who traveled Safavid Iran in 1628, mentions that certain religious men had "seeds and charms to make women fruitfull [*sic*]."[72] In a satirical manner, the *ʿAqāyid al-nisāʾ*[73] (*Beliefs of Women*; seventeenth century) describes how the physician (*ṭabīb*), the fortune-teller (*rammāl*), the prayer-writer (*duʿā-nivīs*), the magician (*jādūgar*), and the necklace-seller (*galūband-furūsh*) figure among the persons considered *maḥram* for women.[74] Indeed, according to du Mans, fortune-tellers (*rammāl*) not only foretold the future but also inscribed amulets on metal.[75] In addition, the *ʿAqāyid al-nisāʾ* tells us that some Jewish harness-, lace-, or weapon-sellers (*yarāq-furūsh*), too, wrote amulets.[76] In 1660, du Mans notes that some (Isfahani?) Jews made a living as lapidaries (*ḥakkāk*).[77] And a (albeit pre-Safavid) treatise on the *Medicine of the Imams* states that there was no objection to taking medications from Jews and Christians.[78] It can only be presumed that literate persons wishing to earn some pocket money, for example, students (*ṭullāb*), were ready to write (or copy) amulets; at least Kaempfer reports that some of them copied manuscripts in order to earn themselves some money.[79]

Jean Chardin (*d.* 1713), a French traveler to Safavid Iran, records that in theory, every literate person was able to produce a paper amulet. And yet it follows from his description that ordinary people would not write an amulet for themselves (Herbert, who traveled Iran in 1628, claims: "not one amongst a thousand warriors knows the benefit or use of letters; the Mullayes and Clergy ingrosse that Art").[80] Surviving manuals, however, suggest that every person able to access and read the manual could write amulets for him- or herself; the description of the production of amulets usually starts with the instruction: *Write!*[81] The individual stages of amulet production which Chardin had witnessed with his own eyes are described as follows:[82] first, a piece of paper was chosen which exceeded a cubit (*aune*) in length (≈0.649 m), but usually measured only 5–6 inches (*pouce*) in width (≈12–15 cm). This paper then was brought to forty honest and devout persons, one after another, each of them being asked to write down any prayer on it they considered effective. This is explained by the fact that one can allegedly find among forty persons only one true believer. The prayer typically consisted of one or two verses from the Qur'an and parts of the hadiths. Once this was done, the paper was folded and put into a small sachet.

Since, generally speaking, learning to read and write was a privilege mostly accessible to well-off women only (though both abilities are to be regarded as a continuum rather than absolute categories, of course), the bulk of amulets were presumably produced by men. And yet we should take into account the possibility that certain women wrote/copied amulets; for it is known that women in Safavid Iran were involved in medical treatment and prepared medical products.[83]

4. Clients

Not surprisingly, amulets promised to be beneficial for virtually everyone; they were not just worn by humans but also attached to animals (or their cages), plants, and objects.[84] Amulets with Qur'anic verses on them were, according to du Mans, attached to combat animals (rams, bulls) in order to make them win.[85] High-quality specimens made from precious materials had a higher chance of physical survival; for this reason, those remaining Safavid amulets kept in museums around the world usually originate from a courtly context or were produced for high-ranking members of society.

With regards to the way amulets were worn, common places were the neck, the arm, and the waist. Kaempfer indicates that Shah Sulaymān (*r.* 1666–94) used to wear a "secret seal" around his neck.[86] Chardin states it was most usual to attach amulets to the upper arm.[87] He goes on to report that these amulets, made from paper, were usually kept in small sachets of silk or brocade, the size of a demi-écu (half crown); to a person unfamiliar with Iranian amulet culture, the sachets were not easy to identify as amulets at first sight.[88] Some people wore up to seven or eight of these small sachets sewn on a ribbon as a bracelet.[89] Chardin adds that others kept their amulets in cases worked from gold or silver, and gives two interesting reasons for this: first the better preservation, and second, the wearers never had to take off their amulets, not even for bathing.[90] This is also true of bracelets entirely made of metal and often set with inscribed gemstones. Those were worn on the upper arm; the inscription pointed to the body and was thus invisible. From this point of view, amuletic gems, too, were convenient; a dated chalcedony (1059/1649–50) from Iran, set into a silver brooch, bears the invocation *Nādi ʿAlīyan* on it (see note 6).[91] Another way to hide a paper amulet from the view of others was to place it between the gem and the ring mounting.[92] We certainly have to consider that there were two types of amulets—those meant to be seen by others (e.g., against the evil eye), and those to be hidden, because their purpose was secret or even contrary to the interest of others (e.g., hate or love amulets).

Photographs from later centuries sometimes display (here: Jewish) children and women visibly wearing amulet cases around their neck—even in the street (Figures 9.5 and 9.6). In Figure 9.7 (Safavid manuscript), we see an example of two courtly women wearing what looks like expensive jewelry inside the palace.[93] Here, as is the case with the depiction of a young man, probably from Qazvin (Figure 9.8), it is hard to tell whether these objects are amulets or not.[94] Anyway, an old Persian tradition has it that women had to wear a minimum of nine pieces of jewelry, to which belonged a pendant (*āvīza*), earrings (*gūshvāra*), a chain (*silsila*), a nose-ring (*ḥalqaband*), a necklace (*galūband*), a bracelet on the upper arm (*bāzūband*) and another on the wrist (*nigishtar*), a finger ring (*angushtar*), and an anklet (*khalkhāl*).[95] The wife of Shah Ismāʿīl I (*r.* 1501–24) indeed possessed, according to a jewelry inventory (inter alia),

Figure 9.5 Portrait of a Jewish girl in elaborate costume; Antoin Sevruguin (1851–1933). The Myron Bement Smith Collection, FSA.A.04; Freer Gallery of Art and Arthur M. Sackler Gallery Archives; Gift of Katharine Dennis Smith; Antoin Sevruguin, FSA A.4 2.12.Up.55.

> a pair of large earrings, the pendants set with rubies; 36 unset pearls, each the size of a pear (*sic*); two strings of 24 pearls for the wrists or the ankles; a carved jade plaque inscribed and worked with gold, with a gold chain and a case; an armlet; jeweled rings; a gold seal; and 25 buttons for a gold brocade kaftan.[96]

Of these objects, the inscribed jade plaque accompanied by a chain and a case (amulet case?) could possibly be an amulet. If so, this yet again would confirm that amulets were also popular among women of high society. Recently, Nünlist analyzed four amulet scrolls dating from the sixteenth century; due to their outstanding quality he suggests that they belonged to "members of the inner circle of the Safavid ruling elites."[97] In his view, one of the investigated scrolls perhaps was presented to the Ottoman Sultan Süleiman (*r.* 1520–66) and may have reached his court in connection with the well-known revolt of Alqāṣ Mīrzā (1516–50).[98] Another scroll was, as has already been discussed, given away by a prominent Sunni religious personality of the Ṭahmāsb I and Ismāʿīl II era, Mīrzā Makhdūm.

Figure 9.6 Portrait of two women in elaborate costume; Antoin Sevruguin (1851–1933). The Myron Bement Smith Collection, FSA.A.04; Freer Gallery of Art and Arthur M. Sackler Gallery Archives; Gift of Katharine Dennis Smith.

Safavid amulets served a whole range of purposes:

> In every mischance also, or in sicknesse they use sorcery, prescribing charmes, crosse characters, letters, anticks, or the like, taken most commonly out of their Alcoran.[99]

Rather than giving a comprehensive list of those, I shall limit myself here to a few examples. Miniature Qur'ans and most amulet scrolls were apparently multifunction. The scroll connected to Mīrzā Makhdūm comprises a whole list of objectives the amulet should meet; the titles of the respective prayers (*du ʿā*) and their explanations (*sharḥ*) are given in Persian and contain the warding off of the plague, animals and ferocious beasts, the evil eye, defamers (*badgūyān*), enviers (*ḥasūdān*), and calamities, as well as the wish for fortune (*dawlat*), help to be received by a high-ranking person, and luck in war against the unbelievers.[100] Unlike amulets written for a specific purpose, these multifunctional amulets could be used for a lifetime. Valuable specimens were passed on to generations to come; for instance, a sixteenth-century miniature Qur'an bears the seal impression of Muẓaffar al-Dīn Shāh (*r.* 1896–1907).[101]

Figure 9.7 Detail of *Bahram Gur in the Yellow Palace on Sunday*, Folio 213 from a Khamsa (Quintet) of Niẓāmī; painted by Shaykh-Zāda; Herat, 931/1524–25. Metropolitan Museum of Art; Accession Number: 13.228.7.9.

Temporarily employed amulets served a single purpose, most often even if not exclusively concerning the treatment of mental and physical complaints. Infants were protected against the evil eye by a verse of the Qur'an which was bound on their arm; amulets against the evil eye were sometimes called *lāmcha*.[102] In case of illness, amulets were attached to the aching part of the body; if someone suffered from migraine, for example, the amulet was put on the paining part of the head; in the case of toothache, the amulet was attached to the tooth; and in the event of difficulties in childbirth, to the groin and thigh.[103] The physician Dāvud al-Antakī (*d.* 1599) in his *Taẕkira* recommends to a couple wishing to prevent pregnancy the following procedure and also gives the according formula: "In order to prevent conception a man should write on a piece of paper the following magical formula and then suspend it round the neck of the woman. This done she cannot conceive."[104]

In 1621, Maani, the Christian wife of Pietro della Valle, an Italian traveler to Safavid Iran, fell seriously ill in the city of Mīnā. A maidservant offered her some paper with prayers on it and recommended binding it into her hair; according to the servant's explanation, this prayer had helped many to convalesce before.

Figure 9.8 Young man with jewelry (amulet?), drawn by Shaykh Muḥammad (fl. 1530s–1580s), Qazvin. Metropolitan Museum of Art; Accession Number: 1973.92.

Maani agreed and the paper was bound to a strand of her hair. This account highlights a certain degree of interreligious cooperation in healing; however, when the servant left, Maani immediately asked to have the paper cut off and burned, because it came from a Muslim.[105]

5. Practices

In amulet production, four fundamental elements were—at least theoretically—of utmost importance: time, place, the condition and state of the producer, and the quality of the materials employed. There are, however, considerable differences between the respective instructions we find in manuals and the observations provided by travelogues. It can be assumed that while high-quality amulets for the wealthy were possibly produced in full accordance with all prescriptions handed down to that time, the production of more commonly used amulets went by a bit more pragmatically.

In theory, the writer had to adopt a state of ritual purity. Manuals ask him to fast, observe sexual abstinence for several days prior to the amulet production, and to deliver prayers.[106] And Chardin reveals that amulets were written: "avec de grandes circonspections à l´égard du papier, sur-tout à l´égard du temps et du lieu."[107] The idea that certain months, days, and hours[108] bestowed fortunate effects on amulets (and many other practices) was centuries old in the Middle East. Friday was considered a particularly auspicious day for writing amulets.[109] The Safavid Twelver scholar Muḥammad Bāqir Majlisī (*d.* 1699 or 1700) wrote a whole book on auspicious days (based on the sayings of the imams), the *Ikhtiyārāt*.[110] Astrological constellations, too, could be effective in meeting special purposes; the *Khavāṣṣ-i āyāt* explains that a person who writes down Q I on paper at the very moment of Venus' ascend and wears this amulet on a voyage will be saved from thirst, the horrors of the desert, and all kinds of accidents.[111] Since we are aware that both the Safavid shahs and ordinary people strongly believed in the power of the stars—the court astrologers consequently being one of the most influential groups at court[112]—there is reason to assume that astrological constellations were being respected during amulet production.

Often, the amulet had to be worn a certain number of days, frequently seven.[113] Amulets were probably also fumigated with incense; the existence of so-called *Isfand-gardān*s, who fumigated goods in the bazaars with wild rue in order to bestow them with blessing, *tabarruk* (they probably spoke prayers as well, since they were also called *du ʿā-gū*), is well attested.[114]

Materials on which the amulet texts were to be written had to be fashioned during an auspicious hour (an example: in order to forge alloys, the planets the respective metals were related with had to be in conjunction),[115] and/or they had to match the purpose of the amulet. So, if someone wished to destroy his enemy's life, he had to write an amulet on a small piece of cloth previously worn by his enemy.[116] Or, in order to make an enemy suffer from a terrible headache and render him blind and deaf, his name had to be written on a piece of shroud and buried.[117] It is interesting to note that the author of this last description adds: "If your enemy is a Muslim, you should not do this!" This was probably not respected, but at once makes clear that amulets harming others were not an unproblematic issue to deal with; the "solution" offered by the author is to limit their application to non-Muslims. Obviously he did not have a problem harming people who were not of his religion. At the same time, the idea of harming non-Muslims served as an opportunity and maybe pretext to even discuss this kind of aggressive amulets.

If a husband wanted to find out the truth about his wife, he had to place an amulet made with a piece of cloth worn by a girl who had not yet reached the marriageable age on his sleeping wife's breast and thus she would speak the truth; this had to happen in the night from Sunday to Monday, five hours after the break of dusk.[118] Other materials recommended for having amulet texts written on them are, for example, the leaves of the olive tree, gems, and gazelle parchment (see Figures 9.2a and b).[119] Remaining artifacts, however, show that paper was always deemed a sufficient option.[120] Certain amulet texts were written directly on the client's skin; if, for instance, a person suffered from Quartan fever, he was instructed to write "In the name of Allāh, Jibrāʾīl" on his right hand, "In the name of Allāh, Mīkāʾīl" on his left hand, "In the name of Allāh, Isrāfīl" on his right foot, "In the name of Allāh, therein they shall see neither sun nor bitter cold" (= Q LXXVI: 13) on the left foot, and "In the name of Allāh, the Mighty, the Omnipotent" between the shoulders.[121]

6. Summary

To several sixteenth- and seventeenth-century travelers, amulets seemed a topic interesting enough to comment briefly on. Their accounts to some extent complete our knowledge of lived amulet culture in Iran, which translates images, anthologies, and manuals, but for pragmatic reasons differs in part from the sophisticated amulet descriptions in manuals, at least when it comes to amulet usage outside the court as well as well-off and highly educated circles. On the other hand, remaining artifacts, though they usually reflect the high-end of amulet culture, also bear witness to the different social strata amulet culture permeated. Amulets thus constituted for many people a customary part of daily life, which usually was neither considered strange nor should, on the other hand, be overestimated in its importance. It was just there—and its fascinating material traces have come down to us.

Acknowledgments

The reproduction of two images (*The Myron Bement Smith Collection*) was made possible through a grant by the CRC 933 Material Text Cultures. I am indebted to Konrad Knauber and Laura Willer for organizing the conference "Textual Amulets in a Transcultural Perspective" where a draft of this paper was presented. I would also like to thank Christoffer Theis and Paolo Vitellozzi for preparing this volume. Finally, I extend my gratitude to all conference participants for two lovely and inspiring days.

10

Final Remarks

Toward a Transcultural View of Magical Writing

Christoffer Theis and Paolo Vitellozzi

This volume is not intended as a complete survey of evidence for textual amulets but rather as a comparative description of various traditions of magical writing throughout the centuries in different areas of the world, as they appear from the research experiences of the specialists who participated in the conference.

Many common features have been highlighted in the final discussion, although the diverse cultural traditions examined could initially suggest opposite opinions. In what follows, these features will be summarized, thus showing how the evidence furnished by different areas of research can integrate, providing a more complete view of different aspects of the same phenomenon. Therefore, a more general and synchronic sketch of the way amulets appear in human life can be tentatively provided, as well as of the people who collected and inscribed these amulets, sometimes as amateurs for a small community, some other times as professionals in search of profit, who relied on centuries-old traditions transmitted orally or through handbooks.

Some of the authors have in fact focused on the identity of the individuals who produced textual amulets: some were marginalized people clearly identified as outsiders, but we have also seen that numerous other individuals were part of the community and were able to provide magical devices for protection, healing, or some other benefits. It has been demonstrated that many amulets were easily manufactured, and could therefore be produced within a familiar or at least confined context, inspired at times by long-lasting religious traditions. However, the making of amulets could just as often be entrusted to special categories of professionals: such ritual workers, generally seen as magicians or sorcerers, could produce the amulets by themselves, either relying on an orally transmitted tradition or inspired by models described by magical books, but more often they cooperated with expert scribes and artisans who could master the techniques that the materials required. In some cases, there were women specialists, who embodied the intercultural model of the female healer, but the sources chronicle more about male specialists. The scribes who produced the designs for textual amulets had to be literate to some degree, and perhaps also had to have access to scribal training and to handbooks, as shown by many of the chapters in this volume; however, some of the craftsmen they worked with were probably illiterate, as scribal mistakes seem to suggest.

The presence of magical handbooks containing the archetypal models for textual amulets is in fact recurrent in most of the contexts discussed, and their use was not always tolerated. The owners of magical grimoires were in some cases even persecuted and publicly condemned. An important question arising from the conference was about the relationship between such practices and the official cult, which seems not always intolerant toward the use of amulets, but rather appears controlling, trying to place them under a proper seal of approval.

The amulets observed are made from a variety of natural substances, including durable stones inserted in pendants or finger rings, metal foils (gold, silver, or lead), clay vessels, wood, animal or even human bones, clothes and shoes, and pieces of parchment, up to simple, fragile scrolls of paper often inserted in tubular capsules. All of these material components were thought to have supernatural or divine powers, which were activated by a verbal action attested in various ways in the extant texts; even amulets written on papyrus, paper, or parchment do not defy this logic since, as many of the essays have revealed, writing on paper was subjected to complex ritual procedures, from the selection of inks and writing media up to the ritualization of the writing action itself.

We have seen that the material components were selected not only by virtue of their supposed intrinsic power but also according to the function that objects had in everyday life, which served to create a persuasive analogy for the core of the ritual action.

Some amulets were intended to defend a home or a town, but many of them were worn on the body, inserted in precious jewels or sewn into clothes, tied to one's hair, or even written directly on the parts of the body that one wished to protect.

The artifacts examined in each chapter show outstanding artistry and use of materials: many of such creations originate from cultures of the Near East, while others derive from traditions of Phoenician-Punic origin, as well as from the cultures of the Persian Empire. The scribal cultures of Egypt, Mesopotamia, and Israel, which tend to emphasize the linguistic nature of the divine power, are seen to blend with the Graeco-Roman cultural mindset, thus producing synergies between text and image. In many of the examined contexts, writing becomes itself an image, and this marks an important phase for textual amulets, when the written word transcends the speech acts which originally underlay the action of writing, becoming a graphic sign.

In fact, the most important feature discussed in this volume is the use of writing on amulets, which transformed orally performed prayers, incantations, and other protective or curative speech acts into textual objects that immediately declare their function to the modern observer. As it is evident in the oldest typologies of amulets, writing gradually enters the ritual objects, initially by giving emphasis to their formal characteristics as well as to the images they carry, as if the speech acts employed to activate their supernatural efficacy were made permanent by writing.

If the development of textual amulets was in part encouraged by the need to fix a permanent and never-ending speech act onto a patient or at a doorway, a further important aspect examined in this volume is the transformation, replacement, or disappearance of the rituals that at times accompanied such speech acts: the inscribed object, which makes one or more moments of the ritual permanent, finally replaces the ritual action itself, becoming almost self-referential.

The documentation collected in this volume allows us also to see how protective amulets reflect defensive strategies applied to a number of different boundaries: the city gates, the fields, the house and its door, as well as the various human body parts, such as neck, hips, shoulders, arms, and so on.

A further point that clearly arises from this comparative analysis is that, in the typological diversity of the material media, the basic needs that the users demanded from their amulets through the centuries are surprisingly similar, and clearly visible in the extant texts when not explicitly declared: this, apart from being a comforting aspect of human sensitivity, appears to be a significant feature in the anthropology of religion.

As some chapters in this volume show, house amulets are widely attested in the sources examined, as well as those intended to keep plague and pestilence away from the gates of a city; however, the most intimate circle of defense was not the house, but rather the individual human body, which itself was a complex realm of its own, needing protection and healing.

By tracking the placement of amulets on different parts of the body, we are able to understand how people gauged their vulnerabilities and frailties; in fact, as we have seen, amulets were hung from any limb, worn as finger rings and earrings, sewn into clothes, or even inscribed as pure texts directly on one's skin. A favorite spot for protective amulets seems to have been the front of the body: many were placed on the neck, on the arms, and on the head, although there are many cases of amulets placed between the shoulders—this seems quite common in the Islamic magical tradition, but antecedents of this phenomenon can already be seen in Graeco-Roman magic.

Among individual amulets, a major role is played by the exorcistic ones, heirs of the oldest Israelite tradition continued in many ways both in the East and the West, where it spread mainly through its Christian reinterpretation: the wish to avert evil is therefore primary, either it appears in absolute shapes (from the most severe forms of possession to the simplest manifestations of envy) or it bears the more recognizable features of physical disease (infections, fever, bleeding, inflammations). In the large number of requests concerning the need to be cured, amulets dedicated to female reproductive health, as well as to childbirth and child care, seem to be plentiful in many different cultures. Finally, the need for charisma, which is functional both to the sphere of seduction and that of social success, seems also one of the main trends in the multifarious requests attested by the examined corpora.

Furthermore, our amulets are connected not only by their usage and purposes but also by the ways in which texts are structured: in fact, the basic speech acts underlying their use, as well as many of the graphic strategies employed to write them, can be traced back to some fundamental categories clearly recognized by the scholars.

In fact, we are now able to infer a spoken component or layout to a text written on an amulet, that is a hypothesis relying on the explicit written instructions, style, or analogies that we find in literary sources, and although texts (and especially compilations of texts) may comprise once-oral materials that have been removed from their performative contexts, we can often go back to the original oral performances that lie behind the creation of our artifacts. As we have seen, by following Austin and Searle's theory of speech acts, we are now able to recognize in each kind of textual amulets a category of utterances that under the right conditions were thought to effectively change a situation in real life.

This outline for understanding the true force of speech in reality, which relies on the concept that declarative and other speech acts are more than grammatical expressions but rather expressions of an ideal "action," can now be brought back, as achieved by modern anthropology, to ritual itself and the diverse ways in which metaphor and analogy are used in ritual contexts.

If we correctly employ the linguistic categories elaborated by the scholars, we now have an excellent research template to synchronically frame our textual amulets, beyond their historical context, relying on the pure structure of utterances as well as on agency. By doing this, we have seen that many amulet users expressed their needs in form of a prayer, sometimes simply by uttering divine names in isolation or through enthusiastic acclamations. Such utterances may also hide behind seemingly incomprehensible formulas, which can often be related to languages that are far different from those spoken in the context where certain amulets were produced, and for this reason such formulas contribute to create that sense of otherness that is often taken by the scholars as a distinctive feature of the phenomenon conventionally known as magic.

Inscribed pleas for protection, which are indeed the most common textual typology in all the documents discussed, were most probably spoken aloud by individuals involved in or anticipating a potential danger: inscribed amulets were thought in some way to repeat their request continually to a deity. On some of our amulets, due mainly to a lack of writing space, these inscribed prayers can be extremely brief, consisting for example of bare imperatives, such as the single word "Protect!," but much longer prayers can be found when the writing surface allows the writer to do so. Some amulets, especially those created to protect the body, mention the owner precisely, while others contain generic references to the wearer, thus making it possible, for those belonging to the same community, to pass these amulets from one to another and for the manufacturer to prepare a supply in advance. While some prayers are definitely preventive, other textual amulets seem to have been used after an illness or trouble; in places where endemic diseases were widespread, such objects were probably aimed at curing chronic health problems. Other inscribed amulets imagine relief from an extremely severe disease, while others simply ask for help for their wearer, generally using verbs meaning "to save." Generic requests for rescue and safety are common enough, but amulets employing verbs related more directly to the disease are also found. A further strategy is to ask the divinity to drive away a disease-causing demon that is conceived as wandering and can therefore be removed from one's body as with blood-staunching amulets; in a similar way, some amulets are made to control the anger of other people, which is imagined as a flow of blood.

Furthermore, the authors have provided comment on amulets requesting some specific kind of benefit, such as a generic good disposition of the divinity toward the speaker, or a boost of personal charm that might grant other people's affection. The evidence offered by the contributors shows the continuity in the basic structure of prayers throughout the centuries, despite the many changes to which this genre is subjected in the diverse cultural contexts.

Unlike prayers, where the speaker plays the role of the devoted worshiper, incantations, which are also common on many of the amulets discussed, revolve around a culturally specific belief that music and vocal sounds are endowed with a persuasive power, activated by specific rhythms or tunes. In this way, they address a target directly and contain little reference to the gods, since they rely on the agency of the speaker to modify an unresolved situation. Instead, like prayers, they can aim at protecting and curing but also be a means for seduction and compulsion, and are significantly persistent in history, as the examples shown by the authors have well demonstrated. As perfectly explained by the most recent research, such speech acts, originating from the attempt of averting evil by threat and by means of a command, are often followed by a third-person statement, and in many cases embedded in more complex narrations, commonly known as *historiolae* ("short stories"). Such narrations, providing in the past a comparative model for a wished-for future, seem to ground their agency on a persuasive analogy, which is emphasized through the use of similes. This kind of speech acts, originating from the oldest traditions of Mesopotamia and Egypt, recurs through time and space in many of the textual amulets investigated, sometimes inspired by the mythological repertoire of Greco-Roman (or even Egyptian) antiquity, while most of the later traditions, from Syria to Scandinavia, fully draw from the Bible as well as from the Koranic lore.

The authors have then provided examples that show how incantations are particularly suitable, in many contexts, to be combined with graphic strategies that somehow simulate the expected effect, as we have seen in those wing-shaped calligrams that by diminishing one letter at a time a magical name aim to annihilate the cause of the disease.

The commands that we find at the end of many incantations are similar in many contexts, and include true *topoi* such as the so-called flee-formula, which addresses a demon or a disease in a threatening way. We have then observed true performative speech acts, especially in the genre of exorcism, a near-eastern invention that progressively spreads worldwide both through the Christian and Islamic traditions; this kind of speech acts, consisting essentially in driving a demon out of a human body by putting it under oath, can often include the recourse to a superhuman entity, while the agency is focused on the speaker using direct performatives: some chapters in this volume have shown that the structure of exorcisms is sometimes also extended to iatro-magical amulets such as those protecting the female womb as well as those facilitating childbirth.

By analyzing exorcistic amulets it has been also shown how in the different cultures the reference to the liturgical or sacred language often produces new authoritative classes of powerful speech, simply by association with a particular sacred tradition: this phenomenon has been evidenced for example in those magical formulas derived from foreign languages, as well as in the frequent quotations, reported by many amulets, of the sacred scriptures of the three Abrahamic religions, or even the magic usage of Greek epic poetry, since Homeric language was thought to have, in the Greco-Roman thought of stoic origin, an authoritative power for ritual utterances.

The chapters have also highlighted how the recourse to otherworldly speech, by means of glossolalic speech, vowel sounds, and true nonsense, is recurring in those traditions that place the ground of their authority in a mythical past; this means that magic and its traditions are often presented as if coming from outside social reality, from a mythical world of ancestors and heroes. This has been evidenced in the complex sequences of alphabetical symbols, as well as in cryptography and the various phenomena of pseudo-writing, where foreign, animal, or geometrically configured names or sounds are seen as devices which allow to transcend language itself and to journey toward a linguistic otherness and hence to the divine.

The magical aspects of speech discussed in the nine chapters that constitute this volume seem therefore to contribute to one general principle, that words do not simply transmit information, intentions, or commands but rather are able to deeply change real-life situations by their inner, illocutionary force. This is particularly true in magic rituals, where the authority of compelling tunes and charms, which are possibly also inscribed, allows the participants to experience a metaphysical power. Furthermore, it has been clearly evidenced that, albeit in a plethora of diachronic and geographical varieties, many of the linguistic structures that lie behind the creation of a text, as well as the forms of thought that lead to the use of the examined objects, appear to contain recurring features identical in each of the examined contexts and can therefore be taken as universals of the human religious thought.

Notes

Chapter 1

1 On which, see Gordon (2014).
2 See, e.g., Skemer (2006); Gordon and Marco Simón (2010); Wilburn (2012); Boschung and Bremmer (2015); The Bruyn (2017); Faraone (2018); Frankfurter (2019).
3 Cf. Gordon (2015).
4 See esp. Faraone (2012).
5 Austin(1962); Searle (1969).
6 Frankfurter (2019): 606–25.
7 See Ullmann (1972): 362.
8 Cf. Theis (2014): 377sq.
9 See Forster (2006): 98–100; Ritter and Plessner (1962): 7sq.
10 See Theis (2014): 19–25; Otto (2015).
11 Cf. Kiyanrad, Willer, and Theis (2018): 2.
12 Schnyder (1991): 151.

Chapter 2

1 As it is impossible to provide a complete bibliography on the so-called magical gems, I indicate a short list of studies which have been essential for this chapter: Michel (2001); *SGG I*; *SGG II*; Michel (2004); *Gems of Heaven* (2011); *LIM*; Faraone (2018); Endreffy, Nagy and Spier (2019); Dasen and Nagy (2019).
2 The term "magic" is used here in a purely conventional sense. See Gordon (2011b): footnote 1. On ancient magic in general see recently Frankfurter (2019a). On ancient Greek magic see also Faraone and Obbink (1991).
3 See Faraone (2011); Faraone (2018).
4 Faraone (2012).
5 On this aspect, see in general Mastrocinque (2005); Bohak (2008).
6 Faraone (2011); Faraone (2018).
7 Faraone (2018): 152–5.
8 Galen. *De simpl.* 10.19 (Ed. Kühn XII, 207): Ἰδιότητα δέ τινες ἐνίοις λίθους μαρτυροῦσι τοιαύτην, οἵαν ὄντως ἔχει καὶ ὁ χλωρὸς ἴασπις, ὠφελῶν τόν τε

στόμαχον καὶ τὸ τῆς γαστρὸς στόμα περιαπτόμενον. ἐντιθέασί τε καὶ δακτυλίῳ αὐτὸν ἔνιοι καὶ γλύφουσιν ἐν αὐτῷ τὸν τὰς ἀκτῖνας ἔχοντα δράκοντα, καθάπερ καὶ ὁ βασιλεὺς Νεχεψὼς ἔγραψεν ἐν τῇ τεσσαρακαιδεκάτῃ βίβλῳ ("The testimony of some authorities attributes to certain stones a peculiar quality, which is actually possessed by the light green jasper. Worn as an amulet, it benefits the stomach and the oesophagus. Some set it in a ring and engrave on it a radiate serpent, just as King Nechepso prescribed in his fourteenth book," transl. C. A. Faraone).
It is well known that Chnoubis is often represented on green stone (green jaspers, plasmas, or prases): see the list provided in Michel (2004): 255–63, no. 11. Compare also Faraone (2011): 50–2.

9 Cf. Aët. *Tetrabiblos* 1 serm. 2 c.36: *quidam anulis iaspidem viridem includunt et draconem radios habentem in ipsa sculptum ex praecepto Necepsi regis, qui prosit ventriculo* ("some enclose in their rings a green jasper and a serpent having seven rays, who benefits the belly, as prescribed by King Nechepso"); Marc. Emp. 20.98 (Liechtenhan 1968: 354): *Ad stomachi dolorem remedium physicum sic: in iaspide exculpe draconem radiatum, ut habeat septem radios et claude auro et utere in collo* ("a powerful remedy for pain of the stomach: on a jasper stone carve a radiant serpent, so that it has seven rays; enclose it in gold and employ it on the neck," transl. C. A. Faraone).

10 Marc. Emp. 24.7 (Liechtenhan 1968: 412) *in lapide iaspide frygia aerizusa si nota infra scripta insculpta fuerit, id est SSS, et collo dolentis latus fuerit suspensus, mire proderit.* ("if on a Phrygian jasper stone, pure as the air, is engraved the symbol below, that is SSS, and it is worn around the neck of a patient who has pain in his hip, this will be amazingly helpful."). This type has a close parallel in a milky chalcedony from Aquileia (*SGG II*: 23, pl. 5, no. Aq 33).

11 On gems showing Chnoubis, see in general *SGG* I: 78–82, 242–261; Michel (2004): 166–77, 255–63, no. 11; Mastrocinque (2008); Dasen and Nagy (2012); Quack (forthcoming): § 2.4.3.

12 London, British Museum inv. no. G 260 (EA 56260). See Michel (2001): no. 327 [*CBd*-713].

13 Χνουβίς ναβις βιεννους ὕδωρ δίψῃ ἄρτος πείνῃ πῦρ ῥ{ε}ίγ{ο}<ε>ι.

14 Bonner (1954): 149, no. 36.

15 Ἀποστρέψατε πᾶσαν τάσιν πᾶσαν ἀπεψίαν πᾶν πόνον στομάχου ἀπὸ Ἰουλιανοῦ ὅν ἔτεκεν Νόννα.

16 See esp. Faraone (2011).

17 On persuasive images in the ancient world and the concept of "persuasive analogy," see Faraone (1992): 117–23; Faraone (2018): 106–12.

18 Kotansky (2019): 508sq.

19 Faraone (2018): 118–21.

20 Faraone (2018): 40sq.

21 Michel (2004): 280sq, no. 23.1. For a detailed discussion, see Faraone (2013).

22 Εἰς λίθον Μηδικὸν γλύψον Ἡρακλέα ὀρθὸν πνίγοντα λέοντα καὶ ἐγκλείσας εἰς δακτυλίδιον χρυσοῦν δίδου φορεῖν. Alex.Trall. VIII (IV, p. 80 Brunet).

23 London, British Museum, inv. no. GR 1894, 1101.458.

24 Faraone (2011): 52–4.

25 Paris, Cabinet des Médailles, inv. no. 58.2220 bis. See *LIM*: no. 403 [*CBd*-3638].

26 Grk. ἀναχώρ(ε)ι, κόλε, τὸ θ(ε)ῖον σε δι<ώ>κει.

27 Dasen (2008).

28 See, e.g., Paris, Cabinet des Médailles, inv. no. AA.Seyrig.121 (red jasper, bearing on the rev. the inscription: στάθητι μήτρα, "Uterus, stay!"): *LIM*: no. 425 [*CBd*-3658]. See also Dasen (2008): 265–81; Faraone (2016): 109sq.

29 See, e.g., Verona, Musei Civici d'Arte: Museo di Castelvecchio (inv. no. 26737). Pink coral: obv. Gorgon's head / rev. Hekate. See *SGG* II: no. Vr 26 [*CBd*-4109].

30 Ἐκλήθη δὲ οὗτος καὶ ὑπό τινων γοργόνιος, διὸ εἰς αὐτὸν εἰσχαράσσουσι Γοργόνα καὶ κατακλείουσιν ἐν χρυσῷ ἢ ἀργύρῳ. Καὶ τελεσθείς ἐστι μέγιστον φυλακτήριον πρὸς πάντα φόβον καὶ ἐπήρειαν πονηρῶν ἀνθρώπων καὶ μάλιστα ἐν ταῖς ὁδοιπορίαις πρὸς ἐφόδους πονηρῶν καὶ πρὸς ἑρπετὰ παντοῖα· ἔστι γαρ ὁ λίθος Ἑρμοῦ. Ποιεῖ δὲ καὶ ἐπὶ τῶν ὀνείρων καὶ φαντάσματα ἀπωθεῖται τῇ ἰδίᾳ ἀντιπαθείᾳ. Μέγιστον δὲ φυλακτήριον καὶ πρὸς ὀργὴν δεσπότου γλυφέντος ἐν αὐτῷ ζωδίου Ἑκάτης ἢ Γοργόνος προτομῆς. *Orphei Lithica Kerygmata* 20. 12–16.
"This stone is even called *Gorgonios* by some and on account of this they carve a Gorgon into it and set in gold or silver. And, if it is consecrated, it is the greatest phylactery against every fear, against the abuse of wicked persons, and most of all for those in a journey against the attacks of the wicked and all the creeping things. It is in fact the stone of Hermes. It also works for dreams and repels ghosts thanks to its own antipathy. It is also the greatest phylactery [i.e., for slaves] against the anger of masters, if the image of Hekate is carved into it or the frontal head (*protome*) of the Gorgon" (Transl. C. A. Faraone).

31 Boston, Museum of Fine Arts, inv. no. 1997.174. See Bonner (1954): no. 42; Faraone (2013): 327–32, no. 1 [*CBd*-2813].

32 Γοργών. Ἀχιλλεύς Ὀάλιο<ς>(?) τοῦ Ταύρου Ἰουλίς. <ὅτ>αν λαλῶ{ω}σιν Ἀλ<ε>ξίῳ μὴ <π>ιστευέσθωσαν. Χνουβί<ς>. On this text, see especially Faraone (2013): 327–32.

33 See Gordon (2011a). On the relationship between magical gems and magical papyri, see esp. Bonner (1946): 25sq. (discrepancies); Preisendanz (1966): 388sq. (*PGM* and gem parallels); Wortmann (1975): 80 (parallel); Smith (1979); Schwartz (1981); Brashear (1995): 2412–18; Nagy (2002) (complete list of occurrences); G. Sfameni Gasparro in *SGG* I: 28–43; Vitellozzi (2018).

34 See recently Faraone (2012); Faraone (2018): 177–237; Frankfurter (2019b).

35 See especially: Poccetti (2002); Faraone and Kropp (2010).

36 Such procedures are widely described in Faraone (2012); see also Frankfurter (2019c).

37 See Michel (2004): 152sq.; Faraone (2009); Faraone (2012): 35–49.

38 On the so-called *charaktêres*, see Gordon (2011b); Dzwiza (2013); Gordon (2014); Dzwiza (2015); Dzwiza (2019).

39 Luc. *Philops*. 24. See A. Mastrocinque in *SGG* I: 54–58.

40 On this problem, see recently Thissen (1988); Bohak (2003); Quack (2019). For a wider analysis on the most common magical names and formulas, see Brashear (1995): 3576–603; Versnel (2002); Martin (2005): 215–21; A. Mastrocinque in *SGG* I: 90–112; Michel (2004): 481–7.

41 Zosimus, *On the letter Omega*, 9. See Cox Miller (1986): 495–9.

42 Nagy (2015): 207sq.

43 *AGD* III K: no. 127.

44 Good examples of this can be found in Faraone (2010): 215–18; Mastrocinque (2017).

45 See, e.g., Henig and McGregor (2004): 127, no. 13.29 [*CBd*-1177], Μέγας Σάραπις ("Great is Sarapis!"). For further examples, see Faraone (2018): 182–5.

46 See, e.g., Michel (2001): no. 69 [*CBd*-447], ωραρα νικᾷ Ἑκάτη ὑποτάσσ<ε>ι ("Orara conquers, Hecate subdues!").

47 Perugia, Museo Archeologico Nazionale dell'Umbria (inv. no. 1771): Vitellozzi (2010): no. 466 [*CBd*-4280]. Obv.: εἷς θεός ἐν οὐρανῷ φιλάνθρωπος, Ζηο / rev.: κύριος εἰς τοῦς αἰῶνας.

48 For a glossary on the most common magical *logoi*, see Brashear (1995): 3576–603; A. Mastrocinque in *SGG* I: 90–112; Michel (2004): 481–7.

49 Searle (1969).

50 A comparison between the developments of these two genres of magic has been formulated by Faraone (2018): 177sq.

51 Faraone (1991).

52 Kagarow (1929).

53 "These [performative sentences] consist of a performative verb used in the first-person present tense of the indicative mood. [. . .] In uttering a performative sentence a speaker performs the illocutionary act [i.e., a statement, question, command or promise] [. . .] named by the performative verb by way of representing himself as performing that act" [Searle and Vanderveken (1985): 2sq].

54 "Occasionally [. . .] third-person passive imperative." See Faraone (1991): 6.

55 Which corresponds to Kagarow's "Wunschformel."

56 Kropp (2008). In Kropp (2010) the two taxonomies are compared.

57 Austin (1962): 14sq.

58 "Manipulationsformel," see Kropp (2008): 145sq. English definitions used in the text are provided by Kropp herself. See Kropp (2010).

59 These are, for example, latin *ligo*, *obligo* (= Grk. καταδῶ, καταδεσμεύω), *defigo* (= Grk. καταπατταλεύω), *immergo*.

60 "Übergabeformel," see Kropp (2008): 146sq.
61 For example Latin *do, trado* (cf. Grk. παραδίδωμι), *commendo, mando, dono, dedico, devoveo, desacrifico.*
62 "Aufforderungsformel," see Kropp (2008): 147–9.
63 On which, see Faraone (2018): 229–36.
64 See also Gordon (1995): 371.
65 Poccetti (2002).
66 Cf. Greek terms like ποιεῖν, πράσσειν, πράξις.
67 Faraone (2018).
68 Faraone (2018): 221–37.
69 That is, a speech act by which the performer, speaking in first person, hopes to direct the action on his target in an automatic way.
70 Berlin, Staatliche Museen zu Berlin, Ägyptisches Museum, Inv. no. 9871. Carnelian: obv. Ouroboros snake and characteres / rev. Inscription. See Philipp (1986): no. 196 [*CBd*-2148].
71 ιαηεηιαιωηαβαθιγαωρ|αφεσινηηαεωγαρβαθα|γιαμμηφιβαχνηνεω|επικαλουμαισετ ονπσι|λαμπονταπαντατην||ηκουμενηνκαιαναζω|πυρουντατaυ *character* την|κ υισιναβλαθαναλβα|αβρανειαουαβριαω|βαναβοιαναρχοακιζω||οαραθαραυτη ησφρα|γηαυτηητινησφρα|γεισηνγραφομενη → ιαη εη ια ιωη Ἄβα Θιγάωρ ἄφεσιν ηηαεω γαρβαθαγιαμμηφιβαχνηνεω ἐπικαλοῦμαί σε τὸν πσι λάμποντα πάντα τὴν ἠκουμένην καὶ ἀναζωπυροῦντα τὰ ὑ[.] τὴν κύισιν αβλαναθαναλβα αβραν ειαου αβρ ιαω βανα βοι αίαρχοακίζω ὁ Ἀραθάρ· αὕτη ἡ σφραγή αὐτη ἥτιν ἡ σφραγεὶς ἦν γραφομένη.
72 Faraone (2018): 222–9.
73 Paris, Cabinet des Médailles (Inv. Froehner 2829). See Michel (2004): no. 28.2.a_2 = *LIM*: no. 677 [*CBd*-3909].
74 ἐξορκίζω σε θεὸν τὸν μέγαν Βαρβαθ Ἰηαὼθ τὸν Σαβαὼθ θεὸν τὸν καθήμενον ἐπάνω τοῦ ὄρους παλαμνάιου θεὸν τὸν καθήμενον ἐπάνω τοῦ βάτου θεὸν τὸν καθήμενον ἐπάνω τοῦ Χερουβί. Αὐτός ἐστι παντοκράτωρ. Λέγει σοι πάν<τ>α ἐὰν καὶ συν<ά>ντημα Μαρμαραυὼθ Ἰηαώθ. Ὁρκισμὸς οὗτος ἐστ<ι> Σαβαὼθ Ἀδωναῖ τοῦ μὴ ἐγγίσαι ὁτι Κυρίου θεοῦ Ἰσραὴλ Ἀκραμμαχαμαρεὶ Βρασαυ Ἀβραβλαιν. Ἐξορκίζω θεὸν Ἑναθιάω Φαβαθαλλον Βαβλαια Ἰάω Θαλαχ Ερου Ῥωσαρ Βὼς Θοῦθ μὴ παρακούσῃς τὸ ὄνομα τοῦ θεοῦ.
75 *Enunciati desiderativo-iussivi* in Poccetti's classification.
76 See, e.g., *AGWien* III: no. 2246 = Michel (2004): no. 36.1.a_12 [*CBd*-2490], βοήθει Αβαλβαπαχαχρη κύριε / "Help, Abalbapachachre, Lord!"; Michel (2004): no. 27.1.b_9 = *LIM*: no. 107 [*CBd*-3278], βοήθ<ε>ι μοι / "Help me!"
77 See, e.g., Schwartz and Schwartz (1979): no. 34 = Michel (2004): no. 41.5_2 [*CBd*-1780], φύλα<ξ>ον ἀπὸ παντὸς κακοῦ τὸν φορ<οῦντα> / "Protect the wearer (of this amulet) from all evil"; Michel (2004): no. 11.3.e_2 = *LIM*: no. 259 [*CBd*-2943]

φύλα<ξ>ον ὑγ{ε}ιῆ στομάχον Πρόκλου / "Keep Proclos' stomach healthy!" (Transl. C. Bonner).

78 See, e.g., Boardman and Wagner (2003): no. 263 [*CBd*-1256], σῷζε με Ἰάω / "Save me, *Yhwh*"; Vitellozzi (2010): no. 526 = *SGG* II: no. Pe 25 [*CBd*-4274], ορω[ρ]ιουθ σ[ῷζε] Ζενώριαν ἣν ἔτεκεν Δομιτία / "Orôreiouth, s[ave] Zenobia whom Domitia bore."

79 See, e.g., Michel (2001): no. 120 = Michel (2004): no. 19.1.c_1 [*CBd*-1256], δὸς χάριν τῇ Ζυρουᾳ / "give charm to Zyroua"; Michel (2001): no. 134 = Michel (2004): no. 19.3.b_2 [*CBd*-534], Δός χάριν Θεανοῦτι πρὸς Σεραπάμμωνα / "Grant Theanous favor in the eyes of Serapammon"; Bonner (1950): 206 = Michel (2004): no. 19.4.a_5, δὸς χάριν φοροῦντι / "Grant favor to the wearer"; *SGG* II: no. Na 18 = Michel (2004): no. 6.2_3 [*CBd*-2205], Φρῆθ δὸς ν{ε}ίκην, χάριν, ὄλβον / "Phreth! Give victory, kindness, wealth!"

80 Mouterde (1930–1931): no. 11.

81 Faraone (1991): 5.

82 A rock crystal in the Boston Museum of Fine Arts (Inv. no. 01.7556) showing the lion-headed god bears, for example, the following inscription: ΖΕΘ ΑΦΟΒΕΤWΡ ΘΡΟΨΜΕW ΜΙΘΟΡΟΝ ΦΑWΧΙ ΕΙΑΕΟϹ ΤΗ ΕΜΕ ΨΥΧΗ ΚΑΙ ΤΟΥϹΕΜΟΥϹ ΤΕΚΝΥϹ → Ζεθ ἀφοβέτωρ θροψμεω μιθορον φαωχι ἵλεως τῇ ἐμῇ ψυχῇ καὶ τοὺς ἐμοὺς τέκνους (τοῖς ἐμοῖς τέκνοις) / "Zeth, fearless-hearted, Thropsmeô Mithoron Phaôchi, (be) well disposed to my soul and my children." See Bonner (1950): 234 = Michel (2004): no. 37.B.1.b_1 [*CBd*-1417].

83 Oxford, Ashmolean Museum, inv. no 2003.129. See Henig and MacGregor (2004): no. 13.10 = Michel (2004): no. 39.6.a_4 [*CBd*-1158].

84 Αρπονχνουφιβριντατηνωφριβρισκυλμαρυζαβαραμεσενκριφινιπτουμιχμουμαω: all the *voces* refer to the solar deity, and they include the well-known αρπονχνουφι-logos. See Michel (2004): 483.

85 Graf (1991): 192.

86 St. Petersburg, Hermitage Museum. Inv. no. Ж.157 (GR-21714). Nicolo: obv. Perseus / rev. Inscription ΦΥ[--] / ΠΟΔΑΓΡΑ / [-]ΕΡΣΕΥΣΣ / ΕΔΙWΧΙ (Φύγε ποδάγρα, Περσεύς σε διώχι). See Nagy (2015): 220–32.

87 A similar gem once in a private collection at Susa in Tunisia (Bonner 1950: 97; *SEG* 19.12.818) shows the sun god drawing his bow and on the reverse: μὴ θιγῃς μου, βασκοσύνη, διώκει σε Ἥλιος ("Don't touch me Envy, Helios pursues you!"). See Faraone (2018): 211.

88 *LIM*: no. 350 = Michel (2004): no. 5.3.b_4 [*CBd*-3552].

89 Grk. Φθόνε ἀτύχι (*LIM*: no. 467).

90 Cambridge (MA), Harvard Art Museum (inv. no. TL38193.10) = Michel (2004: 266sq., pl. 88.2 [*CBd*-3085]. Obv.: suspended woman / rev.: inscr. Βλαρθαρ εἰμὶ Αραχθα τὴν συγγεινομένην πυρὶ φλέξατε ὡς Αρβαθαιρας.

91 See Faraone (2013): 338–41, no. 5.

92 See *CBd*-3085.

93 Inv. no. G 241 (EA 56241). See Michel (2001): no. 8 = Michel (2004): no. 39.1.f_2 [*CBd*-387]. Here Fig. 2.11.

94 Michel (2004): nos. 47.1.b_2-3 = *LIM*: nos. 464–465 [*CBd*-3692 and 3693].

95 See Faraone (2018): 95sq.

96 See, e.g., Michel (2001): no. 425 = Michel (2004): no. 47.1.a_4 [*CBd*-783], σχίων / "for the hips"; *LIM*: no. 211, μητρικ<ὴ>ν θ<ε>ραπ(ε)ίαν / "therapy for the womb"; Michel (2001): no. 402 = Michel (2004): no. 43.1_2, στομάχου / "for the stomach"; Michel (2004): no. 1.2_2 [*CBd*-4003], πρὸς κωλάνεμον / "against wind from the rectum." Compare Faraone (2018): 95.

97 *SGG* II: no. Pe 1= Vitellozzi 2010: no. 510 [*CBd*-4250].

98 *PGM* IV 2705–2707.

99 See, e.g., *LIM*: no. 618 [*CBd*-3842], obv.: καὶ τότε δὴ χρύσεια πατὴρ ἐτίταινε τάλαντα / "then it was that the Father lifted up his golden scales" (Hom. *Il.* 7.69 and 22.209).

100 E.g., New York, MMA, inv. no. 17.190.491. See Bol and Breck (1983): no. 165 [*CBd*-1123], καὶ ἡ γυνὴ οὖσα [ἐν] ῥύσει αἵματος ἔτη, καὶ πολλὰ παθοῦσα ἦν καὶ ἐδαπάνησα μηδὲν ὠφεληθεῖσα ἀλλὰ μᾶλλον ἦν δραμοῦσα ἐξηράνθη ἡ πηγὴ τοῦ αἱματησμοῦ αὐτῆς ἐν τῷ ὀνόματι τῆς πίστεως αὐτῆς. "There was a woman afflicted with hemorrhages for years. She had suffered greatly and had spent all that she had. Yet she was not helped but only grew worse. Her flow of blood dried up in the name of her faith" (Cf. *Mk* 5.25-34).

101 Faraone (2018): 231.

102 Compare n. 93. See Faraone (2016): 111sq.

103 Obv.: Ἡμέρας γόνος Μέμνων κοιμᾶται κραβαζαζηραβιραθκηβα Ἰάω εω. / "Memnon, the son of Hemera is asleep (*voces magicae*)." Rev.: Φιλίππας γόνος Ἀντίπατρος κοιμᾶται κραβαζαζηραβιραβιραθκηβα Ἰάω εω; Ἐγὼ ὁ ὤν. / "Antipatros, the son of Philippa is asleep (*voces magicae*), *Iaō*; *eō*, I Am the Existing One."

104 For a magical hiss inscribed on a gem, see Vitellozzi (2019: 290).

105 Cox Miller (1986): 481–6.

106 Pl. *Crat.* 387–427.

107 See Vitellozzi (2018): 182sq.

108 Staatliche Museen zu Berlin, Ägyptisches Museum, inv. 9876. See Philipp (1986): no. 118 = Michel (2004): no. 50.2.b_1 [*CBd*-2091].

109 On which see Michel (2004): 484.

110 *PGM* XII 270–7.

111 Faraone (2012).

112 Malibu, The J. Paul Getty Museum. Inv. no. 73.AN.1. Brown and white agate. Obv.: variant of the Ἀβλαναθαναλβα palindrome, inscribed in *pterygoma* / rev.:

῾Απάλλαξον Γαΐ<α>ν τοῦ πυρετοῦ [καὶ] το<ῦ>τε ῥ{ε}ι[γους κε] πάσης [τῆς ὀ]δού [νης τῆς] κεφ[αλῆς.].

113 See Kotansky (1980); Faraone (2012): 12, fig. 1.4, 17, appendix no. 6.

114 Seren. *Liber Medicinalis*, 935–40.

115 London, British Museum, inv. no. G 386 (EA 56386). Jasper (Green and red). See Michel (2001): no. 553 [*CBd*-912].

Chapter 3

1 See the most prominent titles of Bonner (1950); Michel (2001); Michel (2004); Zwierlein-Diehl (1992).

2 For example, on various pieces at the British Museum in London published by Michel (2001): 66–89 (nos. 102–135). For an overview, see *The Campbell Bonner Magical Gems Database* [Online www2.szepmuveszeti.hu/talismans/visitatori_salutem; June 7, 2021].

3 For example, on various pieces at the British Museum in London published by Michel (2001): 12–16, 89–92 (nos. 17–24; 136–142).

4 See the compilation by Michel (2004): 235–345 and for Chnoubis Quack *in preparation*.

5 See Theis *in preparation*, chapter 4sq.

6 See Theis (2018).

7 E.g., First (2011): 57 ("relatively small number").

8 E.g., Michel (2005): 142 and Sfameni (2010): 443sq.

9 See Caylus (1761) and Chiflet (1657).

10 See, for example, Kaplony (1963): pl. 6 (no. 7); pl. 25 (no. 56 and 57); pl. 26 (no. 62); pl. 99 (no. 423); Kaplony (1981): pl. 153 (no. 10); Teissier (1987): 30 (fig. 2a–f); Theis (2017).

11 See the depiction by Hawass (2006): 123; Hornung (1963a): pl. 6; Hornung (1997a): 122; Hornung (1997b): 116sq). However, the name is not mentioned in all documents, cf. Hornung (1963b): 119.

12 See Hornung (1963a): pl. 11; Hornung (1963b): 26b.

13 At least, with Bonner (1950); Delatte/Derchain (1964) and Michel (2001); Michel (2004) there are some larger compilations available.

14 See Theis *in preparation*.

15 See Theis (2018).

16 E.g., the gem Coll. De Clercq, 3470, made of red jasper, size 3.15 × 2.3 × 0.4 cm, see De Ridder (1911): 779, pl. 29; Cambridge, Fitzwilliam Museum, S 37 (CM), made of brown chalcedony, size 1.80 × 1.40 × 0.25 cm, see Henig (1994): 29 (no. 47); London, British Museum, Inv. G 454 (EA 56454), made of serpentine, size

3 × 2.5 × 0.4 cm, see Michel (2001): 180sq. (no. 288); or Slg. Sa'd, Gadara, Jordan, no. 424, made of heliotrope, size 1.4 × 1.2 cm, see Henig/Whiting (1987): 39 (no. 424).

17 Bonner (1950): 297sq. (no. 267); Michel (2001): 302 (no. 494).

18 Bonner (1950): 297, pl. 13 (no. 264); Michel (2004): 288 (sub 27.4.c); corresponds to *The Campbell Bonner Magical Gems Database* 1441.

19 This common medical term describes one being with two heads on two necks; cf. Boemke et al. (1939): 435; Buck (1889): 20 and Wingert (1984): 179.

20 For example, depicted by Hawass (2006): 105; Hornung (1963a): 192, pl. 12; Hornung (1997a): 128; Hornung (1997b): 186sq. In some cases, a comparable being is pictured directly behind the sun bark; see Schmidt (1919): 156, fig. 860. Similarly, in Egypt anthropomorphic gods have been depicted with other bird heads, such as the statuette with two bronze falcon heads, today Florence, Museo Archeologico, without no., see Hornemann (1951): no. 160. This piece looks almost like a statuette from al-Musawwarat as-Sufra, today Paris, Louvre, E. 5704, see Hintze/Hintze (1967): fig. 138 and Hornemann (1957): no. 310; identical with Lanzone (1886): pl. 119 (no. 3).

21 Cf. Hieroglyphs by Hornung (1963): 203. Cf. Sadek (1985): 287 and Schulman (1964): 275–9.

22 For example, on Bern, Historical Museum, AE.10, which comes from the region of Thebes, see Küffer/Renfer (1996): 39 and Daressy (1907): 28; or on the sarcophagus of *Nś-M'w.t*, today Neuchâtel, Musée d'ethnographie, Eg. 184a–e, see Küffer/Siegmann (2007): 53, fig. 7.

23 De Garis Davies (1953): pl. 24.

24 Quack *in preparation*, chapter 2.4.2; cf. also Sadek (1985): 287.

25 This font P39 is used especially for the inscriptions on gems because it reminds the features of the inscriptions.

26 This formula can also be found on other gems; for example, London, BM, G 257 (EA 56257), see Michel (2001): 78 (no. 120); London, BM, G 365 (EA 56365), see ead. (2001): 261 (no. 416); Oxford, AM, 2003.129, see Henig/MacGregor (2004): no. 13.10.

27 See, for example, Michel (2001): 373; Michel (2004): 483, with older literature.

28 Cf. Meeks (1977): 1011; see also Quack (2004): 476. Since this epithet is documented from ancient Egyptian sources, this should be preferred to the interpretation of Delatte/Derchain (1964): 106 and Mastrocinque (2003): 105 as *Ḥr pꜣ ꜥnḫ nfr*, which is not attested in ancient sources.

29 For example, on London, BM, G 541 (EA 43115), see Michel (2001): 10 (no. 15); London, BM, G 316 (EA 56316), see ead. (2001): 60 (no. 91); London, BM, G 516 (EA 56516), see ead. (2001): 85 (no. 130); London, BM, G 513 (EA 56513), see ead. (2001): 94 (no. 145); or London, BM, G 568 (EA 56526), see ead. (2001): 171sq. (no. 277).

30 Cf. Michel (2001): 374; Michel (2004): 483 with older literature for the interpretation of "*Iaô fꜣ i̯=f rn ỉmn ꜥḏ mr (=rw) Rꜥ-(m)-kꜣr=f*" "Iaô is the bearer of the secret name, the lion of Ra, safe in his shrine" ("'Iaô ist der Träger des geheimen Namens, der Löwe des Re, wohlbehalten in seinem Schrein").

31 Cf. the text García Valdés, Llera Fueyo and Rodríguez-Noriega Guillén (2006): 279.

32 Mastrocinque (2003): 240 (no. 147); Zazoff (1970): 242, pl. 109; formerly Coll. Capello.

33 For example, Michel (2004): 318 titles this gem in this way.

34 Michel (2004): 332, pl. 59, 2. This gem corresponds to coll. Sossidi, no. 10.

35 See Theis (2019); Theis (2020); in press.

36 Depicted by Hornung (1984): 246sq., pl. 11; Hornung (1997a): 140; Hornung (1997b): 282sq.

37 Golénischeff (1877): pl 1.

38 See the text by C. Schmidt (1905): 207.

39 Coptic text after C. Schmidt (1925): 318sq.; translation by Mead (1896): 320 and C. Schmidt (1905): 207.

40 Bonner (1951): 332, pl. 98 (no. 45); King (1872): pl. 9 (no. 2); Michel (2001): 110sq. (no. 173); Michel (2004): pl. 40 (no. 3). Formerly collection George Eastwood; corresponds to *The Campbell Bonner Magical Gems Database* 571.

41 Preisendanz (2001a): 174–7; specifically for this Theis (2014): 356sq. and the translation by Betz (1986): 98sq.

42 Cf. Preisendanz (2001a): 64.

43 Preisendanz (2001a): 175. For the heads, one can compare Pap. London, BM gr. CXXII, col. I, 3sq. = PGM VIII, 9sq., see id. Preisendanz (2001b): 45. Here, in a love-binding magical spell, four figures are described in the four cardinal points, of which one represents an ibis in the east and a dog-headed monkey in the west; the sparrowhawk is not mentioned here.

44 It is not possible to equate the word "ⲂⲒⲬⲰ" with a decan βιχοουθ, because this identification requires the postulate of substantial corruption. Especially the reversal formation ⲬⲰⲂⲒ, and also the possible Egyptian background of these words, rather speaks against an equation with the decan. My thanks to Joachim F. Quack for his help and his suggestions concerning this topic.

45 For example, as suggested by Michel (2001): 110.

46 Scott (1992): 160sq. (no. 111).

47 Kaper (2012): 68 (no. M-24); Passeri (1750): 172. On the back, a seated youth with a stylized crown, holding a keychain in his right hand and a sceptre in his left, is depicted.

48 For further pieces, see the compilation by Kaper (2003); Kaper (2012).

49 Hoey Middleton (1998): 67–70 (no. 55).

50 Cf. Hoey Middleton (1998): 69. Contrary to the meaning of ead. (1998): 69, this depiction seems not to be identical with the third decan of cancer ♋, according to

the tradition of Hermes, *Liber Hermetis Trismegisti de triginta sex decanis* I, 15 [. . .] *In medio vero duarum dearum est draco habens quattuor capita, cuius duo capita tendunt sursum et duo flectuntur hinc inde circa pinum* "[. . .] But in the middle of the two goddesses is a serpent that has four heads. Two of their heads stretch upwards and two curls around here and there around a pine cone," see Feraboli (1994); likewise, the third decan of the constellation Aries ♈ is, according to the Latin tradition of Hermes Trismegistos, *Liber Hermetis Trismegisti de triginta sex decanis* I, 6, of another depiction [. . .] *tenens serpentem quadricapitem super baculo* [. . .] "[. . .] She is holding a four-headed snake on a wand [. . .]," see Feraboli (1994): 4. To this topic, see Quack *in preparation.*

51 Cf. Bonner (1950): 201.

52 Depicted by Hawass (2006): 119; Hornung (1997a): 120; Hornung (1997b): 94sq.; Michalowski (2001): no. 444. Cf. the two-headed snake (Amd. 347) in the fifth hour of Amduat, see Hornung (1963): 80sq., pl. 5; Hornung (1997a): 121; Hornung (1997b): 102sq.

53 Michel (2001): 109sq. (no. 172); Michel (2004): pl. 6 (no. 2).

54 See, for example, Theis (2011): 103sq.

55 Steindorff (1946): 158, pl. 103 (no. 715).

56 Published by Kitchen (1980): 184, 5sq. (= KRI III, p. 184, 5sq.).

57 Published by Chassinat (1909): 2sq.; depiction on the Aenigmatic wall by Darnell (2004): 328–33, pl. 15; Hornung (1984b): 227, 236; Hornung (1997a): 87sq., 156.

58 Published by De Wit (1958): 112, l. 12.

59 For the different epithets, see Theis *in preparation*, chapter 4.5sq.

60 Delatte/Derchain (1964): 50sq. (no. 43); Chabouillet (1858): 287 (no. 2170).

61 Cf. literature mentioned by Delatte/Derchain (1964): 50.

62 See Theis *in preparation*, chapter 4.8.1.

63 Cited after Assmann (1999): 299 (no. 129, ll. 158–162); text by De Garis Davies (1953): pl. 32, middle, l. 31.

64 Cf. Bonner (1950): 200; text by Preisendanz (2001b): 23.

65 Text by Preisendanz (2001b): 175; for this part cf. Fauth (2014): 26.

66 Cf. Ryhiner (1977): 134–6.

67 For the god *Twtw*, see Kaper (2003); Kaper (2012).

68 Bonner (1950): 297 (no. 266); corresponds to *The Campbell Bonner Magical Gems Database* 1129.

69 Bonner (1950): 297 (no. 265); Michel (2004): pl. 31,1; Schwartz/Schwartz (1979): 170sq., pl. 36 (no. 25); formerly collection Edward T. Newell 38.

70 On the back is a seated Harpocrates with one hand on his mouth and a flagellum on a lotus flower. He wears the side-bell on the left side and has a nimbus around his head with six sunrays and the inscription ΖΑΓΟΝΡΗ. In front of Harpocrates stands an ithyphallic monkey with the head of a dog, who has raised his arms in adoration to Harpocrates. Above both figures are three scarabs, which are partly

broken off today, as well as three lions; on the left end are still parts of three falcons, which carry sun discs on their heads, as well as a single crocodile. On the right side, you can still see the abdomen of another animal, which may be a dog or a jackal.

71 Cf. Michel (2001): 374; Michel (2004): 483 with older literature.

72 Philipp (1986): 79 (no. 106); formerly collection Osman Nury Bey. Made of red ironstone, size 2.0 × 1.65 × 0.28 cm. Depicted is a ram with four ram heads on a neck on a papyrus bark.

73 Gabra (1944): 178sq. Four ram heads were shown under a *Hmhm*-crown, on each side of which a uraeus snake rears up. The ram heads emerge from a kind of neck in the middle, as it is the case with the other objects.

74 Delatte/Derchain (1964): 172sq. (no. 228); Mastrocinque (2014): 64 (no. 151).

75 For example Michel (2004): 373; earlier, for example, Budge (1904): vol. II, p. 270. For example, one can mention the gem Ann Arbor, Special Collections Library (CBd-1038), which depicts Hecate, but around the goddess, is written ΑΒΡΑCΑΞ and ΒΑΙΝΧѠѠΧ, see Bonner (1950): 263sq. (no. 64); Theis (2018): 170.

76 For Ἰάω, see the many possibilities mentioned by Fauth (2014): 126–8.

77 Naples, MAN, Inv. 27265/1403 (CBd-2208) shows an Anguipedes with the inscription ΙΑѠ, see Mastrocinque (2003): 353 (no. 310); this is also the case with an Anguipedes on the gem coll. Skoluda, MN001 (CBd-1689), see Michel (2001): 63sq. (no. 61); Michel (2004): 278. On the gem Paris, Bibl. nat., coll. Blanchet the goddess Hecate is depicted with the inscription ΙΑѠ ΧΟΧΜΑΙ, see Delatte/Derchain (1964): 191 (no. 253); Michel (2004): 277; Mitropoulou (1978): no. 61d; Theis (2018): 171 and Werth (2006): 405sq. (no. 246).

78 This is the case with a gem depicted by Chiflet (1657): I, pl. 14, 56.

79 Published by Michel (2004): 278. Made of hematite; size 6.9 × 1.5 × 1.3 cm.

80 Published by Maaskant-Kleibrink (1978): 353 (no. 1110); Michel (2004): 277; Theis (2018): 172 and Werth (2006): 411sq. (no. 261). Made of grey hematite; Size 1.3 × 1.2 × 0.2 cm. This is also the case with Ann Arbor, Special Collections Library (CBd-1038), see Bonner (1950): 263sq. (no. 64). Made of red jasper; size 1.3 × 1.0 × 0.3 cm.

81 Kaper (2012): 68 (no. M-24); Passeri (1750): 172.

82 At least, Ereškigal appears as a name on gems, for example, on Baltimore, W.A.G., Inv. 42.874 with ΕΡΕCΧΕΙΓ//ΑΛ, see Bonner (1950): 263 (no. 63); Michel (2004): 277, pl. 80, 1 and Werth (2006): 407 (no. 249); and London, BM, Inv. G 28, EA 56028 (CBd-445) as Ε//ΡΕC//****//CΧΙ//ΓΑΛ, see Michel (2001): 43sq. (no. 66); Michel (2004): 277.

83 Theis *in preparation*, chapter 4.

84 For example, Werth (2006); Theis (2018).

85 For example, Binsfeld (1956). Plinius, *Naturalis Historiae* XXXV, 14 mentioned these depictions with “He (sc. Antiphilos) painted a man named Gryllus of ridiculous appearance on amusing panels; therefore, this painting genus is called

Grylloi" (*Idem (sc. Antiphilos) iocosis nomine Gryllum deridiculi habitus pinxit unde id genus picturae grylli vocantur*), see the Latin text by Mayhoff (1998): 271. Against this term Hammerstaedt (2000): 45; earlier Binsfeld (1965): 52sq. According to Jürgen Hammerstaedt, the term "Grylloi" is related to impersonal representations of ridiculous human figures. Roes (1935): 233–5 wanted to derive the motive of compiling animals and masks from the Persian area.

86 Cf. TAMBIAH (1978): 284.

87 The inscription ωΡΑΡ//ΑΝΙΚΑ//ΙΕΚΑ//ΤΗΥΠΟ//ΤΑCCΙ//Ι is written on the backside, where the name ΕΚΑ//ΤΗ as Ἑκάτη is clearly visible, see Michel (2001): 46 (no. 69); Michel (2004): 277; Theis (2018): 173. Made of red jasper; size 1.9 × 1.6 × 0.3 cm.

88 An overview of the extant instructions for cutting gem pictures in magic papyri is offered by Vitellozzi (2018): 196sq. with further literature.

89 Preisendanz (2001b): 66.

90 See Halleux/Schamp (1985): 171 (no. 36).

91 See the compilation of the sources by Quack *in preparation*.

92 Zwierlein-Diehl (1992): 79sq., pl. 14; Zwierlein-Diehl (2007): 461 (no. 802). The offered statement by Halleux/Schamp (1985): 171, note 1, that this type is not proven, can be rejected with the gem Cologne, Inst. für Altertumskunde der Universität, no. 18.

Chapter 4

1 E.g., Frankfurter (1994); Gordon (2002); Bohak (2008): 250sq.

2 Small, thin sheets of metal, with text inscribed on them using a sharp point.

3 E.g., Meyer and Smith (1994); de Bruyn and Dijkstra (2011).

4 E.g., Spier (2007).

5 E.g., Gager (1992).

6 Zografou (2010): 27.

7 Segal (2000): 27sq.

8 Angel (2009): 794.

9 Swartz (1990): 166.

10 Frankfurter (1994).

11 Moriggi (2014): 1sq.

12 Brodie (2014): 19.

13 Peters (1897): 153; Montgomery (1913): 14.

14 E.g., Müller-Kessler (2005): 220; Brodie and Kersel (2014).

15 "Section E," in *Policy of Professional Conduct*, approved by the *American Schools of Oriental Research Board of Trustees* on April 18, 2015. Cited August 25, 2020.

Online: http://www.asor.org/about/policies/conduct.html. The Society of Biblical Literature (SBL) adopted the same principles from 2017 (*SBL Policy on Scholarly Presentation and Publication of Ancient Artifacts*, September 3, 2016. Cited August 25, 2020. Online: https://www.sbl-site.org/assets/pdfs/SBL-Artifacts-Policy _20160903.pdf).

16 Hunter (1987): 85–8; Hunter (1990): 355sq.

17 E.g., Hunter (2009); Hunter (2015).

18 Hunter (2012): 302–4; Hunter (2013): 23.

19 E.g., Dabbs (1963).

20 E.g., Hunter (2012); Hunter (2013); Hunter and Dickens (2014).

21 Hunter (2012): 23; see also Hunter (2013): 304sq.

22 E.g., Moriggi (2014): 65.

23 E.g., Moriggi (2014): 140.

24 There are, however, a few instances in Jewish and Mandaic bowls: Segal notes three Jewish bowls where the persons acting through the text seem to be named (2000): 25, and Edwin Yamauchi also includes a Mandaic bowl where the scribe's name is given (1967): 49.

25 Moriggi (2014): 36sq.

26 Sørensen (1984): 7.

27 Gager (1992): 26.

28 I use transliterations of the Syriac text into Latin script, following the current convention in studies on the late antique material (Moriggi 2014: 4). Studies of the medieval and early modern amulets often use Syriac fonts, either *estrangelo* or *serto* depending on what most closely resembles the script in the manuscripts. Here, however, I use transliteration throughout the chapter for consistency.

29 Moriggi (2014): 140. This bowl, AO 207964-O, belongs to the Smithsonian Institution in Washington, DC, and is held at the National Museum of Natural History. It was acquired in 1900/1, following its purchase from the Rev. Gabriel Oussani, and hails from Hillah, the capital of Babylon Province south of ancient Babylon ("Incantation Bowl, inscribed in Syriac," Smithsonian Institution, Washington, DC, Entry last modified: December 7, 2016. Entry read: September 20, 2020. URL: https://www.si.edu/object/incantation-bowl-inscribed-syriac :nmnhanthropology_8046135).

30 Hunter (1996): 222sq.

31 Moriggi (2014): 32sq. CBS 9008 is now held at the University of Pennsylvania Museum of Archaeology and Anthropology. It was found in the excavations at ancient Nippur by the University of Pennsylvania Expedition in 1888/9, and part of the finds donated to the university by the Ottoman sultan following the excavation (Moriggi 2014: 32).

32 Moriggi (2014): 139. See note 29 of this chapter for ownership and provenance.

33 Graf (1991): 188sq.
34 Moriggi (2014): 60sq.
35 Moriggi (2014): 60sq. CBS 9010 is now held at the University of Pennsylvania Museum of Archaeology and Anthropology. It was found in the excavations at ancient Nippur by the University of Pennsylvania Expedition in 1888/9, and part of the finds donated to the university by the Ottoman sultan following the excavation (Moriggi 2014: 60).
36 Montgomery (1913): 42.
37 Frankfurter (2015).
38 Gordon (1941): 199.
39 Shaked, Ford, and Bhayro (2013): 8.
40 Müller-Kessler (1999): 199.
41 Hunter (1996): 226. For more on the apotropaic use of figurines in ancient Mesopotamian, see Braun-Holzinger (1999) or Feldt (2015). While parallels between the bowls and ancient Babylonian incantations are acknowledged, other scholars caution that they cannot be considered direct parallels—rather they show the starting and end point of a long and complex route of transmission (Bhayro 2013: 190).
42 Shaked, Ford, and Bhayro (2013): 30. It would be misleading to speak of a mass production, with today's connotations of industrial scale production.
43 Segal (2000): 29.
44 Montgomery (1913): 32.
45 E.g., Müller-Kessler (1998): 331–3; Levene (2003): 24.
46 E.g., Levene (2003): 28.
47 Levene (2003): 26; Shaked (2011): 204sq.
48 Hunter (2013); Hunter and Dickens (2014).
49 Hunter (2013): 24.
50 Hunter (2013): 24.
51 Hunter (2012): 303–6; Hunter (2013): 23.
52 Moriggi (2016).
53 E.g., Sanzo (2017).
54 Hunter (2013): 29–31.
55 Gollancz (1912); Hunter (1987): 83.
56 Hunter (2013): 25. Syr HT 330 is held at the Staatsbibliothek zu Berlin-Preussicher Kulturbesitz and was excavated at Shuipang in Turfan by Albert von le Coq and Albert Grünwedel in 1904/5 (Hunter 2013: 23).
57 Syr HT 330 [Recto], in Hunter (2013): 26.
58 Hunter (2013): 31sq.
59 Gollancz (1912): 22, xlvi. What he calls codex A and codex B were in Gollancz' private possession and are only available through his publication (Hunter 1987: 83 n.2). Gollancz writes that he first presented them at a conference in Paris in 1897 (1912: ix),

but not how or where he acquired them. Codex A has an ownership inscription in Syriac with the date 1889 (Gollancz 1912: x), so it is likely that it came to London and Europe some years after that, along with the many manuscripts that were bought by Western missionaries to Iraq and Kurdistan during these decades (Hunter 1987: 83).

60 #6 Codex B, in Gollancz (1912): lxvii.

61 Hunter (1987): 86–8; Hunter (2013): 31sq.

62 Hunter (1987): 85.

63 Hunter (1987): 88.

64 Gollancz (1912): xi; Hunter (1987): 83.

65 Hunter (2009): 189sq.

66 Gollancz (1912): x–xi; Hunter (1987): 85 n. 5.

67 #54 Codex A, in Gollancz (1912): lvii–lx.

68 #54 Codex A, in Gollancz (1912): 34, lix.

69 Gollancz (1912): xxv–xxix.

70 Hunter (1987): 91.

71 #15 Codex C, in Gollancz (1912): 85, lxxxi. What Gollancz calls codex C is Cambridge Ms. Syr. 3086, held at the University Library at Cambridge (Gollancz 1912: ix–x; Hunter 1990: 356). It was donated by Prof. W. R. Smith in 1892, who bought it from the widow of Rec. Percy Badger, who had served as the Archbishop of Canterbury's delegate to the Eastern Churches among the Syrians in Kurdistan. It is not known how Badger came to acquire the codex (Hunter 1990: 355).

72 #5 Codex A, in Gollancz (1912): 3, xxvi.

73 Hunter (1987): 90.

74 Hunter (1987): 92.

75 Hunter (1987): 90.

76 Gollancz (1912): 3 n. 2.

77 Gollancz (1912): xxv n. 2.

78 Gollancz (1912): 87, lxxxiii.

79 Hunter (1987); (1990).

80 Hunter (1987): 97.

81 #5 Codex A, in Gollancz (1912): 3, xxvi.

82 Hunter (1987): 95.

83 Hunter (1990): 355–68.

84 Hunter (1987): 95.

85 Hunter (1990): 362.

86 E.g., Bradshaw (1993).

87 Hunter (1987): 97.

88 E.g., Shaked (2011); Shaked, Ford, and Bhayro (2013): 8–13.

89 Hunter (2009): 188.

90 E.g., MacMullen (2009); Connerton (2011); Rebillard (2012).

Chapter 5

1 On bracteats with runic or other inscriptions, see mainly Düwel (1988): 70–110.

2 Published in Knirk (1998): 476–507, 500, and Simek (2004): 180.

3 A different, and now superseded, reading was given by Düwel (1989): 43–82.

4 Cf. Leidig (2004): 60.

5 See McKinnell, Simek, and Düwel (2004): 50sq.

6 Cf. Eriksson and Zetterholm (1933): 129–56; Düwel (2001)a: 135sq.

7 In some detail, but by no means exhaustive Schulz (2000): 65–70.

8 For a detailed discussion of this particular type of charm, see Simek (2019): 375–89.

9 Simek (2019): 387, n. 29.

10 Edited in McKinnell, Simek, and Düwel (2004): 187sq.

11 The version here taken from: *Rituale Romanum Pauli V. pontificis maximi . . .* Tournai (1840): 389sq.

12 Cf. Simek (2011): 25–52.

13 Stoklund (1996): 282–4.

14 Stoklund, Imer, and Steenholt Olesen (2004): 4–6; Steenholt Olesen (2010): 165sq.

15 Imer and Uldum (2015): 14sq.

16 See http://runer.ku.dk/Search.aspx (accessed February 20, 2021).

17 Düwel (2001b): 227–302.

18 Cf. Düwel (2001b): 239.

19 Düwel (2001b): 227–302.

20 Stoklund, Imer, and Steenholt Olesen (2004): 4–6; Steenholt Olesen (2010): 165sq.

21 Imer and Dørup Knudsen (2019): 64–7: the transcript is taken from Imers' photos and redrawing, as she unhelpfully only gives a Danish (!) translation of the Latin text instead the text itself.

22 Transcription taken (with ligatures ignored) from Muhl and Gutjahr (2013): 33–5.

23 For the nature of these illnesses, see Simek (2019).

24 Muhl and Gutjahr (2013): 42.

25 Muhl and Gutjahr (2013): 26sq.

26 Muhl and Gutjahr (2013): 20sq.

27 Imer and Uldum (2015): 6.

28 In 2004, we could only name the Odense lead amulet. The Lurekalven lead amulet from Norway, and a Bergen wooden amulet: McKinnell, Simek, and Düwel (2004): 159–61.

29 Cf. McKinnell, Simek, and Düwel (2004): 161.

30 Vollmann (1987): 162.

31 McKinnell, Simek, and Düwel (2004): 161; see also Imer and Uldum (2015): 9–15.

32 However, while the Alpha is executed as an upper case letter, the Omega is in lower case!

33 See my comments in n. 21.

34 That the various names of god had apotropaic functions is testified to even in Old Norse literary texts, cf. Foote (1981): 139–54.

Chapter 6

1 Ms Harley 585, f. 165a [*Lacnunga*], eleventh century; G. Storms, *Anglo-Saxon Magic*, La Haye (1948): n° 44, p. 282.

2 Ms Cotton Caligula A XV, f. 140b, eleventh century; G. Storms, n° 69, p. 300sq.

3 Ms Cotton Vitellius E XVIII, f. 13b, eleventh century, G. Storms, n° 86, p. 311.

4 Ms BL Sloane 962, f. 135v, fifteenth century; Hunt (1990): 96.

5 Ms Durham Cathedral Chapter Library, Hunter 100, f. 118; Skemer (2006): 80, n. 11.

6 Ibid., f. 117.

7 Ms Harley 978, f. 34v; ed. in Hunt (1990): 124.

8 Ms Oxford, Bodleian e. Musaeo 243, f. 3; ed. Sheldon (1990): 175.

9 *Médecinaire liégeois*, ms Darmstadt, f. 166v, thirteenth century; ed. Haust (1941): n° 100, p. 17.

10 Ms Auch, AD du Gers I 4066, f. 75, ed. Corradini Bozzi (1997): 242.

11 Ms Auch, AD du Gers I 4066, ed. Corradini Bozzi (1997): n° 40, p. 242.

12 Ms Princeton, Garrett 80, f. 11, ed. Corradini Bozzi (1997): n° 100, p. 176.

13 Ms Gand, Bibl. de l'Université, ms 1272, f. 148v; Lecouteux (2002): 90.

14 Ms Auch, AD du Gers I 4066, ed. Corradini Bozzi (1997): n° 48, p. 219.

15 *Médecinaire liégeois*, ms Darmstadt, f. 159, ed. Haust (1941): n° 38, p. 99.

16 Ms Auch, AD du Gers I 4066, ed. Corradini Bozzi (1997): n° 54, p. 245.

17 Ms Paris, BnF, ital. 1524, f. 143v-144; Grévin and Véronèse (2004): 368, n. 177.

18 Ms London, BL Sloane 3550, f. 224, ed. Hunt (1990): 139.

19 Skemer (2006).

20 Aymar (1926).

21 Cf. Olsan (2003): 343–66.

22 Ms London, BL Sloane 56, f. 2, ed. Olsan (2003): 365.

23 Ms London, BL Harley 2558, f. 125v, ed. Olsan (2003): 366.

24 Zanone (2010): 39–54.

25 Ceppari Ridolfi (1999): 42.

26 Luc (1938): 374–402.

27 Dobschütz (1910): 428.

28 Scot (1584).

29 Dobschütz (1910): 423.

30 Bozoky (2013): 112sq.; cf. also ead. (1991): 84–92.

31 Bonser (1963): 245: "Charms in a foreign or unintelligible language were considered to be of special potency."

32 Frankfurter (1994): 199–205.
33 Betz (1992): 307.
34 Betz (1992): 3.
35 Betz (1992): 191.
36 Betz (1992): 192.
37 Schnyder (1991): 151: . . . *cum tacitum pactum propter verba ignota et caracteres signati cum demone initur et demon occulte se ingerit et optata procurat ut tandem ad peiore alliciat.*

Chapter 7

1 The concept of minority is different from "marginals," and the difference lays in the will to live collectively as it is already set up in Vincent (1979).
2 Two essential readings about the Morisco question in the Spanish Catholic Monarchy are Caro Baroja (2000) and Domínguez Ortiz and Vincent (1985).
3 Bernabé Pons (1994): 322–32.
4 Villaverde Amieva (2010): 91–128.
5 Those interested in a wider view on this topic can consult my doctoral dissertation, also available online: Fernández Medina (2014).
6 Doutté (1984): 147.
7 Barceló and Labarta (2009); López-Baralt (2009).
8 A few extant Andalusian examples can be found in Martínez Núñez (2007): 310–13, 320sq., 344sq.
9 The practice of healing illnesses via written talismans is described by the cleric Pedro Ciruelo who authored a manual for inquisitors:

> We should condemn those kinds of "ensalmos" [prayers] which using words are doing no profitable things and have no natural virtue to heal, and also those individuals who use a piece of paper, or linen, or any other thing as they use, because this way of healing does not go by natural course and it is exercised with vain things. And so, it is superstitious and diabolical. (Ebersole 1978: 81)

10 Dieleman (2015): 23.
11 The Most Beautiful Names of Allah, *al-Asmā' al-Ḥusnà*, are ninety-nine epithets to name the Islamic deity, see Gimaret (1988). For a deeper understanding of the significance of enigmatic and magical script, see my doctoral dissertation: Fernández (2014): 77–104.
12 Hamès (2007).
13 Forshaw (2015): 357–78.
14 Instructions in Arabic to lower a fever from the trial of Jaime Bolaix, Inquisition of Valencia, (1585), Archivo Histórico Nacional, Leg. 549, nº 11.
15 Ibid.

16 Ibid.
17 García-Ballester (1984): 65.
18 Porter (2004): 187.
19 Labarta (1993): 126; the manuscript is accessible to the readers in the Manuscripta site of the CSIC http://simurg.bibliotecas.csic.es/viewer/image/CSIC001227532/1/ (last access September 19, 2021).
20 *Libro de dichos maravillosos.* Ms. 16th.c., Aljamiado / Arabic (M-CCHS RES RESC/22). Biblioteca Tomás Navarro Tomás (CCHS-CSIC), f. 351r-v.
21 Savage-Smith (2004): XV.
22 Trial of Leonés Benali. Archivo Histórico Nacional, Inquisition of Valencia, (1585), Leg. 549, nº 8.
23 García-Arenal (2010): 57–71.
24 AHN, Inquisition of Valencia, (1585), Leg. 549, nº 8.
25 Trial of Leonor de Mendoza. Archivo Histórico Nacional, Inquisición de Granada, año 1593, Leg. (1953) nº 28, ff. 59v-60r.
26 Ibid.
27 "Herce." Sixteenth century?, Ms. V25 (II/9416, caja nº 25) BRAH, loose paper. I give here my own translation despite the intended or unintended mistakes present in the text.
28 Álvarez de Morales and Girón Irueste (1992).
29 Trial of Rafaela Mayor. Archivo Histórico Nacional, Inquisición de Valencia, año (1589), Leg. 553/I, nº 6.
30 Trial of Isabel de Lopo. Archivo Histórico Nacional, Inquisición de Zaragoza, año (1595), Lib.1000, f. 117r.
31 Trial of Diego de Vargas. Archivo Histórico Nacional, Inquisición de Granada, 1586, Leg. (1953), nº83.
32 Ibid.
33 Trial of Antonio de Piedrahita. Archivo Histórico Nacional, Inquisición de Valencia, Lib. 968, nº 30, año (1599), f. 449r.
34 Butler (1947): 48.
35 About the sympathetic function of magical seals reproducing the authority of their original owners, see Porter (2004): 179–200. And, specifically about the Seal of Solomon, my own contribution Fernández Medina (2012): 175–87.

Chapter 8

1 More information about his life can be found in the book by Dankoff (2006).
2 Dankoff and Kreiser also wrote about the Evliya's travel log in another book (Dankoff and Kreiser 1992).

3 That is an early description of a natural phenomenon which occurs once in a year when the endemic Van fish, which thrives in a lake that is inhospitable to other forms of fresh water and marine fish, travels upstream to lay its eggs.
4 Ruska and de Vaux (2000): 500.
5 https://www.etymonline.com/word/talisman#etymonline_v_4337; accessed February 2021.
6 Apollonius of Tyana was an ancient Greek Pythagorean philosopher. He lived in the first and second centuries AD in Cappadocia and is known in the Orient as ṣāḥib aṭ-ṭilasmat "the Lord of talismans" (cf. Ullmann 1972: 378).
7 EI (1934), 830.
8 İA (2012), 91.
9 Redhouse (1999): 1244.
10 Pakalin (1946).
11 Meninsky (1680): 626.
12 Al-Būni (née in Algeria, died in 1225) possessed manyfold works on magic, magic squares, and talismans. He influenced many Islamic countries on occult knowledge with his most popular work *Shemsü l-ma ʿārifi l-kübrā.*
13 Ullmann (1972): 364.
14 Cf. Nestroy (2002).
15 Tawada (1996).
16 Ṯaʿlabī (2006): V–VI.
17 Arberry (2018): 254.
18 https://quranx.com/Hadith/Muslim/USC-MSA/Book-24/Hadith-5218.
19 Winkler (1930): 116.
20 Winkler (1930): 127.
21 Gruber (2020): 233.
22 Hammer-Purgstall (1848): 2.
23 Cf. Pakalin (1993): 585.
24 Pakalin (1993): 585.
25 Onay and Kurnaz (2007): 191.
26 Cf. B. 1 Pakalin (1946), 750.
27 And (2012): 47.
28 Cf. Çelebi (2012): 553.
29 Tezcan (2011).
30 Halûk Perk Müzesı (2010): 24.
31 Halûk Perk Müzesi (2010): 24.
32 Kiyanrad (2017): 198.
33 Manuscript Nr: Bağdat Köşkü 305 in the Topkapı Palace library Ms. Y237v3-21 (E. Çelebi).
34 Manuscript Nr IÜTY 5973 from the library of the University of Istanbul MS. 80a (E. Çelebi).

35 Assuan.

36 Şāh-ı mārān.

37 Avicenna.

38 Manuscript Nr: Bağdat Köşkü 304 in the Topkapı Palace library Ms. 188v36–188r8 (E. Çelebi).

39 Erduran (2006): 266.

Chapter 9

1 The illustration and the verses quoted there—the latter being "intended to propound the linkage of *ahl-i bait-i nabi* with Noah's ark, and thus to place the Twelver-Shi῾i legacy within a historical perspective"—are translated and discussed in Shani (2006): 28–30.

2 A tantalizing, though completely speculative, possibility would be the existence of an inscription related to the Seven Sleepers on these amulets, for it was believed that their names once become materialized prevented a ship from drowning; cf. Porter (2007): 126.

3 Canby (2014).

4 Nünlist (2018a); Nünlist (2018b); Nünlist (2020); Berthold (2021). For more information on Iranian amulets, not only made from paper, see also Maddison and Savage-Smith (1997): 132–47; Porter (2011); Vesel (2012); Kiyanrad (2017).

5 It also clearly forms part of the larger Near and Middle Eastern amulet environment. "Despite regional variations, what unites these objects is that they are characterized by the use of a particular and distinctive vocabulary of writings and symbols, which can appear in a variety of combinations, a vocabulary which can be said to have been formalized by the thirteenth century"; Porter, Saif and Savage-Smith (2017): 533. For recent observations and developments, not limited to amulets, see Doostdar (2018). In general, amulets were often used as remedies for severe diseases. The link between oral and literal culture here becomes quite obvious; the community used to pray for their sick persons in order to help them recover, and from this perspective, an amulet is a written prayer. In 1660, a French observer reports that if someone fell ill, the family lit several fires on their home's terrace; passersby would consequently pray for the sick person (Richard 1995: II, 112sq.). Furthermore, Mīrzā Makhdūm (*d.* 995/1587) notes that among the Twelver Iranians "the cursing of the second caliph ῾Umar was even believed to cure diseases and ward off misfortune" (quoted after Arjomand 1984: 165). Other amulets were applied in order to overcome or at least handle exceptional situations and emotions—be it childbirth, the search for a potential wife or husband, envy of the neighbor's greener grass on his side of the fence, or to prevent scorpion stings.

Scorpions were much feared in Safavid Iran anyway. The German traveler Olearius relates that people were especially fearful of being stung by the Kāshān species; thus, if somebody wanted to curse someone else, s/he would say: "Aqrab-i Kāshān ba dastat zanad" ("May the Kāshān scorpion sting your hand"). During his visit to the city, people told Olearius that the scorpion would not pose any danger to him if he said "Man gharībam!" ("I am a stranger!"). However, this obviously failed to have the desired effect, since Olearius was stung by a scorpion at night (Olearius 1971: 495). Jean Chardin's report is similar (Chardin 1811, III: 5). See also Herbert (1638): 213sq. (who remarks: "we found it true [. . .] they never hurt a stranger," Herbert 1638: 214).

6 An inkwell with a well-known Arabic invocation to ʿAlī—*Nādi ʿAlīyan* . . . ("Call upon ʿAlī . . .") and to the twelve imams had already been produced in 919/1513, on which, see Melikian-Chirvani (1982): 282sq. (Cat. 118). The same author (Melikian-Chirvani 1974: 558) states with regards to inscriptions on metalwork: "With the emergence of Safavid power, inscriptions of a militantly Shiʿite content appeared on metalwork, for which I know of no precedent. These were of three categories: litanies calling God's blessing on the names of the twelve imams, or more often on the fourteen pure ones (chahārdah maʿsūm); a prayer naming ʿAlī; and less often, poems celebrating ʿAlī sometimes with burning extremist accents." ʿAlī and the imams were of course venerated in both Sunni and Shi'i circles even before the advent of the Safavids (a phenomenon which has been described as Imamophilism by Melvin-Koushki 2012: 73); hence, a talisman in the *Khalili Collection* (TLS 1966), attributed to fifteenth-century Iran and made from turquoise, is inscribed with *Nādi ʿAlīyan* (https://www.khalilicollections.org/collections/islamic-art/khalili-collection-islamic-art-talisman-tls1966/ [retrieved February 20, 2021]). In consequence, we have to be very careful in determining Twelver aspects of amulets.

7 This does of course not apply to every believer; certain religious scholars opposed the use of (certain) amulets (for an outline of discussions about amulets with Qur'anic verses, see Zadeh 2009: 463–6); Muḥammad Bāqir Majlisī is an example (see Melvin-Koushki 2018a: 143, n. 8). They sometimes intentionally attributed the (alleged) use of amulets and the performance of practices labeled as "magic" to persons (or groups) in order to convince the audience that the respective person behaved in an "unislamic" way and was to be considered a magician rather than a devout believer, let alone legitimate ruler. For instance, in Khunjī Iṣfahānī's *Tārīkh-i ʿĀlam-ārā-yi Amīnī* (1992: 274 [Persian text], 58 [English translation]) Ismāʿīl's father Ḥaydar is called the kind of person who has a hand in *mārbāzī* (snake-charming) and who, instead of distributing *tasbīḥ*s (rosaries), "flung vipers into the faces of those present at his assemblies."

Amulets are, even in academic discourse, often associated with magic. Muravchick (2014): 53 argues in the context of so-called talismanic shirts that "the lack of prolonged attention to these objects can be ascribed to their designation as 'magic' insofar as 'magic' functions as a dustbin for less-convenient examples of divergence in religious practice." She thus decides to use the expression "vernacular religion" instead (Muravchick 2014: 84). See also Kiyanrad (2017); Nünlist (2018a); Nünlist (2018b); Otto (2019).

8 One example is Bandar ʿAbbās, where the locals, according to early-seventeenth-century European travel reports, wore but a piece of linen or went naked and used to "burn round circles in their flesh, to symbolize their pride and love," on which, see Herbert (1638): 123. A friend of mine from this very port city told me that nowadays people sometimes attach small bottles filled with seawater to their entrance doors; they are believed to ward off the evil eye. This is but one example for the impact of regional particularities on amulet culture.

9 We are aware that non-script-bearing amulets and amuletic objects were also being used, especially, it seems, in healing. Membré, a Venetian ambassador to the court of Shah Ṭahmāsb, relates how in 1540, a Turk from Anatolia secretly purchased one of the king's turban-clothes (Membré 1993: 41): "I [Membré; SK] asked him what the cloth was good for, and he told me that it was a *tabarruk*, that is, an object of beneficial effect; and, having a sick father at home, he had seen the said Shah in a dream; and for that reason he wished for the cloth, for his father's contentment, for he would be well." Membré goes on to explain (Membré 1993: 41sq.) that people quite often purchased items that had come in touch with the shah, such as shoes or the water the king had washed his hands with. More than a century later, Engelbert Kaempfer still reports on the shah's (for now, Sulaymān) purported healing powers and the respective use of water that had come in touch with the shah; Kaempfer (1984): 21sq., 275. See also: *A Chronicle of the Carmelites* (1939): I, 50–1. Pieces of (allegedly) cured persons clothes' were apparently being used as amulets as well; (1939): 138. Raphaël du Mans writes in 1660 that some Isfahanis on occasion of the Festival of Sacrifice (*ʿayd-i qurbān*) tore out hairs from a camel that was to be slaughtered and kept the hair on account of its *tabarruk* (Richard 1995 II: 55).

10 Chardin 1811: II, 275, 7 (it is not completely clear if on p. 275 n. 1 Chardin wants to distinguish talismans from amulets); he insists that talismans are closely related to the observation of stars. On the notion of *ṭilism*, see Ruska and Carra de Vaux (2000); Kiyanrad (2017): 197sq.; and also Richard (1995): II, 172; Khvānsārī (2535): 87.

11 Chardin (1811): II, 277; Herbert (1638): 128, 225.

12 Chardin 1811: II, 275. See also Nünlist (2018a), where four amulet scrolls are discussed. They feature, *inter alia*, combinations of (parts of) Q II; III; XIII; XIV; XXXVI; XLVIII; LVIII; LXVII (in once instance, the whole of the Qur'an is cited), some of "God's beautiful names," the names of the four first caliphs and the

"Fourteen Infallibles." Cf. Nünlist (2018b): 261–77. On typical "Elements of the Magical Vocabulary," see Porter, Saif and Savage-Smith (2017): 535–42.

13 Richard (1995): II, 172.

14 Cf. Melikian-Chirvani (1982): 290–2 (Cat. 125); Maddison and Savage-Smith (1997): 88 (Cat. 29), 90 (Cat. 30), 92 (Cat. 31), 93 (Cat. 32), 96 (Cat. 33); Savage-Smith (2003); Farhad and Bağcı (2009): 84sq. (Cat. 5–6); Langer (2013): 41–76; Muravchick (2014): 113–15.

15 Cf. Pavaloi (1993): 115 (fig. 136).

16 http://khgm.razavichto.ir/Default.aspx?get=Zt/SD/lv0fdm1f/lpygp6rb5MFhhkUgr9l0JuNXQBTaYC2pVcfp9sAI81+fFCVE1oPz7ZPja942aLO3W4ih7IesxswkaOAjV3jHoqRjBKRXloP25f9gbshDBG5xZ6Vms (accessed February 20, 2021).

17 Savage-Smith (1997): 119 (Cat. 49).

18 To be more precise, quite often, carnelian is the material of choice. On the properties ascribed to carnelian, see Porter, Saif and Savage-Smith (2017): 543.

19 https://www.khalilicollections.org/collections/islamic-art/khalili-collection-islamic-art-talisman-tls1855/ (retrieved February 20, 2021). A catalogue introducing more than 3,500 amulets kept in the *Khalili Collection* (*The Nasser D. Khalili Collection of Islamic Art, vol. XIII: Seals and Talismans*, by Manijeh Bayani and Ludvik Kalus) is expected in 2021.

20 https://www.khalilicollections.org/collections/islamic-art/khalili-collection-islamic-art-square-talisman-tls3141/ (accessed February 20, 2021).

21 Porter (2011): 140 (Cat. A14); see also 141 (Cat. A 16).

22 Anawati (2000).

23 Cf. Porter (2004).

24 Allan and Gilmour (2000): 307, 309 (G.2).

25 Chardin (1811): II, 277; *Islamic Medical Wisdom* (2007): 25, 33, 116, 125.

26 https://daten.digitale-sammlungen.de/~db/0003/bsb00039626/images/index.html (retrieved September 13, 2021).
I would like to thank Tobias Nünlist for bringing this amulet to my attention.
In his recent study Nünlist states that scroll amulets made of parchment usually measure 4–6 cm in width and not more than 70 cm in length. According to him, most parchment scrolls date to the nineteenth century and feature the names of the "Fourteen Infallibles" (Nünlist 2020: 9).

27 Cf. Richard (1995): II, 300/301. "In Isfahan, paper was produced from rags, making it affordable and more readily available. Paper became the foundation of a new culture of literacy" (Babayan 2021: 10).

28 Berthold (2020: 339–40) suggests to call these objects "amulet Koran or pendant Koran" (being a translation of the Arabic term *muṣḥaf ḥamāʾilī*). Cf. Berthold (2021): 13, 20.

29 Richard (1995): II, 300/301.

30 The writer is Sīmī Nīshāpūrī; quoted after Thackston (1990): 224sq.

31 An example (*Lilly Library*, Indiana University, Bloomington), dating from 958/1551, is discussed in Coffey (2010): 84–6, 96sq. (as well as Fig. 3.4 + 3.5 + 3.11). The manuscript (ca. 6 cm in diameter, 280 folios) contains the "full Qurʾanic text, which terminates in a duʿa-yi khatim, a prayer to be read upon its completion, and a falnama (Book of Divination)" (Coffey 2010: 85sq.). It is on display in the permanent online exhibition *From Pen to Printing Press: Ten Centuries of Islamic Book Arts*, Indiana University Collections; http://www.iub.edu/~iuam/online_modules/islamic_book_arts/exhibit/miniature_manuscripts_and_scrolls/miniature_qur'an_adomeit_mss_12.html (accessed February 20, 2021). Cf. Coffey (2019).

32 Safwat (2000): 70sq. (Cat. 10), 72sq. (Cat. 11); Coffey (2010): 79sq.; Gruber (2011): 38; a number of richly decorated Qur'an cases are depicted in van Regemorter (1961): Pl. 40. Not all miniature Qur'ans comprise the whole revelation text, but some are limited to parts of it. Today, printed miniature Qur'ans are widely used with an amuletic purpose (and often attached to rearview mirrors); a small amulet container made from leather, dating to the twentieth century and purchased in Tehran contained a printed Qur'an, a coin, a leaf-shaped, inscribed amulet and a fruit-shell; Newid and Vasegh Abbasi (2007): 289sq. Berthold (2021: 23) establishes five indicators (concerning content, size, line spacing, mode of usage, and shape) that help to characterize miniature Qur'ans.

33 Allan and Gilmour (2000): 311sq.

34 Richard (1995): II, 98. On the other hand, according to du Mans (Richard 1995), the triangle symbolizes misfortune (*bad yumn*); however, triangular amulet cases are depicted in Safavid manuscripts, see Fig. 9.1b.

35 Berthold (2020): 344; cf. Berthold (2021): 34–39, 87–94.

36 Safwat (2000): 72sq. (Cat. 11).

37 Coffey (2010): 80; see also Nünlist (2018a): 80.

38 Porter (2010).

39 Kaempfer (1984): 173. On the use of Kufi on amulets, see Porter (2010).

40 Reproduced in Babayan (2021): 15.

41 As Muravchick (2014): 107 observes in regards to so-called talismanic shirts.

42 Ebenhöch/Tammen (2019): 171. Yet, in contemporary Iran, book-shaped pendants exist, that is, metal pendants in the codex form imitating the outer appearance of a Qur'an.

43 For block printed amulets, which are not yet attested for Safavid Iran, see Schaefer (2006).

44 Nünlist (2020): 8.

45 Nünlist (2020): 494, 520.

46 Nünlist (2018a): 78.

47 Nünlist (2018b): 251.

48 Nünlist (2020): 7sq.

49 Nünlist (2018a): 79, 92. For later examples with *Nādi ʿAlīyan*, see Porter and Frembgen (2010): 199 (Fig. 123), 204 (Fig. 127). Matthew Melvin-Koushki's forthcoming *The Occult Science of Empire in Aqquyunlu-Safavid Iran: Two Shirazi Lettrists and Their Manuals of Magic* will contain an edition of a treatise by Maḥmūd Dihdār ʿIyānī (*fl.* 1576), in which an invocation of the "Fourteen Infallibles" is explained. For Safavid "magic bowls" with prayers to the twelve imams, see Savage-Smith (2003): 240 (fig. 9.1), 245.

50 https://www.bonhams.com/auctions/20834/lot/56/ (accessed February 20, 2021). The case is made from silver and is 5.2 cm in diameter.

51 For example, on the Ms. Or. Oct. 146 (*Staatsbibliothek zu Berlin*), analyzed in Nünlist (2018a): 86–90 and Nünlist (2020): 469–93. Persian elements can also be observed on a scroll which Nünlist (2018b): 285 attributes to the Ottoman context. A black jade seal ring dated to the fifteenth to sixteenth centuries in the *Khalili Collection* (TLS 2786) is inscribed in Persian and invokes ʿAlī; https://www.khalilicollections.org/collections/islamic-art/khalili-collection-islamic-art-seal-ring-tls2786/ (retrieved February 20, 2021). A brass seal in the same collection (TLS 2708), dated to 1022 (1613–1614), combines a Persian legend with Qur'anic verses and other Arabic elements; https://www.khalilicollections.org/collections/islamic-art/khalili-collection-islamic-art-large-seal-tls2708/ (accessed February 20, 2021). The employment of different languages on scrolls, seals, and script-bearing artifacts in general is a fascinating topic. Two talismanic scrolls from the Turfan region, produced in the late nineteenth century, provide an apt example; they "are written in Chaghatai with Arabic prayers and some Persian specific vocabulary" (Papas 2019: 216). About the second scroll, Papas remarks (Papas 2019: 218): "As regards the uses of Persian what is interesting in this second section, and in the invocation at the end of the scroll, is the rich lexis of love and pain (quite common in Chaghatai), which comes from Persian elegiac poetry. It includes syntagmas like *dard-i firaq* (pain of separation), *diwana-yi shayda* (love madness), *khun-i jigar* (deep affliction), *ʿashiq-i biqarar* (passionate lover), *khar khar* (anxious desire), and so on. Clearly, the language of love is Persian, which here serves the purpose of reification."

52 Nünlist (2018a): 80; Nünlist (2018b): 265; Nünlist (2020): 496. Some Safavid "magic bowls," too, have dates on them; cf. Savage-Smith (2003): 244 (fig. 9.4), 245.

53 Nünlist (2018a): 90; Nünlist (2020): 520.

54 Safwat (2000): 72sq. (Cat. 11).

55 The following examples are quoted after Berthold's recent publication (Berthold 2021: 196sq., 206sq., 210sq., 226sq., 244sq., 254–269, 272–279): *Bibliothèque Nationale de France*, Paris, MS Arabe 449 (copied by Shaykh Najab b. Shaykh Faraj

b. Shaykh Manṣūr in 990/1582); *British Library*, London, MS Or. 2200 (copied 950/1543 in Shiraz); *Bayerische Staatsbibliothek*, Munich, Cod. Arab. 2620 (copied by Ḥājjī Shaykh Ḥasan b. Shaykh Amīn al-Dīn in 985/1577); *The David Collection*, Copenhagen, Inv 41/1999 (copied in 1081/1671); Sotheby's Auctions, London, sale October 2008, lot 22 (copied by Ibrāhīm b. Ḥājjī ʿAbd al-Jalīl Shirvānī in 1037/1627); *Topkapı Sarayı Müzesi*, Istanbul, MS E. H. 440 (copied in 1076/1665-66); *Topkapı Sarayı Müzesi*, Istanbul, MS E. H. 442 (copied by Bahāʾ al-Dīn ʿAlī Nūr al-Dīn Aḥmad in 957/1547); *Topkapı Sarayı Müzesi*, Istanbul, MS E. H. 451 (copied in 984/1576-77); *Topkapı Sarayı Müzesi*, Istanbul, MS E. H. 454 (copied by Niẓām b. ʿImād al-Dīn Najjār in 972/1564-65); *Topkapı Sarayı Müzesi*, Istanbul, MS E. H. 461 (copied on 957/1550-51); *Topkapı Sarayı Müzesi*, Istanbul, MS E. H. 477 (copied by Muḥammad Aṣghar b. Muḥammad b. Muḥammad b. ʿAlī b. Ḥaṭīb al-Sabzivārī in 965/1557-58); *Topkapı Sarayı Müzesi*, Istanbul, MS E. H. 479 (copied by Muḥammad Sharīf in 962/1554); *Topkapı Sarayı Müzesi*, Istanbul, MS E. H. 482 (copied by Ibrāhīm b. Mihr b. Manṣūr in 1037/1627-28); *Topkapı Sarayı Müzesi*, Istanbul, MS E. H. 491 (copied in 1003/1594-95); *Topkapı Sarayı Müzesi*, Istanbul, MS E. H. 492 (copied in 974/1566-67); *Topkapı Sarayı Müzesi*, Istanbul, MS E. H. 499 (copied in 994/1586); *Topkapı Sarayı Müzesi*, Istanbul, MS E. H. 507 (copied in 978/1570-71); *Topkapı Sarayı Müzesi*, Istanbul, MS E. H. 533 (copied by Ḥasan b. Muḥammad al-Hāshimī in 944/1537-38); *Topkapı Sarayı Müzesi*, Istanbul, MS E. H. 543 (copied by 'Kalb-i Āstān-i ʿAlī' ʿUmrānī Asad Allāh Shaykhū Simnānī in 987/1579-80); *Topkapı Sarayı Müzesi*, Istanbul, MS E. H. 548 (copied by Ibn al-Ḥājj Qāsim Muḥammad Ṭāhir in 981/1574); *Topkapı Sarayı Müzesi*, Istanbul, MS Y. 16 (copied by ʿImād al-Dīn Ḥasan b. Ibrāhīm in 1004/1595-96).

56 Nünlist (2018a): 78, 95. See also Nünlist (2018b): 250, 288; Nünlist (2020): 65–141.

57 Nünlist (2018a): 90, 93sq.; Nünlist (2020): 520, 531sq.

58 Chardin (1811): II, 278sq.

59 An Ottoman talismanic shirt dating from 1532 has the name of the twelfth-century Persian Sufi ʿAbd al-Qādir al-Jīlānī (Muravchick 2014: 223, Cat. 14), which shows that the latter's name (or allegedly his re-used *khirqa*) was intended to bestow the shirt with his *baraka*; see also Muravchick (2014): 25 n. 43, 194, 235 (cat. 25), 239 (cat. 29), 241 (cat. 31).

60 Melvin-Koushki (2020): 265sq.

61 Babayan (2021): 75.

62 Babayan (2021): 75.

63 Nünlist (2018a): 87; Nünlist (2020): 482. This Mīrzā Makhdūm (also known as Ibn Sayyid Sharīf Muʿīn al-Dīn Ashraf) completed his *al-Navāqiḍ fī radd al-ravāfiḍ*, a polemic against the Qizilbāsh, in 1580; Eberhard (1970): 56–60, 180–90. Details about his life, with a focus on his exile in the Ottoman Empire, are provided by Ghereghlou (2019).

64 Safwat (2000): 72sq. (cat. 11).
65 Berthold (2021): 77sq.
66 In one example, "On seeking an audience with kings," quoted in Melvin-Koushki (2020): 267sq., it is described how to inscribe a square and certain numbers on gold. See also the example Melvin-Koushki (2020) quotes on 268.
67 Richard (1995): II, 172.
68 Babayan (2021): 13 (+ Fig. 0.3).
69 Cf. Melvin-Koushki (2020): 264sq.
70 Chelebi (2010): 56.
71 Chelebi (2010): 57.
72 Herbert (1638): 267.
73 This book was supposedly written in the era of Shah Sulaymān (*r.* 1666–1694) by the cleric Āqā Jamāl Khvānsārī (*d.* 1710). The *ʿAqāyid al-nisāʾ* reveals, although in an exaggerated and ultimately critical manner, details about female beliefs in amulets (in Isfahan); for a general introduction, see Babayan (1998).
74 Khvānsārī (2535): 93sq.
75 Richard 1(995): II, 172. For the sixteenth-century manual on *raml* by Shāh Mullā Munajjim Shīrāzī, erstwhile written for Shah Ṭahmāsb and possibly later rededicated, see Melvin-Koushki (2018b): 169sq.
76 Khvānsārī (2535): 94.
77 Richard (1995): II, 151.
78 *Islamic Medical Wisdom* (2007): 75. We are aware of the existence of Iranian amulets inscribed in Hebrew; to my knowledge, they have not yet been studied systematically. According to the texts mentioned earlier we may assume that Muslims, too, approached Jewish amulet-writers who were most probably able to write amulets in Arabic (and Persian) as well. Material evidence clearly attests to the similarities and mutual influences of Arabic and Hebrew amulets from Iran on each other. Cf. Carmeli (2014): 153–5.
79 Kaempfer (1984): 147.
80 Herbert (1638): 225; see also 235.
81 See for example *Islamic Medical Wisdom* (2007): 11.
82 Chardin (1811): II, 278.
83 Cf. de Thévenot (1772): III, 301 ("par toute la Perse ce sont les femmes qui preparent les medecines").
84 Chardin (1811): II, 277. As concerns the miniature Qur'ans examined by Coffey (2010): 80, the author suggests that "some specimens appear to have a courtly provenance, others clearly speak to humbler origins." Amulets were sometimes hung up in shops (to attract customers, for example), or attached to ceremonial objects, as Coffey (2010): 85 suggests with regards to a Safavid Qur'an case. The *Xavāṣṣ-i-āyāt* (1920): 33sq. describes how amulets could be suspended on trees (so that they may bear fruits). And the *Islamic Medical Wisdom* (2007): 125 has an

invocation "for an old and noble mare" which was to be written "on the parchment of a gazelle" and fastened to her groin at the time of delivery. See also *Islamic Medical Wisdom* (2007): 125–7. For obvious reasons, warriors often made use of amulets; cf. Ekhtiar and Parikh (2016).

85 Richard (1995): II, 173.

86 Kaempfer (1984): 63. A seal belonging to Shah Ṭahmāsb (3.1 × 2.4), made from rock-crystal and inscribed with Allāh, Muḥammad, ʿAlī, and a few lines of poetry is preserved in the *Khalili Collection* (TLS 2714); https://www.khalilicollections.org/collections/islamic-art/khalili-collection-islamic-art-seal-of-shah-tahmasp-tls2714/ (retrieved February 20, 2021).

87 Chardin (1811): II, 276. See also Richard (1995): II, 172.

88 Chardin (1811): II, 276sq.

89 Chardin (1811): II, 277.

90 Chardin (1811): II, 277. Comp. *Islamic Medical Wisdom* (2007): 116.

91 Porter (2011): 164 (Cat. A109).

92 Chardin (1811): II, 277.

93 Depicted in Dimand (1930): 37; Chelkowsi (1975): 78; discussed and depicted in Jenkins and Keene (1983): 100sq. (fig. 8). Several illustrations related to the story of *The Seven Princesses* show courtly women with large necklaces; see Chelkowski (1975): 85, 87 (detail), 90, 97, 99 (detail), 101, 107. See also Bothmer (1982): 44sq. (cat. 13).

94 On this drawing, see Jenkins and Keene (1983): 102sq; Swietochowski and Babaie (1989): 56sq. (cat. 23).

95 Elgood (1970): 203sq.

96 Cited after Spink (2013): 562.

97 Nünlist (2018a): 79.

98 Nünlist (2018a): 85; Nünlist (2018b): 266–70; Nünlist (2020): 512–4 (an alternative possibility is discussed on p. 511sq.).

99 Herbert (1638): 232. In a similar manner, Chardin (1811): II, 277 writes: ". . . il faut observer qu´il y en a pour être gardé contre toute sorte de maux, et pour obtenir toute sorte de bien." Christensen gives a list of purposes listed in the *Xavāṣṣ-i-āyāt* (1920): 8–11; he mentions, inter alia, headache, fever, epilepsy, back pain, serpent sting, healing of a person obsessed by a jinn, prevention of fear, protection against thieves, increase of income, winning the love of a woman, harming an enemy . . . .

100 Nünlist (2018a): 90; Nünlist (2020): 475–82. Especially miniature Qur'ans were taken to the battlefield as amulets. These artifacts have become known as *sancak* Qur'ans; but Coffey (2010): 80 warns against this tradition's "application to newly discovered specimens as a predetermined explanation."

101 Safwat (2000): 70 (cat. 10).

102 Elgood (1970): 275. However, according to the *ʿAqāyid al-nisāʾ*, which has a whole chapter on amulets against the evil eye (*Dar bayān-i taʿvīẕ va chishm-zakhm*)

they were also called *ta'vīẕ*. None of the described amulets, among which figure a panther's nail, blue beads, or stones (*muhra*), is script-bearing; Khvānsārī 2535: 87–90. Children as wearers of amulets are also mentioned in *Islamic Medical Wisdom* (2007): 116. For more recent examples of Iranian amulets, inscribed with Q LXVIII: 51–52 and thus possibly meant to serve against the evil eye, see Newid and Vasegh Abbasi (2007): 272–5, 277sq., 290.

103 *Islamic Medical Wisdom* (2007): 11, 17, 34sq., 120sq., 125–7.

104 Quoted after Elgood (1970): 239.

105 Della Valle (1981): 132.

106 See *Xavāṣṣ-i-āyāt* (1920): 12; Kiyanrad (2017): 305–9; Melvin-Koushki (2020): 269.

107 Chardin (1811): II, 276.

108 The amulet text quoted in Melvin-Koushki (2020): 268 asks to be written down "at an auspicious hour."

109 *Xavāṣṣ-i-āyāt* (1920): 13.

110 Third edition, Tehran: 1383. Compare also the "Invocations for days of the week" in *Islamic Medical Wisdom* (2007): 43–9.

111 *Xavāṣṣ-i-āyāt* (1920): 28sq. This manual (actually *Khavāṣṣ-i āyāt va manāfi'-i suvar-i nabiyyāt* ["The qualities of the [Qur'anic] verses and the benefits of the prophetic surahs"]) rests on a tradition attributed to the Shi'i imam Ja'far al-Ṣādiq and was translated into Persian in 926/1520 by a certain 'Abdallāh b. Muḥammad b. Ḥusayn.

112 Many travelogues give information about their standing and power, on this see for example Richard (1995): I, 218, 225sq. and II, 16; Kaempfer (1984): 108.

113 *Islamic Medical Wisdom* (2007): 25sq.

114 Richard (1995): II, 169. On fumigation practices in medieval Arabic "magic rituals," see Coulon (2016).

115 Richard (1995): II, 172.

116 *Xavāṣṣ-i-āyāt* (1920): 32sq.

117 *Xavāṣṣ-i-āyāt* (1920): 33.

118 *Xavāṣṣ-i-āyāt* (1920): 35.

119 *Islamic Medical Wisdom* (2007): 17, 25, 33, 34, 125. Even talismanic charts dating to the Pahlavi I era could still be made from gazelle skin (Tanāvulī 1387 [2008]: 36 speaks of "pūst-i āhū").

120 It is also mentioned in manuals, such as *Islamic Medical Wisdom* (2007): 11, 35, 89, 120sq., 149. The standard work on Block printed amulets inscribed in Arabic and made from paper is Schaefer (2006).

121 *Islamic Medical Wisdom* (2007): 58.

Bibliography

Chapter 1

Austin, J. L. (1962), *How to do Things with Words. The William James Lectures Delivered at Harvard University in 1955*, Edited by J. O. Urmson, Oxford: Clarendon Press.

Boschung, D. and J. N. Bremmer (eds.) (2015), *The Materiality of Magic* (Morphomata, 20), Paderborn: Wilhelm Fink.

De Bruyn, T. (2017), *Making Amulets Christian: Artefacts, Scribes and Contexts*, Oxford: University Press.

Faraone, C. A. (2012), *Vanishing Acts on Ancient Greek Amulets: From Oral Performance to Visual Design*, London: Institute of Classical Studies, School of Advanced Study – University of London.

Faraone, C. A. (2018), *The Transformation of Greek Amulets in Roman Imperial Times*, Philadelphia: Penn University Press.

Forster, R. (2006), *Das Geheimnis der Geheimnisse. Die arabischen und deutschen Fassungen des pseudo-aristotelischen Sirr al-asrār, Secretum secretorum* (Wissensliteratur im Mittelalter, 43), Wiesbaden: Reichert.

Frankfurter, D. (ed.) (2019), *Guide to the Study of Ancient Magic*, Leiden/Boston: Brill.

Gordon, R. L. (2014), "*Charaktēres* between Antiquity and Renaissance: Transmission and Re-Invention," in V. Dasen and J.-M. Spieser (eds.), *Les savoirs magiques et leur transmission de l'antiquite a la Renaissance*, 253–300, Florence: Edizioni del Galluzzo.

Gordon, R. L. (2015), "From Substances to Texts: Three Materialities of 'Magic' in the Roman Imperial Period," in D. Boschung and J. N. Bremmer (eds.), *The Materiality of Magic* (Morphomata, 20), 134–76, Paderborn: Wilhelm Fink.

Gordon, R. L. and F. Marco Simón (ed.) (2010), *Magical Practice in the Latin West: Papers from the International Conference Held at the University of Zaragoza, 30 Sept.–1 Oct. 2005* (Religions in the Graeco-Roman World, 168), Leiden/Boston: Brill.

Kiyanrad, S., L. Willer, and C. Theis (2018), "(Schrift-)Bildliche Magie," in S. Kiyanrad, C. Theis, and L. Willer (eds.), *Bild und Schrift auf 'magischen' Artefakten. Images and Texts on "Magical" Artifacts* (Materiale Textkulturen, 19), 1–13, Berlin/Boston: De Gruyter.

Otto, B.-C. (2015), *Magie: Rezeptions- und diskursgeschichtliche Analysen von der Antike bis zur Neuzeit* (Religionsgeschichtliche Versuche und Vorarbeiten, 57), Berlin/Boston: De Gruyter.

Ritter, H. and M. Plessner (1962), .*"Picatrix": Das Ziel des Weisen von Pseudo-Maǧrīṭī*, London: The Warburg Institute.

Searle, J. R. (1969), *Speech Acts. An Essay in the Philosophy of Language*, London: Cambridge University Press.

Schnyder, A. (ed.) (1991), Malleus Maleficarum *von Heinrich Institortis (alias Kramer) unter Mithilfe Jakob Sprengers aufgrund der dämonologischen Tradition zusammengestellt. Wiedergabe des Erstdrucks von 1487*, Göppingen: Kümmerle.

Skemer, D. C. (2006), *Binding Words. Textual Amulets in the Middle Ages*, University Park: The Pennsylvania State University Press.

Theis, C. (2014), *Magie und Raum. Der magische Schutz ausgewählter Räume im alten Ägypten nebst einem Vergleich zu angrenzenden Kulturbereichen* (Orientalische Religionen in der Antike, 13), Tübingen: Mohr Siebeck.

Ullmann, M. (1972), *Die Natur- und Geheimwissenschaften im Islam* (Handbuch der Orientalistik, I/VI.2), Leiden/Köln: Brill.

Wilburn, A. T. (2012), *Materia Magica: The Archaeology of Magic in Roman Egypt, Cyprus, and Spain*, Ann Arbor: The University of Michigan Press.

Chapter 2

Austin, J. L. (1962), *How to Do Things with Words. The William James Lectures Delivered at Harvard University in 1955*, Edited by J. O. Urmson, Oxford: Clarendon Press.

Boardman, J. and C. Wagner (2003), *A Collection of Classical and Eastern Intaglios, Rings and Cameos*, Oxford: Archaeopress.

Bohak, G. (2003), "Hebrew, Hebrew Everywhere? Notes on the Interpretation of Voces Magicae," in S. B. Noegel, J. Walker, and B. M. Wheeler (eds.), *Prayer, Magic, and the Stars in the Ancient and Late Antique World*, 69–82, University Park: Pennsylvania State University Press.

Bohak, G. (2008), *Ancient Jewish Magic. A History*, Cambridge: Cambridge University Press.

Bol, P. and H. Breck (eds.) (1983), *Spätantike und frühes Christentum* - Exhibition catalogue, Frankfurt am Main: Haßmüller.

Bonner, C. (1946), "Magical Amulets," *Harvard Theological Review*, 39: 24–5.

Bonner C. (1950), *Studies in Magical Amulets. Chiefly Graeco-Aegyptian*, Ann Arbor: The University of Michigan Press.

Bonner, C. (1954), "A Miscellany of Engraved Stones," *Hesperia*, 23(2): 138–57.

Brashear, W. (1995), "The Greek Magical Papyri: An Introduction and Survey; Annotated Bibliography (1928–1994)," in W. Haase (ed.), *Aufstieg und Niedergang der römischen Welt II.18.5*, 3380–684, Berlin: De Gruyter.

Cox Miller, P. (1986), "In Praise of Nonsense," in A. H. Armstrong (ed.), *Classical Mediterranean Spirituality: Egyptian, Greek, Roman* (World Spirituality, 15), 481–505, New York: Crossroad.

Dasen, V. (2008), "Le secret d'"Omphale," *Revue Archéologique*, 46(2): 265–81.

Dasen, V. and Á. M. Nagy (2012), "Le serpent léontocéphale Chnoubis et la magie de l'époque romaine impériale," *Anthropozoologica*, 47(1): 291–314.

Dasen, V. and Á. M. Nagy (2019), "Gems," in D. Frankfurter (ed.), *Guide to the Study of Ancient Magic*, 416–55, Leiden/Boston: Brill.

Dzwiza, K. (2013), *Schriftverwendung in antiker Ritualpraxis. Anhand der griechischen, demotischen und koptischen Praxisanleitungen des 1.–7,* Jahrhunderts: Universität Erfurt (thesis).

Dzwiza, K. (2015), "Insight into the Transmission of Ancient Magical Signs: Three Textual Artefacts from Pergamon'', *MHNH*, 15: 31–56.

Dzwiza, K. (2019), "Magical Signs: An Extraordinary Phenomenon or just Business as Usual? Analysing Decoration Patterns of Magical Gems," in K. Endreffy, Á. M. Nagy, and J. Spier (eds.), *Magical Gems in Their Context*, 59–83, Rome: L'Erma di Bretschneider.

Endreffy, K., Á. M. Nagy, and J. Spier (eds.) (2019), *Magical Gems in Their Context*, Rome: L'Erma di Bretschneider.

Faraone, C. A. (1991), "The Agonistic Context of Early Greek Binding Spells," in C. A. Faraone and D. Obbink (eds.) *Magika Hierà, Ancient Greek Magic and Religion*, 3-32, New York: Oxford University Press.

Faraone, C. A. (1992), *Talismans and Trojan Horses. Guardian Statues in Ancient Greek Myth and Ritual*, Oxford/New York: Oxford University Press.

Faraone, C. A. (2009), "Does Tantalus Drink the Blood, or Not? An Enigmatic Series of Inscribed Hematite Gemstones," in U. Dill and C. Walde (eds.), *Antike Mythen Medien, Transformationen und Konstruktionen – Ancient Myth. Media, Transformations and Sense-Constructions*, 248–73, Berlin/Boston: De Gruyter.

Faraone, C. A. (2010), "Notes on Some Greek Amulets," *Zeitschrift für Papyrologie und Epigraphik*, 172: 213–19.

Faraone, C. A. (2011), "Text, Image and Medium. The Evolution of Graeco-Roman Magical Gemstones," in C. Entwistle and N. Adams (eds.), *'Gems of Heaven': Recent Research on Engraved Gemstones in Late Antiquity, AD 200–600,* 50–61, London: The British Museum Press.

Faraone, C. A. (2012), *Vanishing Acts on Ancient Greek Amulets: From Oral Performance to Visual Design*, London: Institute of Classical Studies, School of Advanced Study – University of London.

Faraone, C. A. (2013), "Notes on Some Greek Magical Gems in New England," *Greek, Roman, and Byzantine Studies*, 53: 326–49.

Faraone, C. A. (2016), "Some Further Remarks on Greek Magical Gems," in A. Szabo (ed.), *From Politês to Magos: Studia György Németh sexagenario dedicata* (Hungarian Polis Studies, 22), 105–15, Budapest/Debrecen: University of Debrecen.

Faraone, C. A. (2018), *The Transformation of Greek Amulets in Roman Imperial Times*, Philadelphia: Penn University Press.

Faraone, C. A. and A. Kropp (2010), "Inversion, Aversion and Perversion in Imperial Roman Curse-Tablets," in R. L. Gordon (ed.), *Magical Practice in the Latin West: Papers from the International Conference Held at the University of Zaragoza, 30 Sept.–1 Oct. 2005* (Religions in the Graeco-Roman World, 168), 381–98, Leiden/Boston: Brill.

Faraone, C. A. and D. Obbink (eds.) (1991), *Magika Hierà, Ancient Greek Magic and Religion*, New York: Oxford University Press.

Frankfurter, D. (ed.) (2019a), *Guide to the Study of Ancient Magic*, Leiden/Boston: Brill.

Frankfurter, D. (2019b), "Spell and Speech Act: The Magic of the Spoken Word," in D. Frankfurter (ed.), *Guide to the Study of Ancient Magic*, 608–25, Leiden/Boston: Brill.

Frankfurter, D. (2019c), "The Magic of Writing in Mediterranean Antiquity," in D. Frankfurter (ed.), *Guide to the Study of Ancient Magic*, 626–58, Leiden/Boston: Brill.

Gordon, R. L. (1995), "The Healing Event in Graeco-Roman Folk-Medicine," in H. F. J. Horstmanshoff, P. J. van der Eijk and P. H. Schrijvers (eds.), *Ancient Medicine in Its Socio-Cultural Context, Volume 2. Papers Read at the Congress Held at Leiden University, 13–15 April 1992*, 363–76, Amsterdam/Atlanta: Brill.

Gordon, R. L. (2011a), "Archaeologies of Magical Gems," in C. Entwistle and N. Adams (eds.), *'Gems of Heaven': Recent Research on Engraved Gemstones in Late Antiquity, AD 200–600*, 39–49, London: The British Museum Press.

Gordon, R. L. (2011b), "*Signa Nova et Inaudita*. The Theory and Practice of Invented Signs (Charaktēres) in Graeco-Egyptian Magical Texts," *MHNH*, 11: 15–44.

Gordon, R. L. (2014), "*Charaktēres* between Antiquity and Renaissance: Transmission and Re-Invention," in V. Dasen and J.-M. Spieser (eds.), *Les savoirs magiques et leur transmission de lantiquite a la Renaissance*, 253–300, Florence: Edizioni del Galluzzo.

Graf, F. (1991), "Prayer in Magical and Religious Rituals," in Faraone, C. A. and D. Obbink (eds.) (1991), *Magika Hierà, Ancient Greek magic and religion*, 188–213, New York: Oxford University Press.

Henig, M. and A. MacGregor (2004), *Catalogue of the Engraved Gems and Finger-Rings in the Ashmolean Museum, II. Roman*, Oxford: Archaeopress.

Kagarow, E. G. (1929), *Griechische Fluchtafeln* (Eos Suppl., 4), Lwow/Paris: Les Belles Lettres.

Kotansky, R. (1980), "Two Amulets in the Getty Museum: A Gold Amulet for Aurelia's Fever. An Inscribed Magical-Stone for Fever, "Chills," and Headache," *J. Paul Getty Museum Journal*, 8: 181–8.

Kotansky, R. (2019), "Textual Amulets and Writing Traditions in the Ancient World," in D. Frankfurter (ed.), *Guide to the Study of Ancient Magic*, 507–54, Leiden/Boston: Brill.

Kropp, A. (2008), *Magische Sprachverwendung in vulgärlateinischen Fluchtafeln (defixiones)*, Tübingen: Gunther Narr Verlag.

Kropp, A. (2010), "How Does Magical Language Work? The Spells and Formulae of the Latin *defixionum tabellae*," in R. L. Gordon and F. Marco Simón (eds.), *Magical Practice in the Latin West: Papers from the International Conference Held at the*

University of Zaragoza, 30 Sept.–1 Oct. 2005 (Religions in the Graeco-Roman World, 168), 357–80, Leiden/Boston: Brill.

Liechtenhan, E. (1968), *Marcelli De medicamentis liber, post Maximilianum Niedermann iteratis curis edidit Eduard Liechtenhan, in linguam Germanicam transtulerunt Jutta Kollesch et Diethard Nickel* (Corpus medicorum Latinorum, 5), Berlin: Akademie Verlag.

Martin, M. (2005), *Magie et magiciens dans le monde gréco-romain*, Paris: Errance.

Mastrocinque, A. (2005), *From Jewish Magic to Gnosticism* (Studien und Texte zu Antike und Christentum /Studies and Texts in Antiquity and Christianity, 24), Tübingen: Mohr Siebeck.

Mastrocinque, A. (2008), "Un'altra immagine transculturale: Chnoubis," in S. Estienne, D. Jaillard, N. Lubtchansky, and C. Pouzadoux (eds.), *Image et religion dans l'antiquité gréco-romaine* (Actes du colloque de Rome, 11–13 décembre 2003), 392–7, Naples: Centre Jean Bérard.

Mastrocinque, A. (2017), "Invocations to Hermes and Aphrodite on two engraved gems in Leiden," in B. J. L. van der Bercken and V. C. P. Baan (eds.), *Engraved Gems. From antiquity to the Present.* (Papers on Archaeology of the Leiden Museum of Antiquities, 14), 93–8, Leiden: Sidestone Press.

Michel, S. (2001), *Die magischen Gemmen im Britischen Museum*, London: The British Museum Press.

Michel, S. (2004), *Die magischen Gemmen. Zu Bildern und Zauberformeln auf geschnittenen Steinen der Antike und Neuzeit* (Studien aus dem Warburg-Haus, 7), Berlin: Akademie Verlag.

Mouterde, R. (1930–1931), "Le glaive de Dardanos: Objets et inscriptions magiques de Syrie," *Mélanges de l'Universite Saint-Joseph*, 15: 53–87.

Nagy, Árpád M. (2002), "*Gemmae magicae selectae.* Sept notes sur l'interprétation des gemmes magiques," in A. Mastrocinque (ed.), *Gemme gnostiche e cultura ellenistica.* Atti del Convegno, Verona, 22–23 ottobre 1999, 153–79, Bologna: Pàtron.

Nagy, Árpád M. (2015), "Engineering Ancient Amulets. Magical Gems of the Roman Imperial Period," in D. Boschung and J. N. Bremmer (eds.), *The Materiality of Magic* (Morphomata, 20), 205–40, Paderborn: Wilhelm Fink.

Philipp, H. (1986), *Mira et Magica, Gemmen im Ägyptischen Museum der Staatlichen Museen, Preussischer Kulturbesitz, Berlin-Charlottenburg*, Mainz am Rhein: Philipp von Zabern Verlag.

Poccetti, P. (2002), "Manipolazione della realtà e manipolazione della lingua: alcuni aspetti dei testi magici antichi," in R. Morresi (ed.), *Linguaggio – Linguaggi. Invenzione – Scoperta* (Atti del Convegno. Macerata-Fermo, 22–23 ottobre 1999), 11–59, Rome: Il Calamo.

Preisendanz, K. (1966), Rev. of A. Delatte and P. Derchain (1964), "Bibliothèque Nationale. Les Intailles magiques gréco-égyptiennes," *Byzantinische Zeitschrift*, 59: 388–92.

Quack, J. F. (2019), "From Egyptian Traditions to Magical Gems. Possibilities and Pitfalls in Scholarly Analysis," in K. Endreffy, Á. M. Nagy, and J. Spier (eds.), *Magical Gems in Their Context*, 233–49, Rome: L'Erma di Bretschneider.

Quack, J. F. (forthcoming), *Beiträge zu den ägyptischen Dekanen und ihrer Rezeption in der griechisch-römischen Welt* (Orientalia Lovaniensia Analecta), Leuven: Peeters.

Smith, M. (1979), "Relations Between Magical Papyri and Magical Gems," in J. Bingen and G. Nachtergael (eds.), *Actes du xve Congrès international de papyrologie, III. Problèmes généraux. Papyrologie littéraire* (Papyrologica Bruxellensia, 18), 129–36, Brussels.

Searle, J. R. (1969), *Speech Acts. An Essay in the Philosophy of Language*, London: Cambridge University Press.

Searle, J. R. and D. Vanderveken (1985), *Foundations of Illocutionary Logic*, Cambridge: Cambridge University Press.

Schwartz, J. (1981), "Papyri Magicae Graecae und magische Gemmen," in M. J. Vermaseren (ed.), *Die orientalischen Religionen im Römerreich* (Études préliminaires aux religions orientales dans l'Empire romain, 93), 485–509, Leiden: Brill.

Schwartz, F. M. and J. H. Schwartz (1979), "Engraved Gems in the Collection of the American Numismatic Society: 1. Ancient Magical Amulets," *ANS Museum Notes*, 24: 149–97.

Thissen, H. J. (1988), *Etymogeleien, ZPE*, 73: 303–5.

Versnel, H. S. (2002), "The Poetics of the Magical Charm: An Essay on the Power of Words," in P. Mirecki and M. Meyer (eds.), *Magic and Ritual in the Ancient World* (Religions in the Graeco-Roman World, 141), 105–58, Leiden/Boston/Cologne: Brill.

Vitellozzi, P. (2010), *Gemme e Cammei della Collezione Guardabassi nel Museo Archeologico Nazionale dell'Umbria a Perugia*, Perugia: Volumnia.

Vitellozzi, P. (2018), "Relations Between Magical Texts and Magical Gems Recent Perspectives," in S. Kiyanrad, C. Theis, and L. Willer (eds.), *Bild und Schrift auf 'magischen' Artefakten. Images and Texts on "Magical" Artifacts (Materiale Textkulturen, 19)*, 181–253, Berlin/Boston: De Gruyter.

Vitellozzi, P. (2019), "The Sword of Dardanos: New Thoughts on a Magical Gem in Perugia," in Endreffy, Nagy and Spier 2019: 283–304.

Wortmann, D. (1975), "Neue magische Gemmen," *Bonner Jahrbücher*, 175: 65–82.

Abbreviated References

AGD III B, G, K = Scherf, V., P. Gerke and P. Zazoff (1970), *Antike Gemmen in Deutschen Sammlungen, III. Braunschweig, Göttingen, Kassel.* Wiesbaden: Franz Steiner.

AGWien III = Zwierlein-Diehl, E. (1991), *Die antiken Gemmen des Kunsthistorischen Museums in Wien, III. Die Gemmen der späteren römischen Kaiserzeit, 2. Masken,*

Masken-Kombinationen, Phantasie- und Märchentiere, Gemmen mit Inschriften, christliche Gemmen, magische Gemmen, sassanidische Siegel, Rundplastik aus Edelstein und verwandtem Material, Kameen. Munich: Prestel.

CBd = The Campbell Bonner database: http://classics.mfab.hu/talismans (seen 26.09.2021).

Gems of Heaven 2011 = C. Entwistle and N. Adams (eds) (2011), *'Gems of Heaven': Recent Research on Engraved Gemstones in Late Antiquity, AD 200–600*. London: The British Museum.

LIM = Mastrocinque, A. (2014), *Les intailles magiques du départment des Monnaies, Médailles et Antiques*. Paris: Éditions de la Bibliothèque Nationale de France.

PGM = Preisendanz, K. (ed.) (1928 and 1931), Papyri Graecae Magicae. *Die griechischen Zauberpapyri I–II*. Leipzig: Teubner (2nd edition by A. Henrichs 1973–4, Stuttgart: Teubner).

SEG = *Supplementum Epigraphicum Graecum* (1923–71), New Series, ed. by H. W. Pleket et al. 1976–)

SGG I = Mastrocinque, A. (ed.) (2003), *Sylloge Gemmarum Gnosticarum. Parte I*. Rome: Istituto Poligrafico.

SGG II = Mastrocinque, A. (ed.) (2007), *Sylloge Gemmarum Gnosticarum. Parte II*. Rome: Istituto Poligrafico.

Chapter 3

Assmann, J. (1999), *Ägyptische Hymnen und Gebete* (Orbis Biblicus et Orientalis). 2nd edition, Fribourg/Göttingen: Universitäts-Verlag.

Betz, H. D. (1986), *The Greek Magical Papyri in Translation, Including the Demotic Spells*, Chicago: University of Chicago Press.

Binsfeld, W. (1956), *Grylloi. Ein Beitrag zur Geschichte der antiken Karikatur*, Köln: Dissertation.

Boemke, F. et al. (1939), *Spezielle Pathologie des Skelets und seiner Teile. Unspezifische Entzündungen, metastatische Geschwülste, Parasiten, Wirbelsäule, Becken*, Berlin/Heidelberg: Springer-Verlag.

Bonner, C. (1950), *Studies in Magical Amulets chiefly Graeco-Egyptian*, Ann Arbor: University of Michigan Press.

Bonner, C. (1951), "Amulets Chiefly in the British Museum. A Supplementary Article," *Hesperia*, 20: 301–45.

Buck, A. H. (1889), *A Reference Handbook of the Medical Sciences, Vol. VII*, New York: William Wood & Company.

Budge, E. A. (1904), *The Gods of the Egyptians*, 2 vols, London: Methuen & Co.

Caylus, A. C. P. de (1761), *Recueil d'Antiquités, Egyptiennes, Etrusques, Grecques Et Romaines 4*, Paris: Desaint and Saillant.

Chabouillet, J. M. (1858), *Catalogue général et raisonné des camées et pierres gravés de la Bibliothèque Imperiale suivi de la description des autres monuments exposés dans le Cabinet des Medailles et Antiques*, Paris: Clayde.

Chassinat, É. (1909), *La seconde trouvaille de Deir el-Bahari (Sarcophages)* (Catalogue Général des Antiquités égyptiennes du Musée du Caire, Nos. 6001–6029), Kairo: Institut Français d'Archéologie Orientale.

Chiflet, J. (ed.) (1657), *Ioannis Macarii, Abraxas seu Apistopitus quae est antiquaria de gemmis Basilidianis disquisition*, Antwerp: Off. Plantiniana Balthasaris Moreti.

Daressy, G. (1907), "Les cercueils des prêtres d'Ammon. Deuxième trouvaille de Deir el-Bahari," *Annales du Service des Antiquités de l'Égypte*, 8: 3–38.

Darnell, J. C. (2004), *The Enigmatic Netherworld Books of the Solar-Osirian Unity. Cryptographic Compositions in the Tombs of Tutankhamun, Ramesses VI and Ramesses IX* (Orbis Biblicus et Orientalis, 198), Fribourg/Göttingen: Academic Press.

Delatte, A. and P. Derchain (1964), *Les intailles magiques Gréco-Égyptiennes*, Paris: Bibliothèque Nationale.

Fauth, W. (2014), *Jao-Jahwe und seine Engel. Jahwe-Appellationen und zugehörige Engelnamen in griechischen und koptischen Zaubertexten* (Studien und Texte zu Antike und Christentum, 74), Tübingen: Mohr Siebeck.

Feraboli, S. (1994), *Hermetis Trismegisti – De Triginta sex decanis (Hermes latinus, Tomus IV, Pars 1; Corpus christianorum, continuatio mediaevalis, 144)*, Turnhout: Brepols.

First, G. (2011), "Polymorphic or Pantheistic Deities? – Some Problems with Identification and Interpretation. Contributions to the Manifestation of God in Late Egyptian Religion and Magic," in J. Popielska-Grzybowska and J. Iwaszczuk (eds.), *Studies on Religion: Seeking Origins and Manifestations of Religion* (Acta Archaeologica Pultuskiensia, III), 53–63, Pułtusk: Academy of Humanities.

Gabra, S. (1944), "Un chaton de bague à thème solaire," *Annales du Service des Antiquités de l'Égypte*, 44: 173–8.

García Valdés, M., L. A. Llera Fueyo, and L. Rodríguez-Noriega Guillén (2006), *Claudius Aelianus – De Natura Animalium* (Bibliotheca Scriptorum Graecorum et Romanorum Teubneriana), Berlin: De Gruyter.

Garis Davies, N. de (1953), *The Temple of Hibis III: The Decoration* (Publications of the Metropolitan Museum of Art Egyptian Expedition, 17), New York: Metropolitan Museum.

Golénischeff, V. S. (1877), *Die Metternichstele in der Originalgröße*, Leipzig: Engelmann.

Halleux, R. and J. Schamp (1985), *Les lapidaires grecs*, Paris: Les Belles Lettres.

Hammerstaedt, J. (2000), "Gryllos. Die antike Bedeutung eines modernen archäologischen Begriffs," *Zeitschrift für Papyrologie und Epigraphik*, 129: 29–46.

Hawass, Z. (2006), *Bilder der Unsterblichkeit. Die Totenbücher aus den Königsgräbern in Theben*, Mainz: Von Zabern.

Henig, M. (1994), *Classical Gems. Ancient and Modern Intaglios and Cameos in the Fitzwilliam Museum, Cambridge*, Cambridge: Cambridge University Press.

Henig, M. and A. MacGregor (2004), *Catalogue of the Engraved Gems and Finger-Rings in the Ashmolean Museum, II: Roman*, Oxford: Archaeopress.

Henig, M. and M. Whiting (1987), *Engraved Gems from Gadara in Jordan. The Sa'd Collection of Intaglios and Cameos (Oxford University Committee for Archaeology Monograph, 6)*, Oxford: Oxford University Committee for Archaeology.

Hintze, F. and U. Hintze (1967), *Alte Kulturen im Sudan*, München: Callwey.

Hoey Middleton, S. (1998), *Seals, Finger Rings, Engraved Gems and Amulets in the Royal Albert Museum, Exeter from the Collections of Lt. Colonel L. A. D. Montague and Dr. N. L. Corkill*, Exeter: Exeter City Museums.

Hornemann, B. (1951), *Types of Ancient Egyptian Statuary I*, Kopenhagen: Munksgaard.

Hornemann, B. (1957), *Types of Ancient Egyptian Statuary II*, Kopenhagen: Munksgaard.

Hornung, E. (1963a), *Das Amduat. Die Schrift des verborgenen Raumes. Teil 1: Text* (Ägyptologische Abhandlungen, 7), Wiesbaden: Harrassowitz.

Hornung, E. (1963b), *Das Amduat. Die Schrift des verborgenen Raumes. Teil 2: Übersetzung und Kommentar* (Ägyptologische Abhandlungen, 7), Wiesbaden: Harrassowitz.

Hornung, E. (1984), *Das Buch von den Pforten des Jenseits nach den Versionen des Neuen Reiches, Teil II: Übersetzung und Kommentar* (Aegyptiaca Helvetica, 8), Genf: Ed. de Belles Lettres.

Hornung, E. (1997a), *Altägyptische Jenseitsbücher. Ein einführender Überblick*, Darmstadt: Wissenschaftliche Buchgesellschaft.

Hornung, E. (1997b), *Die Unterweltsbücher der Ägypter*, Düsseldorf/Zürich: Artemis.

Kaper, O. E. (2003), *The Egyptian God Tutu. A Study of the Sphinx-God and Master of Demons with a Corpus of Monuments* (Orientalia Lovaniensia Analecta, 119), Leuven/Paris/Dudley: Peeters.

Kaper, O. E. (2012), "The Egyptian God Tutu: Additions to the Catalogue of Monuments," *Chronique d'Égypte*, 87: 67–93.

Kaplony, P. (1963), *Die Inschriften der ägyptischen Frühzeit* (Ägyptologische Abhandlungen, 8), Wiesbaden: Harrassowitz.

Kaplony, P. (1981), *Die Rollsiegel des Alten Reichs, II: Katalog der Siegel* (Monumenta Aegyptiaca, 3), Bruxelles: Fondation Egypt. Reine Elisabeth.

King, C. W. (1872), *Antique Gems and Rings*, London: Bell and Daldy.

Kitchen, Kenneth A. (1980), *Ramesside Inscriptions III: Historical and Biographical*, Oxford: B. H. Blackwell.

Küffer, A. and M. Renfer (1996), *Das Sargensemble einer Noblen aus Theben*, Bern: Bern Historisches Museum.

Küffer, A. and R. Siegmann (2007), *Unter dem Schutz der Himmelsgöttin. Ägyptische Särge, Mumien und Masken in der Schweiz*, Zürich: Chronos.

Lanzone, R. V. (1886), *Dizionario di Mitologia Egizia V. Tavole*, Turin: Benjamins.

Maaskant-Kleibrink, M. (1978), *Catalogue of the engraved gems in the Royal Coin Cabinet, The Hague. The Greek, Etruscan and Roman collections*, The Hague: Government Publ. Office.

Mastrocinque, A. (2003), *Sylloge gemmarum gnosticarum I* (Bollettino di numismatica: Monografie, 8.2), Rom: Instituto Poligrafico e Zecca dello Stato.

Mastrocinque, A. (2014), *Les intailles magiques du department des Monnaies Médailles et Antiques*, Paris: Éditions de la Bibliothèque nationale de France.

Mayhoff, C. (1998), *Naturalis Historiae: Libri XXXI–XXXVII* (Bibliotheca Teubneriana), Leipzig: Teubner.

Mead, G. R. S. (1896), *Pistis Sophia*, London: Zuubooks.

Meeks, D. (1977), "Harponknuphi," in W. Helck and W. Westendorf (eds.), *Lexikon der Ägyptologie, Band II: Erntefest - Hordjedef*, 1011–2, Wiesbaden: Harrassowitz.

Michałowski, K. (2001), *Die ägyptische Kunst*, Darmstadt: Wissenschaftliche Buchgesellschaft.

Michel, S. (2001), *Die magischen Gemmen im Britischen Museum*, 2 vols, London: British Museum Press.

Michel, S. (2004), *Die Magischen Gemmen. Zu Bildern und Zauberformeln auf geschnittenen Steinen der Antike und Neuzeit* (Studien aus dem Warburg-Haus, 7), Berlin: Akademie-Verlag.

Michel, S. (2005), "(Re)Interpreting Magical Gems, Ancient and Modern," in S. Shaked (ed.), *Officina Magica. Essays on the Practice of Magic in Antiquity*, Institute of Jewish Studies (Studies in Judaica, 4), 141–70, Leiden/Boston: Brill.

Mitropoulou, E. (1978), *Triple Hekate mainly on votive Reliefs, Coins, Gems and Amulets*, Athens: Pyli.

Passeri, G. (1750), "Divinatio in gemmam magicam," in A. F. Gori (ed.), *Thesaurus Gemmarum Antiquarum Astriferarum*, 3 vols., 172–80, Florence: Albizzi.

Philipp, H. (1986), *Mira et Magica. Gemmen im ägyptischen Museum der Staatlichen Museen, Preussischer Kulturbesitz, Berlin Charlottenburg*, Mainz: Von Zabern.

Preisendanz, K. (2001a), *Papyri Graecae Magicae I. Die griechischen Zauberpapyri. Durchgesehen und herausgegeben von Albert Henrichs*, München/Leipzig: Saur.

Preisendanz, K. (2001b), *Papyri Graecae Magicae II. Die griechischen Zauberpapyri. Durchgesehen und herausgegeben von Albert Henrichs*, München/Leipzig: Saur.

Quack, J. F. (2004), "Griechische und andere Dämonen in den spätdemotischen magischen Texten," in T. Schneider (ed.), *Das Ägyptische und die Sprachen Vorderasiens, Nordafrikas und der Ägäis. Akten des Basler Kolloquiums zum ägyptisch-nichtsemitischen Sprachkontakt, Basel 9.–11.* Juli 2003 (Alter Orient und Altes Testament, 310), 427–507, Münster: Ugarit-Verlag.

Quack, J. F. (in preparation), *Beiträge zu den ägyptischen Dekanen und ihrer Rezeption in der griechisch-römischen Zeit* (Orientalia Lovaniensia Analecta), Leiden: Peeters.

Ridder, A. de (1911), *Collection De Clercq, Tome VII: Les bijoux et les pierres gravées, Deuxième Partie: Les pierres gravées*, Paris: Bibliothèque Nationale.

Roes, A. (1935), "New Light on the Grylli," *Journal of Hellenic Studies*, 55: 232–5.

Ryhiner, M.-L. (1977), "A propos de trigrammes panthéistes," *Revue d'Egyptologie*, 29: 125–37.

Sadek, A. F. (1985), *Contribution à l'étude de l'Amdouat. Les variantes tardives du livre de l'Amdouat dans les papyrus du Musée du Caire* (Orbis Biblicus et Orientalis, 65), Fribourg: Universitäts-Verlag.

Schmidt, C. (1905), *Koptisch-gnostische Schriften I: Die Pistis Sophia. Die beiden Bücher des Jeû. Unbekanntes altgnostisches Werk*, Leipzig: Hinrichs.

Schmidt, C. (1925), *Pistis Sophia. Neu herausgegeben mit Einleitung nebst griechischem und koptischem Wort- und Namenregister* (Coptica, 2), Copenhagen.

Schmidt, V. (1919), *Sarkofager, mumiekister, og mumiehylstre i det gamle Aegyptens. Typologisk atlas*, Copenhagen: Frimodts.

Schulman, A. R. (1964), "The God N," *Journal of Near Eastern Studies*, 23: 275–9.

Schwartz, F. M. and J. H. Schwartz (1979), "Engraved Gems in the Collection of the American Numismatic Society: 1. Ancient Magical Amulets," *American Numismatic Society Museum Notes*, 24: 149–97.

Scott, G. D. (1992), *Temple, Tomb and Dwelling: Egyptian Antiquities from the Harer Family Trust Collection*, San Bernardino: California State University.

Sfameni, C. (2010), "Magic in Late Antiquity: The Evidence of Magical Gems," in D. M. Gwynn and S. Bangert (eds.), *Religious Diversity in Late Antiquity* (Late Antique Archaeology, 6), 435–73, Leiden/Boston: Brill.

Steindorff, G. (1946), *Catalogue of the Egyptian Sculpture in the Baltimore, Walters Art Gallery*, Baltimore: Trustees of the Walters Art Gallery.

Tambiah, S. J. (1978), "Form und Bedeutung magischer Akte," in H. G. Kippenberg and B. Luchesi (eds.), *Magie. Die sozialwissenschaftliche Kontroverse über das Verstehen fremden Denkens*, 259–96, Frankfurt: Suhrkamp.

Teissier, B. (1987), "Glyptic Evidence for a Connection between Iran, Syrio-Palestine and Egypt in the Fourth and Third Millennia," *Iran*, 25: 27–53.

Theis, C. (2011), *Deine Seele zum Himmel, dein Leichnam zur Erde. Zur idealtypischen Rekonstruktion eines altägyptischen Bestattungsrituals* (Beihefte zu Studien zur Altägyptischen Kultur, 12), Hamburg: Buske.

Theis, C. (2014), *Magie und Raum. Der magische Schutz ausgewählter Räume im alten Ägypten nebst einem Vergleich zu angrenzenden Kulturbereichen* (Orientalische Religionen in der Antike, 13), Tübingen: Mohr Siebeck.

Theis, C. (2017), "Schminkpaletten mit zwei Köpfen – Reale Vorbilder aus der Natur?," *Göttinger Miszellen*, 253: 131–6.

Theis, C. (2018), "Hekate Triformis auf Gemmen," in S. Kiyanrad, L. Willer, and C. Theis (eds.), *Bild und Schrift auf >magischen< Artefakten* (Materiale Textkulturen, 19), 165–80, Berlin: De Gruyter.

Theis, C. (2019), "Die siebenköpfige Schlange im Vorderen Orient," in Marc Brose, Peter Dils, Franziska Naether, Lutz Popko, and Dietrich Raue (eds.), *En détail – Philologie und Archäologie im Diskurs. Festschrift für Hans-Werner Fischer-Elfert* (Zeitschrift für Ägyptische Sprache und Altertumskunde – Beihefte, 7), 1123–36, Berlin/Boston: De Gruyter.

Theis, C. (2020), "Creatures with Seven Heads in the Revelation of John. A History of the Motif in the Ancient Near East," in Catharina Baumgartner, Patrizia Heindl, Marie-Hélène Lindner, Julia Preisigke-Borsian, and Sarah Schlüter (eds.), *Ideologie und Organisation. Komparative Untersuchungen antiker Gesellschaften* (Distant Worlds Journal 5), 38–58, Munich.

Theis, C. (in press), "Mehrköpfige Wesen in Ugarit in ihrem altorientalischen Kontext," in Reinhard Müller, Hans Neumann and Reettakaisa Sofia Salo (eds.), *Rituale und Magie in Ugarit. Praxis, Kontexte und Bedeutung* (Orientalische Religionen in der Antike), Tübingen: Mohr-Siebeck.

Theis, C. (in preparation), *Der polymorphe Bes – Untersuchungen zu Entwicklung, Devianz und Tradition eines mehrköpfigen göttlichen Konstrukts im alten Ägypten.*

Vitellozzi, P. (2018), "Relations between Magical Texts and Magical Gems. Recent Perspectives," in S. Kiyanrad, L. Willer, and C. Theis (eds.), *Bild und Schrift auf >magischen< Artefakten* (Materiale Textkulturen, 19), 181–253, Berlin: De Gruyter.

Werth, N. (2006), *Hekate. Untersuchungen zur dreigestaltigen Göttin* (Antiquitates – Archäologische Forschungsergebnisse, 37). Hamburg: Kovač.

Wingert, F. (1984), *Snomed – Systematisierte Nomenklatur der Medizin, Band I: Numerischer Index*, Berlin/Heidelberg: Springer-Verlag.

Wit, Constant de (1958), *Les inscriptions du temple d'Opet, à Karnak* (Bibliotheca Aegyptiaca, 11), Bruxelles: Éd. de la Fondation Égyptologique Reine Élisabeth.

Zazoff, P. (Hg.) (1970), *Antike Gemmen in Deutschen Sammlungen III: Braunschweig, Göttingen, Kassel, 2 Bde., bearbeitet von Volker Scherf, Peter Gercke und Peter Zazoff* (Antike Gemmen in Deutschen Sammlungen, III), Wiesbaden: Steiner .

Zwierlein-Diehl, E. (1992), *Magische Amulette und andere Gemmen des Instituts für Altertumskunde der Universität zu Köln* (Papyrologica Coloniensia, 20), Opladen: Westdeutscher Verlag.

Zwierlein-Diehl, E. (2007), *Antike Gemmen und ihr Nachleben*, Berlin: De Gruyter.

Chapter 4

Angel, J. (2009), "The Use of the Hebrew Bible in Early Jewish Magic," *Religion Compass*, 3: 785–98.

Bhayro, S. (2013), "The Reception of Mesopotamian and Early Jewish Traditions in the Aramaic Incantation Bowls," *Aramaic Studies*, 11: 187–96.

Bohak, G. (2008), *Ancient Jewish Magic: A History*, Cambridge: Cambridge University Press.

Bradshaw, P. (1993), "Liturgy and 'Living Literature'," in P. Bradshaw and B. Spinks (eds.), *Liturgy in Dialogue: Essays in Memory of Ronald Jasper*, 138–53, London: SPCK.

Braun-Holzinger, E. B. (1999), "Apotropaic Figures at Mesopotamian Temples in the Third and Second Millennia," in T. Abusch and K. van der Toorn (eds.), *Mesopotamian Magic: Textual, Historical, and Interpretative Perspectives*, 149–72, Groningen: Styx Publications.

Brodie, N. (2014), "Aramaic Incantation Bowls in War and in Peace," *Journal of Art Crime*, 11: 9–14.

Brodie, N. and M. M. Kersel (2014), "Wikileaks, Text, and Archaeology: The Case of the Schøyen Incantation Bowls," in M. T. Rutz and M. M. Kersel (eds.), *Archaeologies of Text: Archaeology, Technology, and Ethics*, 198–213, Oxford: Oxbow Books.

Connerton, P. (2011), *The Spirit of Mourning: History, Memory and the Body*, Cambridge: Cambridge University Press.

Dabbs, J. A. (1963), *History of the Discovery and Exploration of Chinese Turkestan*, The Hague: Mouton & Co.

De Bruyn, T. S. and J. H. F. Dijkstra (2011), "Greek Amulets and Formularies from Egypt Containing Christian Elements: A Checklist of Papyri, Parchments, Ostraka, and Tablets," *BASP*, 48: 163–216.

Feldt, L. (2015), "Monstrous Figurines from Mesopotamia: Textuality, Spatiality and Materiality in Rituals and Incantations for the Protection of Houses in First-Millennium Aššur," in D. Boschung and J. N. Bremmer (eds.), *The Materiality of Magic*, 59–95, Paderborn: Wilhelm Fink.

Frankfurter, D. (1994), "The Magic of Writing and the Writing of Magic: The Power of the Word in Egyptian and Greek Traditions," *Helios*, 21: 189–221.

Frankfurter, D. (2015), "Scorpion/Demon: On the Origin of the Mesopotamian Apotropaic Bowl," *JNES*, 74: 9–18.

Gager, J. G. (1992), *Curse Tablets and Binding Spells from the Ancient World*, Oxford: Oxford University Press.

Gollancz, H. (1912), *The Book of Protection: Being a Collection of Charms*, London: Oxford University Press.

Gordon, C. H. (1941), *The Living Past*, New York: The John Day Company.

Gordon, R. (2002), "Shaping the Text: Innovation and Authority in Graeco-Egyptian Malign Magic," in H. F. J. Horstmanshoff, H. W. Singor, F. T. van Straten, and J. H. M. Strubbe (eds.), *KYKEON: Studies in Honour of H. S. Versnel*, 69–111, Leiden: Brill.

Graf, F. (1991), "Prayer in Magic and Religious Ritual," in C. A. Faraone and D. Obbink (eds.), *Magika Hiera: Ancient Greek Magic and Religion*, 188–213, Oxford: Oxford University Press.

Hunter, E. C. D. (1987), "Saints in Syriac Anathemas: A Form-Critical Analysis of Role," *JSS*, 32: 83–104.

Hunter, E. C. D. (1990), "Genres of Syriac Amulets: A Study of Cambridge Ms. Syr. 3086," in R. Lavenant (ed.), *V Symposium Syriacum, 1988: Katholieke Universiteit, Leuven, 29–31 août 1988*, 355–68, Rome: Pontificum Institutum Studiorum Orientalium.

Hunter, E. C. D. (1996), "Incantation Bowls: A Mesopotamian Phenomenon?," *Orientalia*, 65: 220–33.
Hunter, E. C. D. (2009), "Magic and Medicine Amongst the Christians of Kurdistan," in E. C. D. Hunter (ed.), *The Christian Heritage of Iraq: Collected Papers from the Christianity in Iraq I-V Seminar Days*, 187–202, Piscataway: Gorgias Press.
Hunter, E. C. D. (2012), "The Christian Library from Turfan: Syr HT 41–42–43 An Early Exemplar of the Hudra," *Hugoye*, 15(2): 301–51.
Hunter, E. C. D. (2013), "Traversing Time and Location: A Prayer-Amulet to Mar Tamsis from Turfan," in D. W. Winkler and L. Tang (eds.), *From the Oxus River to the Chinese Shores: Studies on East Syriac Christianity in China and Central Asia*, 23–41, Salzburg: Lit Verlag.
Hunter, E. C. D. (2015), "Two Codex Handbooks of Amulets: Mingana ms syr 316 and Rylands ms syr 52," in S. H. Griffith and S. Grebenstein (eds.), *Christsein in der islamischen Welt: Festschrift für Martin Tamcke zum 60. Geburtstag*, 423–37, Wiesbaden: Harrassowitz Verlag.
Hunter, E. C. D. and M. Dickens (2014), *Syriac Texts from the Berlin Turfan Collection*, Stuttgart: Steiner Verlag.
Levene, D. (2003), *A Corpus of Magic Bowls: Incantation Texts in Jewish Aramaic from Late Antiquity*, London: Kegan Paul.
MacMullen, R. (2009), *The Second Church: Popular Christianity A.D. 200–400*, Leiden: Brill.
Meyer, M. W. and R. Smith (1994), *Ancient Christian Magic: Coptic Texts of Ritual Power*, San Francisco: Harper San Francisco.
Montgomery, J. A. (1913), *Aramaic Incantation Texts from Nippur*, Philadelphia: The University Museum.
Moriggi, M. (2014), *A Corpus of Syriac Incantation Bowls: Syriac Magical Texts from Late-Antique Mesopotamia*, Leiden: Brill.
Moriggi, M. (2016), "'And the Impure and Abominable Priests Fled for Help to the Names of the Devils': Amulets and Magical Practices in Syriac Christian Culture Between Late Antiquity and the Modern World," *Hugoye*, 19(2): 371–84.
Müller-Kessler, C. (1998), "Aramäische Koine - Ein Beschwörungsformular aus Mesopotamien," *Baghdader Mitteilungen*, 29: 331–48.
Müller-Kessler, C. (1999), "Interrelations between Mandaic Lead Rolls and Incantation Bowls," in T. Abusch and K. van der Toorn (eds.), *Mesopotamian Magic: Textual, Historical, and Interpretative Perspectives*, 197–209, Groningen: Styx Publications.
Müller-Kessler, C. (2005), "Of Jesus, Darius, Marduk …: Aramaic Magic Bowls in the Moussaieff Collection," *Journal of the American Oriental Society*, 125: 219–40.
Peters, J. P. (1897), *Nippur: Explorations and Adventures on the Euphrates: The Narrative of the University of Pennsylvania Expedition to Babylonia in the Years 1888–1890*, vol. II, London: G. P. Putnam's Sons.
Rebillard, É. (2012), *Christians and Their Many Identities in Late Antiquity, North Africa, 200–450 CE*, London: Cornell University Press.

Sanzo, J. E. (2017), "Magic and Communal Boundaries: The Problems with Amulets in Chrysostom, Adv. Iud. 8, and Augustine, In Io. tra. 7," *Henoch*, 39: 227–46.

Segal, J. B. (2000), *Catalogue of the Aramaic and Mandaic Incantation Bowls in the British Museum*, London: British Museum Press.

Shaked, S. (2011), "Transmission and Transformation of Spells: The Case of the Jewish Babylonian Aramaic Bowls," in G. Bohak, Y. Harari, and S. Shaked (eds.), *Continuity and Innovation in the Magical Tradition*, 187–217, Leiden: Brill.

Shaked, S, J. N. Ford, and S. Bhayro (2013), *Aramaic Bowl Spells: Jewish Babylonian Aramaic Bowls*, vol. 1, Leiden: Brill.

Sørensen, J. P. (1984), "The Argument in Ancient Egyptian Magical Formulae," *Acta Orientalia*, 45: 5–19.

Spier, J. (2007), *Late Antique and Early Christian Gems*, Wiesbaden: Reichert Verlag.

Swartz, M. D. (1990), "Scribal Magic and its Rhetoric: Formal Patterns in Medieval Hebrew and Aramaic Incantation Texts from the Cairo Genizah," *HTR*, 83: 163–80.

Yamauchi, E. M. (1967), *Mandaic Incantation Texts*, New Haven: American Oriental Society.

Zografou, A. (2010), "Magic Lamps, Luminous Dream: Lamps in *PGM* Recipes," in M. Christopoulos, E. D. Karakantza, and O. Levaniouk (eds.), *Light and Darkness in Ancient Greek Myth and Religion*, 276–94, Plymouth: Lexington Books.

Chapter 5

Düwel, K. (1988), "Buchstabenmagie und Alphabetzauber," *Frühmittelalterliche Studien*, 22: 70–110.

Düwel, K. (1989), "Der runenbeschriftete Holzgriff aus Schleswig – zur Deutung einer rätselhaften Inschrift," in V. Vogel (ed.), *Ausgrabungen in Schleswig. Berichte und Studien 7: Das archäologische Fundmaterial I*, 43–82, Neumünster: Wachholtz.

Düwel, K. (2001a), *Runenkunde*, 3rd edition, Stuttgart/Weimar: Metzler.

Düwel, K. (2001b), "Mittelalterliche Amulette aus Holz und Blei mit lateinischen und runischen Inschriften," in V. Vogel (ed.), *Ausgrabungen in Schleswig, Berichte und Studien 15 (Das archäologische Fundmaterial II)*, 227–302, Neumünster: Wachholtz.

Eriksson, M. and D. O. Zetterholm (1933), "En Amulett från Sigtuna. Ett Tolkningsförsök," *Fornvännen*, 28: 129–56.

Foote, P. (1981), "Nafn guðs hit hæsta," in *Speculum Norroenum*, 139–54, Odense: Odense University Press.

Imer, L. M. and A. Dørup Knudsen (2019), "Jeg besværger jer elvermænd og elverkoner og alle dæmoner ... Blyamuletten fra Møllergade i Svendborg," in K. Risskov Sørensen (ed.), *Fund fortæller. Nye arkæologiske fund på Fyn*, 64–7, Svendborg: Arkaeologi Sydfyn.

Imer, L. M. and O. C. Uldum (2015), "Mod dæmoner og elverfolk," *Skalk*, 2015: 9–15.
Knirk, J. E. (1998), "Runic Inscriptions Containing Latin in Norway," in K. Düwel and S. Nowak (eds.), *Runeninschriften als Quellen interdisziplinärer Forschung. Abhandlungen des Vierten Internationalen Symposiums über Runen und Runeninschriften in Göttingen (4.-9. August 1995)* (Ergänzungsbände zum RGA, 15), 476–506, Berlin/New York: de Gruyter.
Leidig, D. (2004), *Frauenheilkunde in volkssprachigen Arznei- und Kräuterbüchern des 12. bis 15. Jahrhunderts. Eine empirische Untersuchung*, PhD Thesis, Duisburg.
McKinnell, J., R. Simek, and K. Düwel (2004), *Runes, Magic and Religion: A Sourcebook*, Wien: Fassbaender.
Muhl, A. and M. Gutjahr (2013), *Magische Beschwörungen in Blei. Inschriftentäfelchen des Mittelalters aus Sachsen-Anhalt* (Kleine Hefte zur Archäologie in Sachsen-Anhalt, 10), Halle: Landesamt für Denkmalpflege und Archäologie Sachsen-Anhalt.
Schulz, M. (2000), *Magie oder die Wiederherstellung der Ordnung*, Frankfurt/Main: Lang.
Simek, R. (2011), "Elves and Exorcism: Runic and Other Lead Amulets in Medieval Popular Religion," in D. Anlezark (ed.), *Myths, Legends and Heroes: Essays in Old Norse Literature in Honour of John McKinnell*, 25–52, Toronto: University of Toronto Press.
Simek, R. (2019), "Tangible Religion. Amulets, Illnesses, and the Demonic Seven Sisters," in K. Wikström af Edholm et al. (eds.), *Myth, Materiality and Lived Religion in Merovingian and Viking Scandinavia*, 375–89, Stockholm: Stockholm University Press.
Steenholt Olesen, R. (2010), "Runic Amulets from Medieval Denmark," *Futhark*, 1: 165–76.
Stoklund, M. (1996), "Runer 1995," *Arkæologiske udgravninger i Danmark*, 1995: 275–94.
Stoklund, M., L. Imer, and R. Steenholt Olesen (2004), "Arbejdet ved Runologisk Laboratorium, Kobenhavn," *Nytt om runer*, 19: 4–10.
Vollmann, B. K. (ed.) (1987), *Carmina Burana. Texte und Übersetzungen*, Frankfurt: Deutscher Klassiker Verlag.

Chapter 6

Aymar, A. (1926), "Le sachet accoucheur et ses mystères," *Annales du Midi*, 38: 273–347.
Betz, H. D. (ed.) (1992), *The Greek Magical Papyri in Translation including the Demotic Spells*, 2nd edition, Chicago/London: The University of Chicago Press.
Bonser, W. (1963), *The Medical Background of Anglo-Saxon England* (Publications of the Wellcome Historical Medical Library, 3), London: Wellcome Historical Medical Library.

Bozoky, E. (1991), "Mythic Mediation in Healing Incantations," in S. Campbell, B. Hall, and D. Klausner (eds.), *Health, Disease and Healing in Medieval Culture*, 84–92, New York: Palgrave.

Bozoky, E. (2013), "Medieval Narrative Charms," in J. Kapalo, E. Pocs, and W. Ryan (eds.), *The Power of Words. Studies on Charms and Charming in Europe*, 101–15, Budapest/New York: Central European University Press.

Ceppari Ridolfi, M. A. (1999), *Maghi, streghe e alchimisti a Siena e nel suo territorio (1458–1571)*, Monteriggioni: Il Leccio.

Corradini Bozzi, M. S. (1997), *Ricettari medico-farmaceutici medievali nella Francia meridionale*, Firenze: Olschki.

Dobschütz, E. (1910), "Charms and Amulets (Christian)," in J. Hastings (ed.), *Encyclopaedia of Religion and Ethics*, vol. III, 413–30, Edinburgh: Clark.

Frankfurter, D. (1994), "The Magic of Writing and the Writing of Magic: The Power of the Word in Egyptian and Greek Traditions," *Helios*, 21: 189–221.

Grévin, B. and Véronèse, J. (2004), "Les 'caractères' magiques au Moyen Âge (XIIe-XIVe siècle)," *Bibliothèque de l'Ecole des Chartes*, 162: 305–79.

Haust, J. (1941), *Médecinaire liégeois du XIIIe siècle et médecinaire namurois du XVe (manuscrits 815 et 2769 de Darmstadt)*, Brussels/Liège: Palais des académies.

Hunt, T. (1990), *Popular Medicine in Thirteenth-century England*, Woodbridge: Brewer.

Lecouteux, C. (2002), *Le Livre des Grimoires: de la magie au Moyen Âge*, Paris: Imago.

Luc, P. (1938), "Un complot contre le pape Benoît XIII (1406–1407)," *Mélanges d'archéologie et d'histoire de l'Ecole française de Rome*, 55: 374–402.

Olsan, L. T. (2003), "Charms and Prayers in Medieval Medical Theory and Practice," *Social History of Medicine*, 16: 343–66.

Schnyder, A. (ed.) (1991), *Malleus maleficarum*, Göppingen: Kümmerle.

Scot, R. (1584), *The Discoverie of Witchcraft. Being a Reprint of the First Edition Published in 1584*, Totowa: Rowman and Littlefield (réimp. 1930).

Sheldon, S. E. (1990), *Middle English and Latin Charms, Amulets, and Talismans from Vernacular Manuscripts*, Tulane University Ph. D., 1978, Ann Arbor: University Microfilms International, Dissertation Information Service.

Skemer, D. C. (2006), *Binding Words. Textual Amulets in the Middle Ages*, Pennsylvania: The Pennsylvania University Press.

Zanone, E. (2010), "Le 'breve', entre fiction et réalité. Les représentations d'une amulette dans les écrits religieux et les nouvelles en Toscane au XIVe et au XVe siècle," *Cahiers d'études italiennes*, 10: 39–54.

Chapter 7

Álvarez de Morales, C. and F. Girón Irueste (eds.) (1992), *Ibn Ḥabīb, 'Abd al-Mālik. Mujtaṣar fī l-ṭibb* (Compendio de medicina), Madrid: CSIC-ICMA.

Barceló, C. and A. Labarta (2009), *Archivos moriscos. Textos árabes de la minoría islámica valenciana (1401–1608)*, Valencia: Universitat.

Bernabé Pons, L. (1994), "La literatura de los últimos musulmanes de España: Lengua y Literatura de Mudéjares y Moriscos," in B. Bennasar (ed.), *Simposio Internacional «Chrétiens et Musulmans dans la Renaissance». Actes du 37ᵉ Colloque International du CESR*, 322–32, Paris: Champion.

Butler, E. M. (1947), *Ritual magic*, Cambridge: University Press.

Caro Baroja, J. (2000), *Los moriscos del Reino de Granada. Ensayo de Historia Social*, 5th edition, Madrid: Itsmo.

Dieleman, J. (2015), "The Materiality of Textual Amulets in Ancient Egypt," in D. Boschung and J. N. Bremmer (eds.), *The Materiality of Magic* (Morphomata, 20), 23–58, Munich: Wilhelm Fink.

Domínguez Ortiz, A. and B. Vincent (1985), *Historia de los moriscos. Vida y tragedia de una minoría*, Madrid: Alianza Editorial.

Doutté, E. (1984), *Magie et religión dans l'Afrique du Nord*, Paris: Maisonneuve et Geuthner.

Ebersole, A. V. (ed.) (1978), *Ciruelo, Pedro. Reprobación de las supersticiones y hechicerías*, Valencia: Albatros.

Fernández Medina, E. (2012), "The Seal of Solomon: From magic to messianic Device," in I. Regulski et al. (eds.), *Seals and Sealing Practices in the Near East. Developments in Administration and Magic from Prehistory to the Islamic Period* (Orientalia Lovaniensia Analecta, 219), 175–87, Louvain: Peeters.

Fernández Medina, E. (2014), *La magia morisca entre el cristianismo y el islam*, Universidad de Granada, https://digibug.ugr.es/handle/10481/35183, last consulted 01/23/20.

Forshaw, P. J. (2015), "Magical Material & Material Survivals: Amulets, Talismans, and Mirrors in Early Modern Europe," in D. Boschung and J. N. Bremmer (eds.), *The Materiality of Magic* (Morphomata, 20), 357–78, Munich: Wilhelm Fink.

García-Arenal, M. (2010), "La Inquisición y los libros de los moriscos," in A. M. Paramio (ed.), *Memoria de los moriscos. Escritos y relatos de una diáspora cultural*, 57–71, Madrid: SECC.

García-Ballester, L. (1984), *Los moriscos y la medicina. Un capítulo de la medicina y la ciencia marginadas en la España del siglo XVI*, Barcelona: Labor.

Gimaret, D. (1988), *Les Noms Divins en Islam. Exégèse lexicographique et théologique*, Paris: Cerf.

Hamès, C. (ed.) (2007), *Coran et talismans. Textes et pratiques magiques en milieu musulman*, Paris: Karthala.

Labarta, A. (ed.) (1993), *Libro de dichos maravillosos. Misceláneo morisco de magia y adivinación*, Madrid: CSIC-AECI.

López-Baralt, L. (2009), *La literatura secreta de los últimos musulmanes de España*, Madrid: Trotta.

Martínez Núñez, Mª A. (2007). *Epigrafía Árabe* (Publicaciones del Gabinete de Antigüedades de la Real Academia de la Historia, I, Antigüedades, 1.3), Madrid: RAH.

Porter, V. (2004), "Islamic Seals: Magical or Practical?," in E. Savage-Smith (ed.), *Magic and Divination in Early Islam*, 179–200, Aldershot: Ashgate.
Savage-Smith, E. (2004), "Introduction," in E. Savage-Smith (ed.), *Magic and Divination in Early Islam*, 1–20, Aldershot: Ashgate.
Villaverde Amieva, J. C. (2010), "Los manuscritos aljamiado-moriscos: Hallazgos, colecciones, inventarios y otras noticias," in A. M. Paramio (ed.), *Memoria de los moriscos. Escritos y relatos de una diáspora cultural*, 91–128, Madrid: SECC.
Vincent, B. (dir.) (1979), *Les Marginaux et les exclus dans l'histoire*, Paris: UGE.

Inquisition trials (in order of appearance)

Jaime Bolaix. Archivo Histórico Nacional, Inquisición de Valencia, 1585, Leg. 549, nº 11.
Leonés Benali. Archivo Histórico Nacional, Inquisición de Valencia, 1585, Leg. 549, nº 8.
Leonor de Mendoza. Archivo Histórico Nacional, Inquisición de Granada, 1593, Leg. 1953, nº 28.
Rafaela Mayor. Archivo Histórico Nacional, Inquisición de Valencia, 1589, Leg. 553/I, nº 6.
Isabel de Lopo. Archivo Histórico Nacional, Inquisición de Zaragoza, 1595, Lib.1000.
Antonio de Piedrahita. Archivo Histórico Nacional, Inquisición de Valencia, 1599, Lib. 968, nº 30.
Diego de Vargas. Archivo Histórico Nacional, Inquisición de Granada, 1586, Leg. 1953, nº 83.

Aljamiado-Arabic manuscripts

Libro de dichos maravillosos. Ms. 16th.c., Aljamiado / Arabic (M-CCHS RES RESC/22). Biblioteca Tomás Navarro Tomás (BTNT), CCHS-CSIC, Madrid, Spain.
Loose paper. 'Herce', 16th.c.?, Ms. V25 (II/9416, caja nº 25). Biblioteca de la Real Academia de la Historia (BRAH), Madrid, Spain.
مجموعة مؤلفات في الأمداح النبوية [Maŷmū'at mu'allafāt fī l-amdāḥ al-nabawiyya]. Ms. 19th c.? Arabic (GR-EEA ms4). Biblioteca de la Escuela de Estudios Árabes (EEA), Granada, Spain.

Chapter 8

And, M. (ed.) (2012), *Minyatürlerle Osmanlı-İslâm mitologyası*. 4. baskı. Yapı Kredi yayınları 2572, Istanbul: YKY, Yapı Kredi Kültür Sanat Yayıncılık.
Arberry, A. J. (2018), „The Koran Interpreted," https://ia801007.us.archive.org/15/items/QuranAJArberry_201805/Quran-A%20J%20Arberry.pdf (accessed September 21, 2021).

Çelebi, A. (2012), "Tılsım," in T. D. Vakfı (ed.), *İslâm Ansiklopedisi* 41: 91, Istanbul: Türkiye Diyanet Vakfı İslâm Araştırmaları Merkezi.

Çelebi, E. (o. J.), *Seyāḥatnāme. Handschrift Nr. IÜTY 5973.* Bd. 10.

Çelebi, E. (o. J.), *Seyāḥatnāme. Handschrift Nr: Bağdat Köşkü 304.* Bd. 1, 2.

Çelebi, E. (o. J.), *Seyāḥatnāme. Handschrift Nr: Bağdat Köşkü 305.* ar 305. Bd. 3,4.

Dankoff, R. (2006), *An Ottoman Mentality: The World of Evliya Çelebi* (Ottoman Empire and its heritage, 31). 2nd rev. edition, Leiden/Boston: Brill.

Dankoff, R. and K. Kreiser (1992), *A Guide to the Seyāḥat-nāme of Evliya Çelebi: bibliographie raisonnée* (Beihefte zum Tübinger Atlas des Vorderen Orients Çelebi, 2), Wiesbaden: Reichert.

Erduran, Z. (2006), *Evliya Çelebi Seyahatname'sine göre İstanbul'da esnaf, zanaat ve ticaret* (Yüksek lisans tezi), Kırklereli: Kırklereli Üniversitesi Tarih Kürsüsü.

Gruber, C. (2020), *Osmanlı-Islam Sanatında Tapınma ve Tılsım. Übersetzt von Erdem Gökyaran*, Kitapyurdu: Yapi Kredi Yayınları.

Halûk Perk, Müzesi (ed.) (2010), *Halûk Perk koleksiyonu: Osmanlı tılsım mühürleri*, Istanbul: Zeytinburnu Belediyesi, Halûk Perk Müzesi.

Hammer-Purgstall, J. von (1848), *Abhandlung über die Siegel der Araber, Perser und Türken (vorgetragen in der historisch-philologischen Classe am 9. März 1848)*, Wien: Hof- und Staatsdruckerei.

Kiyanrad, S. (2017), *Gesundheit und Glück für seinen Besitzer: schrifttragende Amulette im islamzeitlichen Iran (bis 1258)* (Kultur, Recht und Politik in muslimischen Gesellschaften, 36), Würzburg: Ergon Verlag.

Meninsky, F. (1680), *Thesaurus linguarum oriental. (arabisch-türkisch-persisches Wörterbuch)*, Wien.

Nestroy, J. (2002), *Der Talisman: Posse mit Gesang in drei Akten. Um Anmerkungen ergänzte Ausgabe* (Universal-Bibliothek, 3374), Stuttgart: Reclam.

O. A. (1934), "Tılsam," in *Enzyklopädie des Islams. Geographisches, ethnographisches und biographisches Wörterbuch*, 4, 830, Leiden/Leipzig: Brill.

Onay, A. and C. Kurnaz (2007), *Açiklamali Divan Şiiri Sözlüğü.* 1. Baskı, Ankara: Birleşik.

Öz, M. (2012), "Zülfikar," in T. D. Vakfı (ed.), *İslâm Ansiklopedisi* 44: 553, Istanbul: Türkiye Diyanet Vakfı İslâm Araştırmaları Merkezi.

Pakalın, M. Z. (1946), *Osmanlı Tarih Deyimleri ve Terimleri Sözlüğü*, Istanbul: Millî Eğitim Basimevi.

Pakalın, M. Z. (1993), *Osmanlı tarih deyimleri ve terimleri sözlüğü*, Istanbul: Milli Eğitim Basımevi.

Redhouse, J. W. (ed.) (1999), *Redhouse Türkçe/Osmanlıca-İngilizce sözlük: Redhouse Turkish/Ottoman-English dictionary. 17. Basım*, Istanbul: SEV Matbaacılık ve Yayıncılık.

Ruska, J. and C. de Vaux (2000), "Tılsam," in H. A. R. Gibb (ed.), *The Encyclopaedia of Islam New Edition, Bd. 10*, 500, Leiden: Brill.

Ṯaʿlabī, Abū-Isḥāq Aḥmad Ibn-Muḥammad Ibn-Ibrāhīm aṯ. (2006), *Islamische Erzählungen von Propheten und Gottesmännern: Qiṣaṣ al-anbiyā' oder 'Arā'is al-mağālis. Herausgegeben von Hartmut Bobzin, Übersetzt von Heribert Busse* (Diskurse der Arabistik 9), Wiesbaden: Harrassowitz.

Tawada, Y. (1996), *Talisman: Yoko Tawada*, Tübingen: Konkursbuch.

Tezcan, H. (2011). *Topkapı Sarayı Müzesi koleksiyonundan tılsımlı gömlekler*, Istanbul: Timaş Yayınları.

Ullmann, M. (1972), *Die Natur- und Geheimwissenschaften im Islam* (Handbuch der Orientalistik. Abt. 1: Der Nahe und der Mittlere Osten. Ergänzungsband 6, Abschnitt 2), Leiden: Brill.

Winkler, H. A. (1930). *Siegel und Charaktere in der muhammedanischen Zauberei* (Studien zur Geschichte und Kultur des islamischen Orients Zwanglose Beihefte zu der Zeitschrift "Der Islam," 7), Berlin/Leipzig: De Gruyter.

Chapter 9

[A Chronicle of the Carmelites 1939] *A Chronicle of the Carmelites in Persia and the Papal Mission of the XVIIth and XVIIIth centuries*, 2 vols, London: Eyre and Spottiswoode.

Allan, J. and B. Gilmour (2000), *Persian Steel. The Tanavoli Collection*, Oxford: Oxford University Press.

Anawari, G. C. (2000), "BĪRŪNĪ, ABŪ RAYḤĀN v. Pharmacology and Mineralogy," *Encyclopædia Iranica*, online edition, https://www.iranicaonline.org/articles/biruni-abu-rayhan-v (accessed July 28, 2021).

Arjomand, S. A. (1984), *The Shadow of God and the Hidden Imam. Religion, Political Order, and Societal Change in Shiʿite Iran from the Beginning to 1890*, Chicago: University of Chicago Press.

Babayan, K. (1998), ""The "Aqāʾid al-Nisāʾ": A Glimpse at Ṣafavid Women in Local Iṣfahānī Culture," in G. R. G. Hambly (ed.), *Women in the Medieval Islamic World. Power, Patronage, and Piety*, 349–81, New York: St. Martin's Press.

Babayan, K. (2021), *The City as Anthology. Eroticism and Urbanity in Early Modern Isfahan*, Stanford: Stanford University Press.

Berthold, C. (2020), "The Word of God in One's Hand: Touching and Holding Pendant Koran Manuscripts," *Das Mittelalter*, 25(2): 338–57.

Berthold, C. (2021), *Forms and Functions of Pendant Koran Manuscripts*, Wiesbaden: Harrassowitz.

Bothmer, H.-C. Graf von (1982), *Die islamischen Miniaturen der Sammlung Preetorius*, München: Lipp.

Canby, S. R. (2014), "The Material World of Shah Tahmasp," in S. R. Canby (ed.), *The Shahnama of Shah Tahmasp. The Persian Book of Kings*, 21–60, New York: The Metropolitan Museum of Art.

Carmeli, O. (2014), "The Material Culture and Ritual Objects of the Jews in Iran," in H. M. Sarshar (ed.), *The Jews of Iran. The History, Religion, and Culture of a Community in the Islamic World*, 144–72, London/New York: I. B. Tauris.

Chardin, J. (1811), *Voyages du Chevalier Chardin en Perse, et autres lieux de l'Orient*, Edited by L. Langlès, Paris: Le Normant.

Chelebi, E. (2010), *Travels in Iran and the Caucasus, 1647 & 1654*, Translated by H. Javadi and W. Floor, Washington: Mage Publishers.

Chelkowski, P. J. (1975), *Mirror of the Invisible World. Tales from the Khamseh of Nizami*, New York: The Metropolitan Museum of Art.

Coffey, H. (2010), "Between Amulet and Devotion: Islamic Miniature Books in the Lilly Library," in C. Gruber (ed.), *The Islamic Manuscript Tradition: Ten Centuries of Book Arts in Indiana University Collections*, 78–115, Bloomington/Indianapolis: Indiana University Press.

Coffey, H. (2019), "Diminutive Divination and the Implications of Scale: A Miniature Qur'anic *Falnama* of the Safavid Period," in K. Myrvold and D. Miller Parmenter (eds.), *Miniature Books – The Format and Function of Tiny Religious Texts*, 72–107, Sheffield/Bristol: Equinox Publishing Ltd.

Coulon, J.-C. (2016), "Fumigations et rituels magiques. Le rôle des encens et fumigations dans la magie arabe médiévale," *Bulletin d'études orientales*, LXIV: 179–248.

Dimand, M. S. (1930), *A Handbook of Mohammedan Decorative Arts*, New York: The Metropolitan Museum of Art.

Doostdar, A. (2018), *The Iranian Metaphysicals. Explorations in Science, Islam, and the Uncanny*, Princeton/Oxford: Princeton University Press.

Ebenhöch, R. and S. Tammen (2019), "Wearing Devotional Books. Book-Shaped Miniature Pendants (Fifteenth to Sixteenth Centuries)," in D. Ganz and B. Schellewald (eds.), *Clothing Sacred Scriptures. Book Art and Book Religion in Christian, Islamic, and Jewish Cultures*, 171–83, Berlin/Boston: De Gruyter.

Eberhard, E. (1970), *Osmanische Polemik gegen die Safawiden im 16. Jahrhundert nach arabischen Handschriften*, Freiburg: Klaus Schwarz Verlag.

Ekhtiar, M. and R. Parikh (2016), *Power and Piety: Islamic Talismans on the Battlefield*, New York: The Metropolitan Museum of Art (digital catalogue).

Elgood, C. (1970), *Safavid Medical Practice or The Practice of Medicine, Surgery and Gynaecology in Persia between 1500 A.D. and 1750 A.D*, London: Luzac & Company Ltd

Farhad, M. and S. Bağcı (2009), *Falnama. The Book of Omens*, London: Thames & Hudson.

Ghereghlou, K. (2019), "A Safavid Bureaucrat in the Ottoman World: Mirza Makhdum Sharifi Shirazi and the Quest for Upward Mobility in the *İlmiye* Hierarchy," *The Journal of Ottoman Studies*, LIII: 153–94.

Gruber, C. (2011), "The 'Restored' Shīʿī muṣḥaf as Divine Guide? The Practice of fāl-i Qurʾān in the Ṣafavid Period," *Journal of Qur'anic Studies*, 13(2): 29–55.

Herbert, T. (1638), *Some Years Travels into Africa & Asia…* London: Jacob Blome and Richard Bishop.

[Islamic Medical Wisdom 2007] *Islamic Medical Wisdom: The Tibb al-A'imma*, Translated by Batool Ispahany, edited by Andrew J. Newman. Qum: Ansariyan.

Jenkins, M. and M. Keene (1983), *Islamic Jewelry in the Metropolitan Museum of Art*, New York: The Metropolitan Museum of Art.

Kaempfer, E. (1984), *Am Hofe des persischen Großkönigs, 1684–1685*, Edited by W. Hinz, Stuttgart: Thienemann.

Khunjī Iṣfahānī, F. Allāh b. Rūzbihān (1992), *Tārīkh-i ʿĀlam-ārā-yi Amīnī. Īrān dar sālhā-yi 1478-1490 mīlādī*, Edited by J. E. Woods, translated by V. Minorsky, London: Royal Asiatic Society.

Khvānsārī, Ā. J. (2535 [1976]), *Kulṣūm Nana*, Tehran: Murvārīd.

Kiyanrad, S. (2017), *Gesundheit und Glück für seinen Besitzer. Schrifttragende Amulette im islamzeitlichen Iran (bis 1258)*, Würzburg: Ergon.

Langer, E. (2013), *Islamische magische Schalen und Teller aus Metall. Medizinschalen und Wahrsageteller sowie Liebesschalen und –teller*, Münster: Monsenstein und Vannerdat.

Maddison, F. and E. Savage-Smith (1997), *Science, Tools & Magic. Part One. Body and Spirit*, Mapping the Universe, Oxford: Oxford University Press.

Melikian-Chirvani, A. S. (1974), "Safavid Metalwork: A Study in Continuity," *Iranian Studies*, 7(3–4), *Studies on Isfahan: Proceedings of the Isfahan Colloquium, Part II*: 543–85.

Melikian-Chirvani, A. S. (1982), *Islamic Metalwork from the Iranian World, 8th–18th Centuries*, London: Her Majesty's Stationery Office.

Melvin-Koushki, M. (2012), *The Quest for a Universal Science: The Occult Philosophy of Ṣāʾin al-Dīn Turka Iṣfahānī (1369–1432) and Intellectual Millenarianism in Early Timurid Iran*, PhD dissertation, Yale University.

Melvin-Koushki, M. (2018a), "How to Rule the World: Occult-Scientific Manuals of the Early Modern Persian Cosmopolis," *Journal of Persianate Studies*, 11: 140–54.

Melvin-Koushki, M. (2018b), "Persianate Geomancy from Ṭūsī to the Millennium: A Preliminary Survey," in N. El-Bizri and E. Orthmann (eds.), *Occult Sciences in Premodern Islamic Culture*, 151–99, Beirut/Würzburg: Orient-Institut.

Melvin-Kushki, M. (2020), "Pseudo-Shaykh Bahāʾī on the Supreme Name, a Safavid-Qajar Lettrist Classic," in J. Elias and B. Orfali (eds.), *Light upon Light: A Festschrift Presented to Gerhard Böwering by His Students*, 256–90, Leiden/Boston: Brill.

Membré, M. (1993), *Mission to the Lord Sophy of Persia (1539–1542)*, Translated with introduction and notes by A. H. Morton, London: Gibb Memorial Trust.

Muravchick, R. (2014), *God Is the Best Guardian: Islamic Talismanic Shirts from the Gunpowder Empires*, PhD thesis University of Pennsylvania.

Newid, M. A. and A. Vasegh Abbasi (2007), "Islamische Amulette Irans als Träger apotropäischer Funktionen im Lichte persischer Quellen," *Eothen*, IV: 246–302.

Nünlist, T. (2018a), "Devotion and Protection: Four Amuletic Scrolls from Safavid Persia," in Y. Kadoi (ed.), *Persian Art: Image-Making in Eurasia*, 78–101, Edinburgh: Edinburgh University Press.

Nünlist, T. (2018b), "Entzauberte Amulettrollen. Hinweise zu einer typologischen Gliederung," in S. Günther and D. Pielow (eds.), *Die Geheimnisse der oberen und der unteren Welt. Magie im Islam zwischen Glaube und Wissenschaft* (Islamic History and Civilization, 158), 247–93, Leiden/Boston: Brill.

Nünlist, T. (2020), *Schutz und Andacht im Islam. Dokumente in Rollenform aus dem 14.–19. Jh* (Islamic History and Civilization, 175), Leiden/Boston: Brill.

Olearius, A. (1971), *Vermehrte Newe Bescheibung der Muscowitischen und Persischen Reyse*, Schleswig 1656, Edited by D. Lohmeier, Tübingen: Niemeyer.

Otto, B.-C. (2019), "Magie im Islam. Eine diskursgeschichtliche Perspektive," in S. Günther and D. Pielow (eds.), *Die Geheimnisse der oberen und der unteren Welt: Magie im Islam zwischen Glaube und Wissenschaft* (Islamic History and Civilization, 158), 515–46, Leiden/Boston: Brill.

Papas, A. (2019), "Lingua Franca or Lingua Magica? Talismanic Scrolls from Eastern Turkistan," in N. Green (ed.), *The Persianate World. The Frontiers of a Eurasian Lingua Franca*, 207–22, Oakland: University of California Press.

Pavaloi, M. (1993), "Sufismus: andere Wege zu Gott," in H. Forkl et al. (eds.), *Die Gärten des Islam*, 106–20, Stuttgart: Mayer.

Porter, V. (2004), "Islamic Seals: Magical or Practical?," in E. Savage-Smith (ed.), *Magic and Divination in Early Islam*, 179–200, Aldershot: Ashgate Variorum.

Porter, V. (2007), "Amulets Inscribed with the Names of the 'Seven Sleepers' of Ephesus in the British Museum," in F. Suleman (ed.), *Word of God, Art of Man. The Qur'an and its Creative Expressions. Selected Proceedings from the International Colloquium, London, 18–21 October 2003*, 123–34, Oxford: Oxford University Press.

Porter, V. (2010), "The Use of the Arabic Script in Magic," In *Proceedings of the Seminar for Arabian Studies, Vol. 40, Supplement: The Development of Arabic as a Written Language. Papers from the Special Session of the Seminar for Arabian Studies held on 24 July, 2009*, 131–40.

Porter, V. (2011), *Arabic and Persian Seals and Amulets in the British Museum*, London: British Museum Press.

Porter, V. and J. W. Frembgen (2010), "Silberamulette mit Inschriften aus Iran und Afghanistan," in J. W. Frembgen (ed.), *Die Aura des Alif. Schriftkunst im Islam*, 192–209, München et al.: Prestel.

Porter, V., L. Saif, and E. Savage-Smith (2017), "Amulets, Magic, and Talismans," in F. B. Flood and G. Necipoglu (eds.), *A Companion to Islamic Art and Architecture*, 521–57, Oxford: Wiley-Blackwell.

Van Regemorter, B. (1961), *Some Oriental Bindings in the Chester Beatty Library*, Dublin: Hodges Figgis.

Richard, F. (1995), *Raphaël du Mans, missionnaire en Perse au XVIIe s., 2 vols. (vol I: Biographie. Correspondance; vol. II: Estats et Mémoire)*, Paris: Éd. L'Harmattan.

Ruska, J. and B. Carra de Vaux (2000), 'Ṭilsam,' *Encyclopaedia of Islam*, X: 500–2, Leiden.

Safwat, N. E. (2000), *Golden Pages: Qur'ans and Other Manuscripts from the Collection of Ghassan I. Shaker*, Oxford: Oxford University Press.

Savage-Smith, E. (1997), "Talismanic Shirts," in F. Maddison and E. Savage-Smith (eds.), *Science, Tools & Magic I: Body and Spirit, Mapping the Universe*, 117–23, Oxford: Oxford Univ. Press.

Savage-Smith, E. (2003), "Safavid Magic Bowls," in J. Thompson and S. R. Canby (eds.), *Hunt for Paradise. Court Arts of Safavid Iran 1501–1576*, 241–7, Milan: Skira.

Schaefer, K. R. (2006), *Enigmatic Charms. Medieval Arabic Block Printed Amulets in American and European Libraries and Museums*, Leiden/Boston: Brill.

Shani, R. Y. (2006), "Illustrations of the Parable of the Ship of Faith in Firdausi's Prologue to the *Shahnama*," in C. Melville (ed.), *Shahnama Studies I*, 1–40, Cambridge: The Centre of Middle Eastern and Islamic Studies, University of Cambridge.

Spink, M. (2013), "Jewellery of the Safavid, Zand, and Qajar Periods," in M. Spink (ed.), *The Art of Adornment. Jewellery of the Islamic Lands. Part Two. With Contributions by J. Ogden, J. M. Rogers, M. G. Kramarovsky and P. Moura Carvalho*, 562–81, London: Nour Foundation.

Swietochowski, M. L. and S. Babaie (1989), *Persian Drawings in the Metropolitan Museum of Art*, New York: The Metropolitan Museum of Art.

Tanāvulī, P. (1387 [2008]), *Ṭilism. Grāfīk-i sunnatī-yi Īrān*, 3rd edition, Tehran: Bungāh.

Thackston, Wheeler M.: "Treatise on Calligraphic Arts: A Disquisition on Paper, Colors, Inks, and Pens by Simi of Nishapur," in: M. M. Mazzaoui and V. B. Moreen (eds.), *Intellectual Studies on Islam. Essays Written in Honor of Martin B. Dickson*, 219–28, Salt Lake City: University of Utah Press.

de Thévenot, J. (1772), *Suite du voyage de Mr. de Thévenot au Levant*, vol. III, Amsterdam: M. C. Le Céne.

Della Valle, P. (1981), *Reisebeschreibung in Persien und Indien, nach der ersten deutschen Ausgabe von 1674 zusammengestellt und bearbeitet von Friedhelm Kemp. Mit Goethes Essay über Pietro della Valle aus dem West-östlichen Divan und einem farbig gedruckten arabischen Alphabet von Josua Reichert*, Hamburg: Maximilian-Gesellschaft.

Vesel, Z. (2012), "Talismans from the Iranian World: A Millenary Tradition," in P. Khosronejad (ed.), *The Art and Material Culture of Iranian Shi'ism. Iconography and Religious Devotion in Shi'i Islam*, 254–75, New York: I. B. Tauris.

[Xavāṣṣ-i-āyāt 1920] *Xavāṣṣ-i-āyāt. Notices et extraits d'un manuscript persan traitant la magie des versets du Coran*, Edited by A. Christensen, Copenhagen: Høst.

Zadeh, T. (2009), "Touching and Ingesting: Early Debates over the Material Qur'an," *Journal of the American Oriental Society*, 129(3): 443–66.

Index of Sources

Æbelholt, Sj 11 74
Aenigmatic wall, tomb of Ramses IX 45, 149
Aëtius, *Tetrabiblos*, 1 serm. 2c. 36 140
Al-Bīrūnī, *Kitāb al-Jamāhir fī ma'rifat al-javāhir* 115
Alexander Trallensis, VIII 14, 141
Amduat
5th hour 149
12th hour 36
287 44
347 149
458 35
759 35
892 36
amulet from Klein-Dreileben, Sachsen-Anhalt 78
Ann Arbor, Kelsey Museum of Archaeology, 26059 36–7, 49, 52–3
Auch, Archives départementales du Gers
MS I 4066 156

Baltimore, Walters Art Gallery
Inv.-No. 42.874 150
Inv.-No. 57.1437 45
Berlin
Aeg. Mus
9871 23, 143
9876 32, 145
16122 49
Staatsbibliothek, Ms. Or. Oct. 146 122, 165
Bern, Historical Museum, AE.10 147
Book of the Gates
11th hour 41
69th scene 41
Boston, Museum of Fine Arts
Inv.-No. 1997.174 141
Bregninge Church, Ærø 74, 76, 78

Cairo, Eg. Mus., CG 6001 46
Cambridge, University Library
Ms. Syr. 3086 154
Cambridge, Fitzwilliam Museum, S 37 146
Cambridge (MA), Harvard Art Museum
Inv.-No. 2012.1.144 40, 52
Inv.-No. TL38193.10 144
Claudius Aelianus, *De natura animalium* XI, 40 39
Coll. De Clercq, 3470 146
Coll. Sa'd, Gadara, Jordan, no. 424 147
Cologne, Institut für Altertumskunde, no. 18 55, 151

Darmstadt
MS 815 156
MS 2769 156
Dublin, Chester Beatty Library, Inv.no. IS 1623 121
Durham, Cathedral Chapter Library, MS Hunter 100 156

Evliyā Çelebi, *Seyāḥatnāme* 101, 108
Exeter, RAMM, Inv. 5/1946,355 44

fibula from Nordendorf I 70

Galen, *De simplicibus medicamentis* X, 19 12, 139
Gand, Bibliothèque de l'Université, MS 1272 156
Ghassan I. Shaker Collection, Qur'an 120
Gollancz' codex
A
spell #5 66, 154
spell #35 64
spell #54 154
B
spell #6 154
C
spell #15 154
spell #20 66

Gospel of Mark, 5.25-34 145

The Hague, Cab. Roy., Inv.-No. 1444 52
Harer Family Trust Collection, No. 111 42–3
Hermes, *Liber Hermetis Trismegisti de triginta sex decanis*
I, 6 149
I, 15 149
Homer, *Iliad*
VII, 69 145
XXII, 209 145

incantation bowl
AO 207964-O 60, 152
CBS 9008 60, 152
CBS 9010 61, 153
Istanbul, Topkapı Palace Library
MS Bağdat Köşkü 304
Ms. 188v36-188r8 110–11, 160
MS Bağdat Köşkü 305
Ms. Y237v3-21 109, 159
Istanbul, University Library
MS IÜTY 5973
Ms. 80r1 109, 159
Ms. 80r6 109, 159
Ms. 80r12 109–10, 159
Ms. 80r16 110, 159
Ms. 80r17 110, 159
Ms. 80r21 110, 159
Ms. 80v1 110, 159

Joshua bar Perahiya-*historiola* 60
Jutland, MJy 32 144

Kassel, Staatliche Kunstsammlung, 176 39, 152
Khalili Collection
TLS 1855 115, 163
TLS 1966 161
TLS 3141 115
Khunjī Iṣfahānī, *Tārīkh-i ʿĀlam-ārā-yi Amīnī* 161
Køge, Sj 14 74

Lacnunga 80, 156
lead amulet
from Blæsinge 72–4
from Bregninge 74, 76, 78
from Halberstadt, Germany 74, 77
from Lille Myregård, Bornholm 74, 77
from Randers 74
from Schleswig 70, 74–5, 77
from Svendborg 77, 79
London, British Library
MS Cotton Caligula A XV 81, 156
MS Cotton Vitellius E XVIII 81, 156
MS Harley 585 80–1, 156
MS Harley 978 82, 156
MS Harley 2558 86, 156
MS Or. 2200 166
MS Sloane 56 86, 156
MS Sloane 962 81, 156
MS Sloane 3550 84, 156
London, British Museum
G 28, EA 56028 150
G 191 (EA 56191) 41–2, 53
G 241 (EA 56241) 30, 145
G 257 (EA 56257) 147
G 260 (EA 56260) 12, 140
G 365 (EA 56365) 147
G 386 (EA 56386) 146
G 454 (EA 56454) 146
G 472 (EA 56472) 36
G 513 (EA 56513) 147
G 516 (EA 56516) 147
G 525 (EA 56525) 44
G 541 (EA 43115) 147
G 568 (EA 56526) 147
G 1986,5-1,111 54
GR 1894, 1101.458 141
GR 1928.5-20.1 17
Lucianus, *Philopseudes*, 24 142

Madla church, Rogaland, Norway 73
Malibu, The J. Paul Getty Museum
Inv.-No. 73.AN.1. 33
Malleus maleficarum 6, 89
Marcellus Empiricus, *De Medicamentis*,
XX, 98 140
XXIV, 7 140
Médecinaire liégeois
f. 159 82, 156
f. 166v. 83, 156
Mīrzā Makhdūm 122, 126–7, 160, 166
New York
American Numismatic Society, no. 25 48–9, 52–3, 149

MMA
17.190.491 145
41.160.642 47–8, 53
50.85 41

Opet I, 112, 12 46
Orphei Lithica Kerygmata, 20, 12-16 15, 141
Oxford
AM, 2003.129 144, 147
BL, MS E. Musaeo 243 82, 156

Papyri
Leiden, Gr. J 384, IV, 17-V, 4 55
London
BM, Gr. CXXI 47
BM gr. CXXII, col. I, 3sq. 148
Paris, Bibl. Nat., suppl. gr. 574, Z. 3125-71 41
Papyri Graecae Magicae (PGM)
IV, 2705-7 145
VII, 498 47
VIII, 9sq. 148
XII, 121-43 55
XII, 270-7 145
XIII, 824-34 88
XXXVI, 351 47, 52
XCVIII, 1–7 87
Paris
Bibliothèque Nationale
2170 46, 52–3
Fr 2896 49, 51–2
Ital. 1524 156
Département des Monnaies, médailles et antiques
58.2220 15, 141
AA.Seyrig.121 141
Froehner 2829 143
Louvre, E. 5704 147
Perugia, Museo Archeologico Nazionale dell'Umbria
Inv.-No. 1248 19
Inv.-No. 1249 13
Inv.-No. 1733 29
Inv.-No. 1741 18
Inv.-No. 1746 25
Inv.-No. 1771 20, 142
Pistis Sophia 126 41
Plato, *Cratylus* 387-427 145
Plinius, *Naturalis Historiae* XXXV, 14 150
Princeton, University Library, MS Garrett 80 156
Pseudo-Aristoteles, *Kitāb Sirr al-Asrār* 156.4-157.6 3
Pseudo-Mağrīṭī, *Ġāyat al-Ḥakīm* 7 3

Qur'an
surah 33:40 104

Ribe Skull Fragment 71
Rituale Romanum of 1614 73
Romdrup church, Northern Jutland 74, 76–7

Saʿdī, *Gulistān* 112
St. Petersburg, Hermitage Museum
Inv.-No. Ж.157 (GR-21714) 27, 144
Serenus, *Liber medicinalis*, 935-40 32, 146
Shah Ṭahmāsb, *Shāhnāma* 112
Skoluda, MN001 52, 150
stone book of Socrates and Dionysius, No. 36 55
Syr HT
99 63
330 153

Tanavoli Collection, Qur'an 115, 118
Ṭaşköprüzāde, *Miftāḥ* I. 277.3 3
TT 183 45

Vokslev, NJy 57 74

Zosimus, *On the Letter Omega*, 9 142

Index of Names

Aba Thigaor (magical name) 23
Ἀβρασάξ/*Abrasax* 41, 52, 80, 89
Abracadabra (magical name) 80, 89
Abraham 86, 104
Achilles (personal name) 15
Adam 104
Adonai 24
Al-Bunį 102
Alexander the Great 104, 109
Alexios (personal name) 15
Alį ibn Abi Tālib 105–6
Allah 93, 104, 111–12, 131, 157
Antipatros (personal name) 145
Antiphilos 150–1
Aphrodite 28
Apollonius of Tyana 104, 159
Arathor (magical name) 23
Arcadius 108
Ardene, John 86
Aristotle 102
Artemidora (personal name) 87–8
Artemis 87
Austin, John L. 3, 21, 22, 135
Avicenna 160
Aymar, Alphonse 85

Βαϊνχωωωχ (magical name) 41, 52, 54
Balthasar 78
Benali, Leonés 94, 158
Bend-i Māhī 109
Benedictus XIII 86
Bes 34, 36, 39, 52–3
Bolaix, Jaime 92, 157
Bonner, Campbell 44, 47

Caesar 104
Canby, Sheila R. 112
Caspar 78
Cassisianus (personal name) 24
Çelebi, Evliyā 100–1, 108–11, 123, 159
Chardin, Jean 124–5, 130, 161–2, 168
Charlemagne 85
Cherubim 24
Chnoubis 12, 15, 34, 55, 140, 146, 172
Clement, St. 87
Cox Miller, Patricia 30
Cynocephalus 41–2

Dasen, Véronique 14
David 73, 75, 78, 87, 104
Develioğlu, F. 102
di Feo, Luca (Ser) 86
Dickens, Mark 59
Dieleman, Jacco 91
Dionysias (personal name) 26
Domitia (personal name) 25, 144
Doutté, Edmond 91
Düwel, Klaus 74

Ereškigal 82
Eros 28
Espinel, Jerónimo 98

Faraone, Christopher A. 10–12, 14, 20–4, 32
Fatima (hand of) 105–6, 115, 120
Fayreford, Thomas 86
Frankfurter, David 57, 61

Gaia/-us (personal name) 32
Gordan, Gordin 6, 78–9
Graf, Fritz 26, 61, 66
Gregory, St. 85
Gruber, Christiane 105

Hammer-Purgstall, Joseph von 105, 107
Harpocrates/Harpokrates 34, 47, 149
Hecate 14, 17, 34, 36, 52–4, 142, 150
Hemera 145
Heracles/Hercules 14–15, 26
Hermanubis 28–9
Hizr 104
Horus 34, 37, 39, 41, 52
Hūd 104
Hunter, Erica C. D. 59–60, 62–8

Ἰάω/*Iaō*/*Iaô* 24, 28, 38, 47, 49, 52, 143–5, 148, 150
Idrįs 104
Ingordan 6, 78–9

Isaac 87
Isis 42, 44
Iulis (personal name) 15

Jesus 41, 65, 75, 77, 86–7, 104
John, St. (the Apostle) 75–6, 79
John, St. (the Baptist) 70
John of Athene 86
Joseph 104
Judah 73, 75
Julian (personal name) 12

Kagarow, Eugen G. 21
Kalavan 109
Khnum 37
Kotansky, Roy 13
Kropp, Amina 20–2

Labarta, Ana 92, 93
Leo, St. 85
Loḳmān 104
Lopo, Isabel de 96
Lot 104

Μιχαήλ 50
Mary 41, 64, 65, 82
Mayor, Rafaela 96
Medusa 14, 15, 26
Meeks, Dimitri 37
Melchior 78
Memnon 30
Mendoza, Leonor de 94
Meninsky, Franciscus 102
Moriggi, Marco 62
Morisco 7, 8, 90–9
Moses 104
Mouterde, René 24
Muhammad 104
Müller-Kessler, Christa 61
Murad IV 110

Nādi ʿAlīyan 114, 125, 161, 165
Nechepso 12, 140
Nessia 71
Nestroy, Johann 103
Noah 104, 112
Nonna (personal name) 12
Nünlist, Tobias 119, 126, 163

Odin 70, 71
Omphale 14
Osiris 25, 28, 29, 41, 44–6, 52, 54

Pakalin, Mehmet Z. 102
Paul, St. 87
Perseus 14, 26, 27, 144
Peter, St. 87
Philippa 145
Phthonos 28
Piedrahita, Antonio de 98
Plato 102
Poccetti, Paolo 24
Psyche 28

Re 148
Redhouse, William J. 102

Samson 104
Sarapis 87, 88, 142
Satan 73, 77
Scot, Reginald 86
Searle, John 21, 22
Şeref H̱an 109
Seth 14
Seven Sisters 6, 72–4, 78, 79
Shaked, Shaul 61
Σαβαώθ 47, 143
Σεμεσιλαμ 47
Solomon 78, 98, 99, 104, 105, 107
Sossidi, Eleftherios 28
Sun ram 46, 47, 51, 52, 54
Swartz, Michael D. 57

Tambiah, Stanley J. 54
Tantalus 16
Tauros (personal name) 15
Tawada, Yoko 103
Theodosius 108
Thor 70
Thouth 24
Ἰιθοής 47
Twtw 43, 47, 53
Typhon 14
Týr 71

Ullmann, Manfred 102

Valios (?) (personal name) 15
Vargas, Diego de 98

Zenobia (personal name) 25, 144
Zeo (=Zeus?) 20

Index of Places

Al-Aqsa 108
Alexandria 34
Almonacid de la Sierra 93
Andalusia 92, 157
Ardabil 123
Athens 108

Babylon 60, 152
Belgrade 109

Cairo 57, 100, 101, 108–10
Constantinople 24
Ctesiphon 104

Danube 109
Denmark 69, 72, 74, 75

Egypt 1, 3, 4, 8, 10, 18, 19, 28, 34–8, 42–5, 47, 50–5, 57, 109, 133, 137, 147
Ephesus 84, 87

Gizeh 108
Granada 94, 97

Hama 108
Hibis 37, 47

Iran 5, 8, 112–14, 116–21, 123–5, 128, 131
Iraq 58, 59, 64
Isfahan 122–4, 161–3, 167
Israel 24, 104, 133, 135
Istanbul 12, 100, 106, 108, 110

Jerusalem 108
Jordan (river) 87

Kurdistan 59, 154

Mecca 116
Medain 104
Mīnā 128
Mosul 59, 66

Norway 69, 70, 73, 74, 155

Schleswig 70, 74, 75, 77
Shiraz 122, 123, 166
Siena 86
Syria 8–9, 58, 137

Turfan 59, 62–4, 67, 153, 165

Urmia (lake) 59, 63, 64

Valencia 92, 94
Van (lake) 101

General Index

99 beautiful names of God 95, 114, 157, 162

ablanathanalba 32
acclamation 20
agate 32, 33, 110
alfaquies 93
Aljamiada 70, 90
alpha and omega 6, 79
αρπονχνουφι βρινταττηνωφρι-formula 37, 39, 52, 144
alphabet 16, 18, 31, 33, 57, 80, 105, 107, 138
anguipede 19, 52, 150
anthropology 1, 134, 135
astrology 31, 102

bāzūband 112, 125
birds 39, 109
bleeding/blood 15, 16, 32, 46, 81, 82, 84, 85, 88, 135, 136, 145
bracteates 69, 155
budūḥ 93

carmina figurata 16
carnelian 14, 23, 24, 143, 163
cédula 97
celandine 80, 81
centipede 110
chalcedony 12, 13, 20, 28, 29, 55, 115, 125, 140, 146
charaktêres/characteres/caracteres 6, 16, 31, 89, 114–15, 118, 143
childbirth 83, 88, 93, 128, 135, 137, 160
Christian cosmology 5, 67, 68
Clavicula of Solomon 98, 99
colics 14
conjuration 71, 73, 75, 76, 78, 79, 82
cross 72, 73, 75, 76, 82
crucifix 86
cryptography 4, 16, 138

demon 6, 24, 25, 28, 32, 74, 88, 89, 136, 137, 157
devil 73, 75, 77, 78
dikephalus 36, 43, 46
dwarf 71, 80, 81

egg(s) 84, 92, 159
envy 28, 135, 144, 160
epigraphy 35
epilepsy 83, 85, 168
evil eye 105, 125, 127, 128, 162, 168, 169
exorcism 6, 73, 74, 79, 137

fever 32, 73, 81, 83, 92, 110, 122, 123, 131, 135, 157, 168
finger rings 12, 17, 125, 133, 134
fire 12, 28, 92, 110, 160
Fourteen Infallibles 115, 120, 163, 165
Futhark 5, 69–71
Futhorc 5, 69, 70

Ghubārī 118, 119, 122
Gorgon 14–15, 17
grimoires 99, 133
grylloi 53, 151

hematite 16, 17, 25, 28, 36, 41, 48, 150
Hand of Fatima 105, 106
Herces 7, 91, 94, 96, 99
heuristic 2, 11
hirz 91
historiola 21, 30, 60
Holy Spirit 72, 75–7
homeric language 29, 138
hymn 47

Iarbatha-logos 31
Imamophilism 161
incantation bowl 57–61, 66, 114, 152
infection 75, 135

infertility 82
inflammation 66, 71, 135

klima 16

Letter of Abgar 84
Letter of Charlemagne 84
Letter of Columba 84
lion 26, 28, 40, 44, 47, 52, 73, 75, 144, 148
logos (magical) 31, 144
longue durée 4, 34

magical formula 1, 15, 17, 22, 85, 87, 92, 128, 138
Mahoma, law of 95
Mandaic 57, 58, 152
Median stone 14
mosque of Zeyrek 108
mummy 25, 28, 30, 41, 44, 45
muska 106

narrative charm 81, 87, 88
navel 81
nazarlık 105, 106
Nemean lion 14, 15, 26
nightmares 28
nómina 97

oath 23, 137
Ouroboros 28, 31, 44, 47, 143

Pahlavi 58, 169
palindrome 16, 25, 32, 38, 49, 52, 145
pars epica 5, 25, 26, 61, 66–8
Parthenon 108
performative utterances 21–3
persuasive analogy 14, 21, 23, 29, 133, 137, 140
phylactery 28, 141
plague 29, 67, 110, 123, 127, 134
plinthion 16
praxeology 1, 2
pseudo-writing 4, 16, 138
pterygoma (see also: wing) 16

reaper 28
runic scripts 5, 69, 70, 74

Safavid amulets 8, 112, 113, 120, 125, 127
salamander 47
santiguador 98
scarab 14, 31, 32, 44, 46
sciatica 28
scorpion 28, 39, 109, 160, 161
Seven Sleepers of Ephesus 84, 104, 108, 160
shoes 105, 162
slaves 110, 141
Solomonic letters 99
speech acts theory 20
square, magical 93, 94, 107, 108
Sūrat al-Baqarah 94
sword 85, 105, 106

technopaignia 12
trikephalos 41
typology 2, 10, 17, 136

Vorlage 62
vowels 16, 30, 44, 47, 48, 53, 54, 87, 88, 138

water (holy) 12, 57, 83, 96, 109, 116, 159, 162
wing formation 16
womb 14, 137, 145

zodiac 114

www.ingramcontent.com/pod-product-compliance
Lightning Source LLC
Chambersburg PA
CBHW061826300426
44115CB00013B/2266
* 9 7 8 1 3 5 0 2 5 4 5 7 2 *